A QUAKER FAMILY IN ZANZIBAR: 186

A Quaker Family in India and Zanzibar 1863-1865

Letters from Elizabeth and Henry Jacob

'Peacock Tails Sprinkled with Diamonds'

edited by
Yvonne Bird
(Great-great niece of Elizabeth)

William Sessions Limited
York, England

ISBN 1 85072 256 0

To my Father

Printed in 11 on 12 point Palatino Typeface
from Author's Disk
by Sessions of York
The Ebor Press
York, England

Contents

List of Illustrations

Introduction and Acknowledgements

Peacock tails and rainbows sprinkled with diamonds - this vivid description by Elizabeth Jacob of the sunlight playing on the sea at Zanzibar is typical of her style, which has made working on this collection of letters such a pleasure. Warm, witty, lively and informative, I have transcribed them almost completely as written, with a only a little punctuation here and there to make them easier to read. Grammar and spelling is as found: for instance color, Hindo, and the names of places current in the 1860s, and a few words which sound as though they were peculiar to the family, such as 'halfish'. Elizabeth's asides are in round brackets, and mine in square brackets for the odd word: in the text for clarity, rather than as footnotes.

The letters were written in Indian ink in a good copperplate hand, and have survived well, especially when you consider that after being read by the immediate family, they were sent all round to the extended family, which was enormous. Probably for this reason too they always stated the relationship of the writer to the recipient, which is very useful to the researcher. A few personal letters from Elizabeth to her mother would have been for private view only. In order to save paper and postage, some of the letters are completed at right angles to the earlier writing, which is a nightmare to transcribe. Although we have only one half of the correspondence, it's a bit like listening to a telephone conversation where you can make a good guess at the half that you don't actually hear. Elizabeth was known to the members of her family by the pet names Eliza, Elisa, Elsie and Lizzie.

****

I would like to acknowledge the help, kindness and enthusiasm of my relatives and friends, in particular my father, Felix (Bob)

Milner for his financial support and encouragement. To Colin Milner for the loan of the letters of Elizabeth and Henry Jacob; to John Milner and William Theophilus for the photo of the oil painting of the Smith family group; to Bruce Milner, Denis Milner, Gladys Milner, Amanda and Steve Shipman, and Lionel and Cicely West. To Roger and Janice Hall and Susan Johnson for information on the descendants of Mary Ann Smith.

To my husband Clifford Bird for his ideas on how he would do it, and in spite of that, his continued support, help and encouragement, and to my brother-in-law Tony Bird for proof reading the first draft and making useful comments.

To Mary Shackleton and Belinda Jacob and the staff of the Friends Historical Library in Dublin for information and photographs of the Jacob family. Also to the Library at Friends House, Euston Road, London, and the Friends Meeting House at Diss. And last, but not least, to William Sessions, who kindly agreed to publish for me and put me in touch with many useful people and sources.

Yvonne Bird, May 2000

Opening the Box

Quite by chance I came upon the letters. My husband and I had dropped in on my cousin Colin Milner at Grange-over-Sands on our way back to Norfolk after a short holiday in the Lake District. We were all talking about our family history when Colin casually said that there was a box of letters in the garage, would I like to see it. Would I! Yes, please!

Out came this little Victorian work box stuffed full with a treasure trove of family memorabilia - hundreds of letters, a great wadge of early postcards, a leather-bound autograph book and a chunky photograph album with brass clasps like an ancient family bible, containing family portraits dating back to the 1860s. The most interesting was a bundle of about 50 letters from Elizabeth Smith, the sister of our great-grandmother Gulielma. My family knew practically nothing about her, except that in 1863 at the age of 23 she went to Kurrachee to marry Henry Jacob. Kurrachee? Where was it? On further reading it was clear that the letters had been sent from Kurrachee in India. Soon it dawned on me that this was Karachi, now in Pakistan since partition in 1947.

So who was Elizabeth Smith? She was born on 10th February 1840, the eldest of the five children of Isabel (1814-93) and Bartholomew Smith (1814-97), who ran a drapery business in Thirsk, Yorkshire, reputed to have been established in 1580 when it was renowned for its excellent breeches. The family was from a long line of Quakers (members of the Religious Society of Friends). Bartholomew Smith was well-liked, a considerable artist and an active member of The British Temperance League and The Anti-vivisection Society. Another cause he felt strongly about was the abolition of slavery, which Elizabeth encountered in Zanzibar. The other four children, frequently mentioned in the letters, are Mary Ann (Pollie) born 1841, Gulielma born 1846, Tom born 1849, and Arthur born 1854. The Quaker emphasis on education and

Elizabeth and Mary Ann Smith (left) painted 1856.

equality applied to their daughters as well as sons and Elizabeth spent two years at Ackworth, the co-educational Quaker school near Pontefract in Yorkshire, which was founded in 1779.

Henry (Harry) Jacob, who married Elizabeth Smith on 31st December 1863, was born of Quaker parents in Ballitore, county Kildare, Ireland on 10th October 1836. The village had been built in the early 18th century by Quakers fleeing from persecution in England, and his parents Henry Jacob (1797-1871) and Lucy Bewley (1802-83) are interred in the Quaker burial ground there. There were twelve children of the marriage whose names can be seen on the family chart of Henry and Lucy Jacob, Henry jnr. being the sixth. His 2nd cousins William and Robert started the famous biscuit firm "W & R Jacob & Co." in 1851. I don't know how Elizabeth and Henry met, but it seems they had a fairly long courtship by correspondence, as he was in Karachi for four years before they were married.

The mid-nineteenth century was a time of technology and change. Elizabeth writes about the laying of the electric telegraph to India and the new sewing machine. She travelled by rail in England, France, Egypt and India. At home gas was available for heating and lighting, and steam power in manufacturing and transport increased industrial output and improved communications. Photography, cheap newspapers and periodicals, and the penny post were widely accessible. Harry was employed as a book-keeper for a company building iron steamships to navigate the River Indus from Karachi, and unusually for Britons in India, he was neither in the Indian Army nor the Indian Civil Service. India under the British Raj in 1863 was comparatively civilised, with its infrastructure of roads and railways and organised government, but Zanzibar, the beautiful and exotic tropical island under Arab rule, was hazardous, unhealthy and primitive.

The history of the British in India began with the The East India Company, which opened up trading opportunities in the far east and became enormously powerful. By the beginning of the 19th century it was no longer merely trading but responsible for ruling large parts of India, assisted by its own army. After the 1857-9 Mutiny, the Crown took over the country's administration and in 1874 the Company was dissolved. As a symbol of the new unity, Queen Victoria was created Empress of India in January 1877.

The Mutiny had dealt a severe blow to British self-confidence in India, and it was only four years later that Elizabeth arrived there, obviously well aware of what had happened, yet there is never the slightest hint that she had any worry or anxiety. There was a racial arrogance amongst the British of which Elizabeth was not exempt, and in their relationships with the native population I expect the Jacobs were typical of most Europeans of the time, although I like to think that Elizabeth was slightly less prejudiced and more liberal-minded. She seems to have treated her servants very reasonably and speaks kindly of them, and was always deter-mined to look on the bright side and see the best in everything.

This book is not just a collection of letters from a long-lost kinswoman. It is about the people who wrote and received the letters and the people mentioned in them; the people whose lives they touched, including mine. It is a snapshot of the personal his-tory of a young woman living far from home in the middle of the 19th century, spoken directly to us through her writing.

The letters – April to December 1863

Who could resist the appeal of this letter written by Henry Jacob to his prospective father-in-law, Bartholomew Smith. Prior to the reforms of the 1860s a Quaker marriage could be delayed or forbidden if the man had not asked parental permission before proposing to his intended wife.

Kurrachee April 7th 1863

My dear Sir

I sit down to write to you with considerable diffidence. Under any ordinary circumstances I am aware I ought to have asked for your consent before proposing to your daughter, but I trust you will take into consideration the rather peculiar nature of our acquaintanceship, and the fact that I have never had the pleasure of seeing you, a fact which no one can regret more than I do.

Henry Jacob 1836-1905. Taken at Bombay.

You are doubtless aware of the whole history of my acquaintance with your daughter, as I know our long correspondence has been no secret to you, and you have perhaps read some of my letters, so that I am perhaps a little better known to you than you are to me - at least I trust that neither you nor Mrs Smith look on me as being entirely a stranger.

Situated as I am many thousands of miles from England, I feel it is no light thing to ask you for your daughter, but Elisa has given me

4

good ground for hoping that she is not altogether indifferent to me, and she tells me that not knowing me, you are willing to leave all to herself. Still you have a right to know something of my position and prospects here, and I can perhaps best explain them by going back a little. For your daughter's sake, I wish they were more brilliant than they are, but the hope of winning her will not be the worst incentive to exertion.

I came out here in 1859/60 as bookkeeper for Messrs. Richardson Duck & Co., who are Contractors for building a fleet of iron steamers for the navigation of the Indus. Owing to the various vexations, delays and interferences on the part of the government this work

Bartholomew Smith 1814-1897.
Father of Elizabeth J.
Photo: J. Navey, Leeds 1860s.

has been much delayed, and four out of the six steamers are still unfinished. Having some spare time on my hands I exerted myself with the object of getting myself better known, and edited one of the local papers here for some time.

By this and other means I have obtained a certain standing which makes me very hopeful for the future, and I have just made an arrangement with [1]Mr Lidbetter (who is Messrs. R D & Co's agent and who carries on business on his own account as a merchant) to divide my time between his office and my original employment, with a view to gaining a better knowledge of mercantile affairs. He guarantees me Rs300 or £30 per month for two years, at the end of which time he holds out a prospect of a partnership. Besides this I hold the office of Secretary to the Chamber of Commerce, which brings me in another Rs100 or £10 a month. My total income at present is therefore £40 per month or nearly Rs500 per annum, and although this is not in India so large a sum as it looks in England yet it is quite sufficient with reasonable economy to marry on.

If Elisa can bring her mind either now or at some future time to come out to me here I can offer her a tolerably comfortable home but this I do not like to press on her. I know it is a great deal to ask of any girl, but the voyage is by no means so formidable as it looks, and I would of course meet her in Bombay. Of course I do not mention this without being in a position to pay the cost of her passage, and will be only too glad to remit you £150 or £200 for that purpose. Should your daughter not be able to bring her mind to such a prospect, we can do nothing but hope for the future, and trust to what it may bring forth.

You can imagine that my inclinations would lead me to England, but I have no prospect of making more than a base livelihood there, and although I should be able to see Elisa, I fear I should not be able to do anything more for perhaps years to come. Still if anything should turn up which would make me to return home with reasonable prospects I shall of course embrace it eagerly.

I do not know that I have anything more to add, I should be very glad to hear from you and learn from yourself that you are not unfavourable to my suit, and I will of course do my best to answer any enquiries you may make. My love for Elisa is founded so entirely on respect and admiration for her character, and is so independent of mere externals, (for as I have told her myself I have the very faintest recollection of her person) that I have no fear of its durability, and I trust that in time she will be able to reciprocate my affection.

I hope I have explained myself to your satisfaction with regard to my prospects here. For the rest I am 27 years of age, or rather I was 26 last October (I believe Elisa is some years younger). I am healthy and active and I hope not destitute of talent. Our tastes moreover are somewhat similar, and while there is no blood relationship between our families, we are connected by marriage, and have to some extent the same friends and acquaintances.

I fear I have not expressed myself very well in what I have written. If so I hope you will try to excuse it and that you will apprehend my meaning even if clumsily expressed.

In conclusion, I feel very deeply the confidence in me which prompts you to accept Elisa's version of my character, and trust I may never do anything to forfeit it. My great regret is my inability to speak instead of writing to you but I can only hope that at some future time this pleasure may be in my power, and that I may have an opportunity of making myself personally known to both yourself and Mrs Smith. Hoping to hear from you in reply, and beg you to believe me,

Yours most sincerely
Henry Jacob

Note:
1. Thomas Lidbetter (1823-1908) was born into the Quaker family of Adam and Lucy Lidbetter of Brighton in Sussex. After an education at Ackworth School (1831-38), he served his apprenticeship with a ship's captain and became a master mariner. In 1848 he married Deborah Wilson from Dudley and there were six children - Maggie and Amy are mentioned in the letters. As captain of *The Swarthmore* he visited Bombay and Calcutta in 1853 then on to Australia to collect a consignment of gold which he succeeded in bringing back to London after many difficulties. *The Swarthmore* was a badly designed ship and on her second voyage she was wrecked in the Bahamas.
   In 1860 he was engaged by Richardson, Duck & Co to build the Indus River Steam Flotilla in Karachi. As Henry Jacob remarks, Thomas Lidbetter was also in business with a firm of Parsee merchants, Doshabhai, Merwangee & Co., but it was ruined by the collapse of the Indian cotton market following the American Civil War (1861-65). In 1866 Captain Lidbetter moved to Bombay and set up as an average adjuster in shipping insurance, also travelling to New Zealand and Australia. In Tasmania he met his second wife, Ellen Louisa Staples, whom he married in 1879 and they had three children. He returned to England in 1889 and died at Wolverhampton in 1908 aged 86.

Sources:
Dictionary of Quaker Biography, Friends House, Euston Road, London.
Sykes, Marjorie *An Indian Tapestry: Quaker threads in the history of India, Pakistan and Bangladesh* (1997).

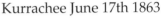

Bartholomew Smith has given consent for Henry Jacob to marry his daughter Elizabeth.

Kurrachee June 17th 1863

Elizabeth Smith c1863.

My dear Friend

I need not tell you how glad I was to receive your letter, and how thankful to find from your own assurance that you have sufficient confidence in me to entrust your dear daughter to me for life. It is a solemn trust, and I assure you I feel it to be so, and I hope I may never prove myself unworthy of it.

Although I have no brilliant prospects to offer her, I believe she will at least find in me a loving and faithful husband, and I know that her comfort and happiness shall always have the first consideration. I feel also my dear friend that it is a very serious thing to ask a father to allow one of his children to link her future with one who is so much of a stranger, and not only that, but to come so many thousands of miles from her home and I can readily understand your reluctance to grant this part of my request. I feel more deeply than I can express what is involved in such a step, and I assure you I feel quite humbled and conscience stricken at the unhappiness I fear I have already caused in your family and the still greater wrench which must attend your daughter's leaving her father's house.

It is fifteen years now since <u>our</u> family was finally broken up, and I shall never forget what we all suffered on that occasion. Were I not bound to think of Elisa as well as of myself, I feel as if I should not have courage to proceed any further. I quite acknowledge the truth of what you say about the advisability of my coming to England and seeing your daughter myself. I need not tell you that this is the course my own inclinations would suggest to me; and the convenience of all parties would be best consulted by it. I

8

would thus get to know you all and I hope would be able to win your esteem and affection.

But at present I frankly confess I cannot see the wildest probability of my being able to undertake such a journey for perhaps years to come. When I have lodged funds in your hands to pay for Elisa's expenses to India and to assist in her outfit, I shall have but a trifling sum left of my savings, not more than enough to purchase a few additional articles to enable me to provide a comfortable home for her. I trust you will not think me mercenary for alluding to these matters. Money is no object to me in such an affair, if I had it. I can do no more however than propose to spend every penny I have in the world, and I am sure you will do me the justice to admit that for a man who has always had to earn his own bread in an ill-paid profession, £200 of savings represents a good deal of carefulness and scraping. It is no trifling sum to me, for it is all the ready money I have got. If however my coming to England is an absolute sine qua non, I can do nothing but wait patiently in the hope that something may turn up which will enable me to meet your wishes and my own.

Lucy and Henry Jacob married 1825. Photo: Chancellor, Dublin 1860s?

It will not however be necessary even under present circumstances for Elisa to come out unattended. By what I cannot help regarding as a most fortunate coincidence, my friend Capt. Lidbetter has gone to England leaving me in charge of his business here. He will be returning towards the fall of the year, and I will write him this mail requesting him if possible to call and see you. I have entire confidence in Capt. Lidbetter and as he is a member of our Society and a father of a family he would form a most suitable escort for Elisa. His protection would I think remove any impropriety in her coming out, and would save her, at little or no trouble to him, from annoyance during the passage. Could you bring yourself to part with her under these circumstances?

I dare not press the matter, knowing how much it involves, but I can see no choice between this and a long delay and separation, perhaps of years. Be assured that I would come and fetch her myself if I could, but I think Capt. Lidbetter will confirm what I have said as to the difficulty of such a step, and I am sure you will consider my last proposal carefully, before coming to an adverse decision. As for my settling in England, I would be deceiving you if I were to hold out any hopes of being able to do so. With or without your daughter, I must work on here, as I have no prospects of success at home, and have already made some little progress in Kurrachee. I do not think I shall ever make my fortune even in India, but settling down in England would imply a more complete separation from Elisa than even my residence here. It would be years and years before I had recovered lost ground, and placed myself in a position of offer her marriage - in all probability I should never be able to do so.

Pray think over all my arguments which I set down without reserve. Whatever decision you may come to, you may rely upon my faithfulness to your dear daughter, whom already I look upon as my wife. If I am to remain separated from her for years it will make no difference in my love for her but it will be a very hard trial for me, and also, I fancy, for her.

Please consider this letter as addressed equally to Mrs Smith to whom, even if I never see her, I trust I may yet prove an affectionate son. Hoping for a speedy answer.

Believe me, my dear friend,

Yours very sincerely
Henry Jacob

Since writing this I have thought it would save you trouble if Capt. Lidbetter would take the needful steps for securing Elisa's passage, in case you give your assent to her coming out with him, and I have accordingly made him a remittance of £120 for that purpose.

From Henry Jacob to Isabel Smith, his future mother-in-law, with further reassurance of his devotion to Elizabeth.

Kurrachee Nov 9th 1863

My dear Mrs Smith

Isabel Smith 1863.

I am sorry to say that all our letters by last mail have been detained a fortnight in Bombay, owing to the steamer from here having been detained on her passage by bad weather, and having arrived after the English mail had been despatched. This letter will therefore reach you in company with one which I wrote dear Elisa and despatched on the 25th ultimo [October] but which, in the event of her having left England I must ask you to be so good as to destroy, as it will not be worth sending back again.

I am much disappointed however to think that a very kind letter which Mrs Lidbetter addressed to yourself by the same opportunity will also reach you a fortnight later than we hoped. I induced her to write it in order to inform you that Mrs L and her family are not likely to leave here before the spring, so that part at least of the former arrangement about Elisa can still hold good. Hearing from your dear daughter by last mail that she still hoped to leave England on the 18th of this month I was much pleased to think that a letter which had been originally written for the purpose of smoothing away any difficulties in the way of her coming out would at all events reach you a day or two after her departure, and tell you that kind and sympathetic friends were waiting to receive her here. This has been prevented by the unfortunate mishap about our letters and you will thus remain another fortnight in some degree of suspense.

I send by this opportunity a <u>copy</u> of a letter which I have addressed to dear Elisa at Suez. It is possible that her plans may have again been altered and that she may be in England when this reaches you, and I wished if possible to provide against the possibility of her being without a letter from me, more especially as you would all have had good reason to think me remiss last mail. If she is really on her way my letter may share the fate of its predecessor. If not, it will explain how it happened that she received none from me by the last opportunity. The probabilities are however that she will get it at Suez, and I write on that hypothesis.

I wish my dear Mrs Smith I could convey to you some idea of my gratitude for the wonderful amount of confidence both you and Mr Smith have bestowed on me, in thus allowing your daughter to come so many thousands of miles to me. It can indeed have been no light matter to part with her, and I have felt very deeply how much I was asking of you. You will believe me I know when I say that if my coming to England could have been in any way arranged I would have let no minor obstacles stand in my way. It is to a certain extent a humiliation to me to sit here quietly while Elisa passes through so many troubles and difficulties to come to me, and it seems a reproach to my manhood to have permitted such an arrangement. But indeed it has been out of my power to act otherwise.

I owe Elisa's parents more than it is possible for me to express, and I can only hope that some day it may be in my power to show you that I am not ungrateful. You have given me indeed what no wealth could purchase - a gift altogether beyond price, and have asked for no pledges, but have trusted in me explicitly as if you had known me always. God grant that I may never show myself unworthy of it. But indeed my dear Mrs Smith, I do think I shall not disappoint you. I can honestly say, now that I have been so many months in close correspondence with your daughter and have discovered so many excellencies in her which I was hardly alive to before - such a wealth indeed of love and affection, such depth and clearness of sincerity of character - that I love her as deeply and truly as if we had had the privilege of more personal intercourse, and had become acquainted with each other in the usual way. When I see her, this feeling must necessarily be intensified, and I am sure I shall love her passionately - passionately as one so noble, so pure and so unselfish deserves to be loved.

After all she has done for my sake you need not fear but that her happiness will always be my first consideration.

Her home is now nearly ready for her, and I only need her assistance in putting the finishing touches. Your husband's kind liberality in bearing the expense of Elisa's passage has placed ample funds at my disposal, and I have felt bound to spend the sum I had set apart for her voyage in providing for her comfort in another way. When she lands she will meet with a warm welcome from Mrs Lidbetter, who with her family are anticipating much pleasure from her visit, and our marriage shall take place as quickly as possible whenever Elisa says she is ready. The season this year promises to be delightfully cool and I am sure that by arriving here in December she will suffer no inconvenience from the climate.

Do send me a few lines when you write to Elisa. I can assure you that I have felt not a little the absence in E's letters of any messages from you or Mr Smith. E tells me the fault has been mainly hers, but I have thought many a time rather sorrowfully that if you had indeed learned to think of me as one of your family that you would sometimes send me a proof of it. Your continued silence has in fact made me feel somewhat of an outcast. You will learn by and by to think of me more as a son will you not, dear Mrs Smith? I shall be uneasy until you assure me of this.

My letter to Elsie has still to be finished so I must say goodbye -

With very kind regards to all your family

Yours very sincerely
Henry Jacob

Elizabeth is writing home to her family in Thirsk, having travelled by train through France to Marseilles to pick up the boat for Alexandria. No date for this letter as the first page has been lost.

.... see this lovely country - the air is wonderfully clear and bright and very warm indeed. The colouring is as intense as any of Harry Moore's sketches - my first view of the Mediterranean this morning with the island of Monte Christo just touched by the sunrise was most glorious - something like this: [little sketch of 'grey sky' then mountains with 'orange over pale blue mist']. Let Father try and paint it with deep blue sea and the clearest and most glowing colours he can get onto his palette.

Yesterday we travelled through most beatifully wooded country - some of the trees quite green yet - and the fields and rivers nearly full of beautiful osiers with glowing crimson and orange stalks - at a distance you can't tell what the lovely colouring is produced by. The vine yards look bare on the hillsides - just long rows of sticks with a few dead leaves. We bought nice grapes yesterday for ten pence a basket holding more than a pound. The villages are beautifully clean and pretty.

These hotels have beautiful court yards square or oval into which you drive and into which many glass doors with lace curtains open, and round which stand plants in vases, orange trees, aloes or cactuses - everything is done so tastily here in France. The interior decorations of these rooms are such as people would go a long way to see in England - gold scroll work in relief round frescoed panels, and bas-reliefs, some of them very beautiful, in the walls.

I think nothing particular has happened besides what I have told you. We have had very little trouble with our baggage. I find my French very useful - rusty as it is from long disuse - a Frenchman told me yesterday that I spoke perfectly! and another said today that I had evidently learnt in France. It is very curious that the poor people here never wear bonnets - they either go bareheaded or wear velvet head-dresses or snowy white capes which look so fresh and pretty. The women in Paris seem to do all the work and the men - hundreds of them - idle about in the squares and streets. Woman drive the carts - sometimes drag them.

14

I have seen nothing yet of any <u>ladies</u> going to India - but I suppose there will be as many as usual. Mr Soares is very kind but very careless in his accounts of which he doesn't keep any. I have great trouble in paying my debts, but I think we are straight so far. It is his own fault if I owe him anything I don't know of. He reminds me often of the Portuguese chief in Dickens story of the [1]Perils of English prisoners - he can look and be so fierce when he is angry - and yet is generally so polite and friendly with his eau-de-cologne and constant smelling salts. He has only lived in England three years altogether.

I hope you are all quite used to being without me - dear ones all - I have hardly had time to feel lonely amongst all this unsettlement - and I quite enjoy travelling. So far I have suffered less than anybody from loss of rest - some of the gentlemen look dreadfully seedy and Mr Soares has dreadful headaches. We are expecting very fine weather in the Mediterranean - it looks like a sea of glass today. We are going out as soon as Mr Soares returns - he has gone out on business and has some letters to write first.

I can't think of any more to tell you. I will try to write a letter every day if I can while at sea, so far of course I have no chance. I always think about you - and long for you to see this lovely place which however I haven't had a good look at yet. I must describe it to you in my next letter. My dear love to you over and over again. Love also to [2]Gilbert and Hannah, Robert and Emma, Sarah Ann etc.

Always your loving daughter
Elisa H Smith

Notes:
1. Charles Dickens: 'The Perils of Certain English Prisoners', a story written for the Christmas issue of Household Words (1857).
2. Gilbert and Hannah: John Gilbert Baker (1834-1920), the son of John Baker, married Hannah Unthank in 1860. The Baker family were also Quakers and close friends of the Smiths, running a drapery business at Castlegate in Thirsk, together with another son, George. Their names appear regularly in the Jacob correspondence.

Letter from Henry Jacob addressed to "Bartholomew Smith Esq. Thirsk, Yorkshire, via Marseilles"

Kurrachee Nov. 21st 1863

My dear Friend

Your letter of the 16th ulto. which reached me safely by last mail, was very welcome - and I lose no time in acknowledging it. I had been thinking it somewhat strange that I had not heard from you before, and the kind tone of your letter has been a considerable relief to me - your silence seemed to me to imply that while you had sufficient confidence in me to trust your daughter to my keeping, you could not think very cordially of me after all - and the feeling appeared to me such a very natural one, considering how little you know of me and how much I have asked of you, that in my heart I could not blame any of you for not writing to me, at the same time that I longed to be able to make you think more kindly of me.

Elisa however tells me that her sister has been to blame in not sending many messages with which she had been entrusted, and indeed Elisa herself admits that she never used to let you know when she was closing her letters to me. I am quite contented however now that you have written me so kindly and cordially.

When this letter reaches you, Elisa will I hope have arrived here, and I do most earnestly hope that I may be able to make up to her in some measure for all that she has gone through for my sake. To you my dear friend, I can do nothing but feebly express an obligation which is too great for words, but I feel sure that the best proof of my gratitude will consist in showing myself worthy of your confidence, and in loving and cherishing your dear daughter, and studying her happiness in every way in my power. It seems to me as if I never could do enough for her and I can honestly say that since our correspondence has become more intimate than it was she has, even without my having seen her, become as dear to me as life itself. However, deeds are better than words, and you shall see.

I told Mrs Smith last mail that Mrs Lidbetter had made up her mind to remain here until the spring. She and her family have just returned to their house which was undergoing repairs, and her

16

great object now appears to be to get everything made as nice and comfortable as possible against your daughter's arrival. I tell you this to show you to what kind friends Elisa is coming, but indeed Mrs Lidbetter is one of the most hospitable of women, and finds her greatest pleasure in making others happy. She seems almost as anxious as I am about Elisa's arrival, and asks eagerly every mail what news I have of her movements. It is an infinite relief to me that she intends remaining here a little longer, as otherwise I really do not know how we should have managed.

Everything that I can do shall be done, to conduct everything as you would wish it if present. A quiet wedding is what I desire above all things, and in Captain Lidbetter's absence anything else would not be decorous even if anybody wished it. I will not fail to write you as soon as your daughter arrives, and I have arranged for a telegram to be despatched from Bombay via Alexandria by the outgoing steamer, by which means you will hear of her safety a fortnight after she lands there.

Please remember me very kindly to Mrs Smith, from whom I hope I shall soon hear again, and believe me

Yours very sincerely
Henry Jacob

Elizabeth is enjoying her journey across the Mediterranean in spite of feeling dreadfully seasick. It was hoped that Captain Lidbetter would be able to chaperone her to India but the arrangement broke down. However, she seems well able to take care of herself and reassures her parents that 'nobody interferes with me'.

On board the [1]*Valetta*
Nov. 22. 1863

My dearest Parents

I have been prevented from writing every day as I intended by a very unexpected reason - viz - by continued sea-sickness - for two days I have not been able to sit up at all, much less attempt writing but this morning I feel a great deal better so far. I am writing in my berth and the great trial - dressing - is yet to come. I made an effort to stay on deck yesterday, the weather was so glorious, but couldn't manage it so came to bed again.

You never saw anything like this Mediterranean weather - cloudless glowing sky - the deepest blue sea, but I must begin in order from where I left off. After finishing my letter in Marseilles we set off to post it - and had the greatest difficulty in finding the post office. I found no letter there for me either from India or England

The Valetta *1863, P&O steam paddler.*

- so I suppose you didn't send my cartes?[2] We had a drive round Marseilles - it is the loveliest town you ever saw, with a perfect climate - it doesn't rain 20 times in a year so that the people nearly live out of doors. There are a great many avenues of trees, fountains etc. and plenty of flowers. I bought a lovely bouquet of crimson roses, sweet violets and orange-blossom off a woman in the street.

We drove to see our steamer in the dock and make arrangements for our luggage going on board when lo! and behold, instead of our expected *Massilia* - we found the *Valetta* - a boat only half the size and with not half the accommodation. The *Massilia* had gone to Toulon, the master said, so we were obliged to pocket our disappointment and go back to the hotel for a six o'clock dinner. I think you would have been amused with this dinner - course after course coming on until I was fairly in despair, I am sure I am under the mark in saying that there were 20 courses. I only tasted 4 or 5 but some people seemed to eat a little of everything. Every guest had 3 bottles of wine set before him and some people drank a good deal, but nobody seemed any [the] worse. Mr Soares complained that French wines are only water and I think it is very well. At 7 o'clock next morning we came on board and found out our great mistake in not bringing chairs where you can lean back, it is a long time before you are fit to sit upright on the ship's benches.

There are many pleasant people on board. I have been introduced to some of them - Mr & Mrs MacFarlane I know best as yet, and my companion Miss Woodington who is going as far as Malta which we expect to reach about 4 today. She is the only other occupant of the cabin - so I shall have it to myself I expect, after today. I am sorry to have so little to tell you owing to my having been in bed nearly all the time. We passed between Corsica and Sardinia yesterday, and I just saw the grand rocky outlines in all shades of sienna colour but couldn't appreciate them. They say the moonlight at night is glorious but that I have yet to see. The ship's officers are extremely kind - always ready to do anything for you. Miss Woodington is very agreeable and so is Mr Soares. If I am well I shall enjoy the voyage extremely, but so far I have felt very poorly indeed and have not eaten anything since I came on board until last night.

We have a good many titled people on board - one of them, [3]Sir Charles Bright is a friend of Mr Soares. He was knighted for laying down the Atlantic Cable and is going to Kurrachee to see about the telegraph being completed between England and India. Though quite a young man, he is married and if no one meets me in Bombay Mr Soares says he will put me under his care to Kurrachee. They have charged me £6.2s.2d for 3cwt. extra baggage, that of course includes what I have here and everything, but it seems a great deal doesn't it.

As it is Sunday we shall have service in the saloon - I hope I may be well enough to sit it out but it is rather trying being downstairs, unless you are lying down.

12 o'clock: I am dressed now and managed to sit the service, so I suppose I may be considered thoroughly convalescent. We have been sailing past Sicily all the morning and I have seen some of the loveliest scenery you can imagine - little towns lying between the high hills and the sea, and beyond all, Mount Etna looking like a white cloud. We are now 92 miles from Malta and the mate has just been to tell me that we shall be there at 8 o'clock this evening.

I am throughly enjoying this delicious day - I wish you could see me sitting under the awning that covers the deck with 50 or sixty people all about, some walking, some talking, some writing - for all are anxious to post at Malta. There are three newly married couples on board - who are beginning to feel happy apparently, now that they have overcome their seasickness. I have been enjoying some sea biscuit for tiffin, in spite of remonstrances with regard to my frugality it is quite a treat to be able to enjoy anything to eat, and one I am able to appreciate.

Sir Charles Bright has just been telling me that he is going to remain several days in Bombay - but that he knows a married gentleman on board who is going on to Kurrachee and that he will put me under his care if nobody meets me in Bombay. I have not found any <u>elderly</u> married lady on board who is good for anything, but I am quite sufficiently well protected and nobody interferes with me, indeed everybody is as pleasant and polite as possible.

I wonder often how you are all getting on at home - now you will be getting dinner. It feels very strange to be so completely thrown out of an old life into a new one, as yet I can hardly realize the difference. Things look quite eastern on board already - some gentlemen have got on their [4]puggarees and white cloth boots. I am comfortable yet in my black silk dress and jacket and white straw hat - the heat is quite pleasant so far although people are beginning to complain.

The telegraph will be quite completed by the end of March so that we can hear from England in 24 hours - won't that be pleasant? There is rather a heavy sea again - but I quite hope not to be ill any more. They are putting up an awning at the sunny side of the vessel in addition to that overhead which makes the deck much cooler.

It has been so rough since I wrote the above that I have laid quite still and consequently have not been sick. The swell is at present immense and I am writing on my back which will account for this bad writing. We shall be in Malta in about two hours so I must close this for the post. My dear love to each one of you - my doubly dear father and mother, brothers and sisters - also remember me to everyone in the house and to Gilbert & Hannah Baker, the Miss Parrys and Robert & Emma especially.

As the light of even this glorious sunset is fading I must say goodbye and am my dear ones,

Your lovingest daughter
Elisa

Notes:
1. The *Valetta*: Registered in June 1853, she was a wooden paddle steamer of 769 tons with a speed of 13 knots, and owned by P&O - the Peninsular and Oriental Steam Navigation Company - for the Marseilles/Alexandria service. She was built of wood because the Admiralty required wooden paddlers for contract mail services to maintain a "uniform high rate of speed" which the authorities did not feel was attainable with an iron hull.
2. Cartes: Carte-de-visite - a small photo (65 x 105mm) which was used as a visiting card and became popular in the 1860s with the advent of photography.

3. Sir Charles Bright (1832-88): the Atlantic cable from Ireland to Newfoundland was completed in 1858, but there were several leaks and breakages and it was 1866 before it was finally operational. London was connected to India (Bombay) by telegraph in 1864, as Elizabeth forecast.

4. Puggaree: the Indian word for turban, a pleated scarf wound round the crown of a sun helmet with the end hanging down behind as protection against the sun.

Elizabeth's journey to India continued by rail - the "Overland Route" - which crossed Egypt from Alexandria to Suez and was established in 1845. The Suez canal was being constructed at this time and completed in 1869. Previously the sea voyage from Southampton to Bombay by the Cape of Good Hope took 84 days, whereas by rail and sea via Egypt it took under four weeks. The boats from England which arrived in India in the autumn at the start of the cold season were unkindly referred to as the "fishing fleet", full of girls hoping to find a husband where European men outnumbered European women by about three to one. It was considered respectable to get married as soon as possible after arrival, often to a complete stranger.

On board S.S. [1]*Malta*
Nov. 28 1863

My dearest Father and Mother

I wasn't able to post anything in Egypt - so left the account of my Egyptian journey until we got near Aden. This evening is dreadfully hot down in the saloon and makes writing quite a labour - but they say it will be hotter tomorrow so I must try to write at least part of my letter tonight.

I enjoyed my Egyptian journey very much indeed. We got to Alexandria about 7 o'clock in the morning, and were very much amused to see the natives come alongside in their boats in all

The S.S. Malta 1863 on the Indian Ocean Service for P&O.

Alexandria.

manner of costume, Turkish, Arabic, Egyptian, etc. We went straight off the boat into the railway carriage so saw nothing of Alexandria except a view of [2]Pompey's Pillar amongst the trees. We went as far as Cairo the first day - at all the stations along the Delta of the Nile were crowds of natives all chattering, shouting and screaming - some of them idling, some selling oranges, sugar canes, water, etc. We got to Cairo about half past four and were taken to [3]Shepheards Hotel in the [P&O] Company's omnibuses - it is a very nice building surrounded by shady gardens - indeed Cairo altogether is a most flowery city with groves of beautiful trees in the squares, avenues of myrtles in flower and masses of large blue convolvulus in bloom - an artist might spend a lifetime in Cairo and find inexhaustible subjects for his pencils.

The groups that pleased me most were those that gathered after dark round the storyteller in the streets. At every corner you might see them with a blazing pan of fuel in the centre and in all manner of costumes and attitudes - listening with breathless interest to the Arab who is telling the story. It was dark as soon as dinner was over, so we left seeing the Mosque until next morning when our [4]dragoman woke us at six o'clock, got us a carriage and we set off in the dewy cool of the morning. I wish I could give you any idea of the dirty, wonderful picturesqueness of the streets - all the shops open to the street and the men busy inside in the midst of the most hopeless disorder - and the street itself crowded by the most wonderful variety of people and donkeys, which the boy who runs before the carriage tries in vain to clear with his stick.

The [5]Mosque is one of the most wonderful buildings in the world - it stands on a hill above Cairo surrounded by the walls of the citadel - it is built outside of white stone but the inside is solid grey veined marble - rising dome within dome to an immense height and carpeted with Turkish carpet of the richest patterns. When I saw it the morning sun shone in through the stained glass windows in the most glorious colours and made the gilding in the half gloom glitter like enchantment. I should tell you that they had red cloth slippers over our boots and most inconvenient things they are. When I came out a man brought me a bouquet of red and white roses and large white jasmine. The view from the platform outside was glorious, close underneath us the picturesque city with its mosques and minarets and masses of green foliage and beyond it the desert with the Nile and pyramids all golden and glowing in the eastern sunrise. There was a very beautiful effect too caused by a sort of mist that hung suspended in the clear air just above the houses and on which the shadow of every minaret and high tower was cast with the utmost distinctness, the houses underneath being visible through.

Cairo from the Citadel (looking west).

25

From Cairo we had a most delicious ride through the desert. There was a gentle refreshing breeze and many fleecy clouds in the sky - just like a glowing June day in England - only the air is so wonderfully light and dry and exhilarating - it makes you feel as if you could fly, almost. There is not the slightest sense of oppression in the heat at this time of the year.

At Suez we had time to dine before we went on board. The dinner was laid out al fresco, under an awning in the square court which all Eastern Inns enclose and which is generally very pretty with its orange trees and creepers and parrots etc. in cages. There I got a letter from Harry telling me what I expect you know already that Mrs Lidbetter is not going to leave India until the spring and that he is not going to meet me in Bombay.

We are many of us sitting writing now in the saloon - with four ⁶punkahs going constantly, I have just had to stop mine as it blows the paper about so. The punkah boys are some of them very pretty and look most picturesque as they stand in the crimson curtained doorways. They wear scarlet turbans and white tunics and are very dark indeed with lovely eyes. I send you a sketch of the one opposite me - he is as graceful as a fawn. Most of the crew of this vessel are black Hindoos and south sea islanders. The captain is a grand looking man, very fierce-looking, but really full of all sorts of fun - they call him Magnificent George in the P. & O.C.

The lady who shares my cabin since we left Suez is called Mrs Pye. She has only been married 3 months and is going out with her husband, she is a nice girl I think.There are a good many ayahs on board taking care of the various babies- they look very comical squatting about wrapped in their striped shawls. We have had very little illness on board considering the heat - one gentleman has had a rather sharp attack of cholera but nothing serious, and he is now well. I bear the heat well, better so far than any newcomer - some of the ladies suffer greatly from headache and lassitude. Last night it came on dreadfully rough and our portholes had to be closed at 3am. so we had no air to breathe and I felt quite poorly this morning but am better now. The temperature in the cabins is 86F with the portholes open so you can imagine the rest.

We have a great deal more fun here than in the other vessel - music and singing in the evening, and one night we tried some quadrilles - but it was so rough that we didn't manage very well. In the morning we play backgammon or chess or cribbage or anything else - unless we are reading or dozing. This is the laziest life you can imagine - I shall be glad to be on shore again. Tonight we shall be in Aden I expect and shall most likely land in the morning for a few hours. Then in 8 more days we shall be in Bombay if all be well. We are all greatly excited today with the prospect of over-taking the French steamer which belongs to the Messagerie Imperiale - she left Suez six hours before us and now we have sighted her - and are going our very hardest to overtake her before we get to Aden. This will be a national triumph and we shall play the National Anthem and cheer immensely and be very proud of our superiority - for we have gained fully an hour every day. Our excitement yesterday was a water wagtail which flew all the way from land and came on board - pretty little thing - I can't tell you how touching a thing of that kind is here.

How very very often I think of you all there is no telling. I was thinking about home last Sunday evening especially and of all the happy Sunday evenings we have spent together, but I hardly ever feel dismal. I am wonderfully cheerful and happy - one would not think that I was a stranger in a strange land. Everybody on board is quite kind and friendly; I know nearly all the ladies and as many gentlemen and like everybody pretty much alike, as my manner is. There are 2 or 3 young ladies going out to be married - one of them, Miss Fricker, to a gentleman whom she has never seen - just think of that, and the worst of it is that she is rather more than usually plain-looking.

It is a general complaint that there is nothing to write about on board ship - so that although I fear my letters will disappoint you I must stop. I shall be able to do a great deal better when I get to India - here there is no settlement and nothing to talk about and the vibration is so great as to render the act of writing a nuisance. I am, my dearest Father, Mother, Pollie, Gulie and all, your most loving daughter, Elsie.

Dear love to Gilbert and Hannah, Robert and Emma and the Miss Parrys.

Notes:
1. In 1840 P&O signed an agreement with the government of India to provide a regular service between Suez and Bombay. The

S.S. Malta was registered with P&O in 1848 as an iron paddler and converted to a screw steamer in 1858 with a new gross tonnage of 1,942 and a speed of 13.5 knots. She sailed with the Company in the Indian Ocean service.

2. Pompey's Pillar, Alexandria: A red granite column about 100 feet high, erected in honour of the Emperor Diocletian in A.D. 296, and still a tourist attraction today.

3. Shepheard's Hotel: Opened in 1841, this was one of the first hotels to be built in Cairo, and the most renowned. In the last century there were many enlarge-ments and rebuilds but it was completely burnt down during the nationalist riots of 1952. The present-day Shepheard's was rebuilt on another site in 1956-7.

4. Dragoman: Interpreter or guide.

5. The Mosque: On top of the Citadel is the Mosque of Mohammed Ali Pasha, famous for its view and the most familiar landmark in Cairo.

6. Punkah: A large swinging cloth fan on a frame.

From Elizabeth to her parents on her arrival in Bombay. The phosphorescence she describes so vividly was a very typical experience for passengers to India.

S.S. *Malta* Dec 10 1863

My dearest Father & Mother

I have not chosen a very good time for writing to you. Seeing that we are expecting to arrive in Bombay in a few hours - and everybody is running about in a fine state of excitement - I have just finished my packing, and have nothing to do now but send you a few lines telling you of my movements. I shall have to wait 24 hours in Bombay for the Kurrachee steamer, but as there are some new steamers on the line we shall get there in 48 hours if weather and everything else favours us.

I had a very bad night last night on account of the cockroaches. Mrs Pye woke me about one o'clock telling me that one had got into her back hair and then run down her back and arm and flown away to my part of the room so we stayed awake a long time and never slept soundly afterwards. You can't imagine the horror of the ship cockroaches. They are quite as big as this [draws insect about 3ins. long plus antennae] and fly as well as walk, some are twice as large but they are exceptions. A gentleman the other day had his ear nibbled and people are constantly getting their hair eaten, but I mustn't talk any more about about them - the very idea nearly makes me sick.

As a contrast to the foregoing, I must tell you how glorious the Phosphorescence was last night. The sea was so smooth that every star had its reflection, but of course we ploughed one deep wave at each side of us and the edges of it curled over in the most dazzling brilliance you can imagine. Then every minute some fish or other shot through the water leaving a silver wake in the darkness - you never saw anything lovelier - it reminded me of the halo and its reflection in "La Martyre" but a hundred times brighter: I stood watching it for an hour I should think.

The other night a flying fish came in at one of the portholes and Mr Price (a missionary who is going somewhere into the interior) got it cooked for me on some rice and he and I and Mr Ranken ate it and very nice it was. Mr Ranken is one of the nicest gentle-

29

men, a widower with one beautiful child whose likeness he showed me the other day. He often plays with me at chess and backgammon. Chess was all the rage yesterday, the different champions playing for the final championship - I haven't heard the result. We stayed an hour or two at Aden and were right glad to get away again. The hills near are all volcanic and the ground is all sand and scoria without a tree or indeed a blade of grass to be seen. Then it was fearfully hot and I got such a headache with the screaming of the natives and the blazing of the sun, that the sea was a positive relief.

I think I told you that a Mr Giles was going to meet me at Bombay and that I am going home with him for the night - I believe it is the same Mr Giles who was such a friend of Willie's at Manchester, he was married about a year ago. Some of the girls on board are going to be married either today or tomorrow, I am not sure which, I don't envy them the fuss and am very thankful that the [1]lines have fallen to me in pleasanter places, also that Harry isn't going to meet me here.

Bombay, Dec 11. We got in yesterday about four o'clock and a gentleman came on board for me who told me that Mr Giles was ill and had gone into the country but that he had been deputed to act for him and was going to take me to his house. His name is Mr Cameron and he, his wife and sister have been exceedingly kind to me. It was quite an exciting scene on board when the vessel stopped - dozens of native boats crowding round each with eager English faces looking out for their friends - husbands for wives, fathers for children and bridegrooms for Miss Palmer and Miss Fricker. One young wife had a first baby that her husband had never seen and it was pretty to see his curiosity as he held it up to look at.

Mr Giles's carriage was waiting at the [2]Bunder to take me to Mr Cameron's, that gentlemen being obliged to go back to his office for the mails. It was a drive of about 3 miles to the bungalow and a very pretty drive too. Bombay is on an island and you hardly ever get away from the sight and sound of the sea. We passed many pretty houses standing amongst the luxuriance of their trees and shrubs but none prettier I think than this one. When I looked out into the courtyard this morning I thought how you all would have liked to see what I saw, especially in December. All the glass of the windows were thrown wide open and most of the lattices, and under the acacia trees the native servants in their scarlet turbans were cleaning the carriage, etc.

The compound is full of lovely flowering shrubs - scarlet, yellow and white, the most brilliant and graceful I ever saw, something like acacias with crowns of flowers. The native huts stand amongst the trees, pretty mat-covered buildings with porches and lattices, and the loveliest clean air and sunshine over all. You get quite a fairy-land impression at first. The interior of this bungalow - the first I have seen - is very handsome, all the doors and windows stand wide open and are provided with dark colored wooden lattices to keep out the heat, which of course stand open too in the delicious cool of the morning. The walls are colored pink - not papered - and hung with pictures. The furniture is all of that heavy carved kind that looks so handsome. The floor is covered with matting with a handsome Turkish carpet in the centre. Mrs Cameron and her sister are very kind to me. The former is very delicate - she lost her health at Calcutta. She looked like a regular Indian last evening in her white muslin wrapper - lying at full length on the carpet with a cushion for her head.

You will have heard by Telegraph of my safe arrival before you get this - I hope. I enjoyed the last half of my journey very much. We are just going down to the Kurrachee steamer, many of my fellow passengers are going up. I am always thinking of you dears, especially yesterday when I first set foot on Indian soil, led carefully up the Bunder steps by Mr Cameron. Mrs Cameron is hurrying me so goodbye my dear dear friends and what a blessing it is that I have got safely so far. In great haste, your loving Elsie.

Notes:
1. Lines: Her marriage lines. She illustrates this with a quote from Psalm 16 v6 "The lines are fallen to me in pleasant places".
2. Bunder: Landing place or harbour.

Karachi, situated on the Indus river, is now the principal seaport and the largest city in Pakistan but in the 1860s was known as Kurrachee, in the Sindh (or Sind) province of India. It has quite a pleasant climate for most of the year. May and June are the hottest months when the temperature rises to over 90F, and the average rainfall of eight inches falls mostly in the months of June, July and August. January and February are the coolest months with an average temperature of about 56F. Following the British defeat in Afganistan, Sindh was annexed by the British in the winter of 1842-43, as a reprisal, it was suggested. The conduct of General Napier in this affair was parodied in "Punch" with the famous pun in which he sends a message to Lord Ellenborough saying "Peccavi" - meaning "I have sinned". Karachi and the Sindh became part of Pakistan after partition with India in 1947, and is a predominantly Muslim country.

On her arrival in Karachi Elizabeth writes excitedly to her sisters, Mary Ann, known as Pollie, and Gulielma.

Kurrachee Dec. 14 1863

My dearest Pollie and Gulie

I feel as though I could write to you now with something like satisfaction which was impossible on shipboard amongst all the shaking and tossing of the boat and the endless chattering and interruptions of the fellow passengers. We made the quickest passage up from Bombay that the boats have ever made - only 50 hours - so that we were in the harbour long before Harry even thought it possible - however he came rushing down in Mr Alsen's dogcart and I hadn't long to wait before he was in my cabin, from which I had determined not to stir until I saw him. Several of the officers on board had been promising themselves great fun from seeing our meeting, but they were disappointed.

I need hardly tell you my dear ones that such was not my case - I was more than repaid for my little journey when I had once heard his voice and seen his face - he is just the same as I remember him - but rather stouter as you may have heard before. He spent a long delightful evening here but we told him not to come this morning as I thought I should be somewhat tired and stupid - and indeed I don't feel quite myself yet. I have a sort of weak feeling with not having taken any exercise for so long - it was generally too rough to walk much on shipboard - a few turns up and down sufficed.

It is rather too soon yet to begin to tell you how happy I am - you will find it out I daresay from time to time, but just at present it is where words cannot reach it. Harry arranged for you to have a telegram from Bombay announcing my safe arrival but I am afraid that Mr Cameron has omitted to forward it - we are very sorry for this - as it would have saved you a week's suspense.

I had a most kind reception from Mrs Lidbetter and Miss Mosley and already feel quite at home with them. The two little girls Maggie and Amy are bright charming children with dark Indian eyes - I slept in their room last night. It is a large airy room and what strikes one very much in an Indian bungalow - the doors are wide open all night - so that we could hear Mrs Lidbetter when she spoke. This morning she came and got into my bed and read some of her English letters - the children sitting on our knees and Miss Mosley running in and out with our coffee and biscuits. Cid the dog slept at the room door and took the opportunity of some bread being left at the top of the stairs to help himself to a good slice of it.

This morning I have been amusing myself greatly as I often did on shipboard with watching the natives at work. For instance, I should like an English carpenter to see the man at work in the verandah making a meat safe for Mrs Lidbetter, sitting on his heels as they always do here and deliberately contemplating one bit of wood and then another and occasionally marking them with a pencil or hammering in a nail. After they had gone on for an hour or two in this way, Mrs Lidbetter came up and found they had done it all wrong, and with a good pull or two - the whole thing came to pieces! But the funniest thing of all was to see the native sailors washing the decks. They balance themselves on their heels with a bit of rag in one hand and a pail of water at some distance to which they continually refer themselves, and dab a few square inches round with the rag then get up and go to the water and so on, but it never seems to strike them that time or trouble are of any value at all.

Dec.17. Did I tell you that all my luggage had been left behind me in Bombay, owing not to any carelessness on my part - for all the

Malta passengers are in the same case. The luggage went to the customs and wasn't passed in time to come on by the Kurrachee - so I am in the pleasant condition of having only this black silk dress to wear morning, noon and night, and it is in a very dilapidated condition, and the worst of it is that I see a great many people, callers etc, - they come in morning and evening - and besides we have company to almost every meal. Mrs Sheldon and her little baby [1]tiffed with us yesterday and Dr & Mrs Bean dined with us at 7, 2 or 3 gentlemen coming in after dinner. We played bagatelle and wandered about the verandah - and at 10 they went away. Today we are going out to dine with Dr & Mrs Skues and are to play "croquet" which has just become fashionable here. Near this bungalow are some holy tombs and consequently numbers of [2]"fakeers" and pilgrims and a great deal of "tom-tomming" which is a detestable sort of kettle drumming.

Harry has taken me one or two drives, once I went to see our bungalow - and into the downstairs rooms. It is a most charming little place, the very prettiest I think in Kurrachee and in the best quarter of the town. It looks something like this outside but I will make you a proper sketch some day. This little projection at the bottom is the porch through which the carriage drive runs. Harry has furnished it beautifully. The drawing room is a charming little room - at least little for India where the rooms are so immense. It has glass doors opening into the verandah with color'd glass panes and a doorway into the next room and that again into another so there is quite a vista. I will tell you more particulars when I have seen more of it - at present of course I have only a confused idea of the contents of the room.

Mr Alsen came in when I was there and he has been to call since. He is very delightful, just the sort of nice looking pleasant man one likes at once - he has been to see me since. A [3]Parsee Gentleman, the broker of Mr Lidbetter, came the other evening to dinner. He has got a beautiful present for me, but I haven't seen it yet. It is a ring with a very fine diamond in it - quite a valuable one. These Parsees are all very rich and can afford to make handsome presents.

Since I came, Harry has been elected a municipal commissioner - that is equivalent to town councillor or something of that kind.

As he did not offer himself he is pleased, and so of course am I - although I can't help thinking that it is more an honour to the municipality than to him! I wrote a note to Mrs Church the other day accounting for the delay in the arrival of her parcel and had a very pleasant note in return this morning - a "chit" we call them here - I am already getting quite an adept in Hindustani in a small way - such as asking for bread and water, etc. We find it quite impossible to fix any day for the wedding until my baggage comes and Harry too has to wait for his clothes from Bombay. I fear that it cannot be managed before the 31st of this month, altho' I have expressed my desire to have it on the day you are keeping it still. Of course it is no use contending against impossibilities - and you will I am sure understand that my great wish was that you should not be disappointed in this matter.

I heard yesterday evening that my baggage had arrived and very glad I am to hear of it, for I am tired of my dirty black silk - the only doubt now is about Harry's clothes coming in time - but it is quite fixed for the 31st. I have a list beside me of 40 people whom Mrs Lidbetter insists upon asking in spite of our united remonstrances but she says that she is quite certain that they will not all come - the list contains 3 doctors, 4 clergymen and some officers and of course all their wives. There are no unmarried ladies here - so that the gentlemen will preponderate dreadfully but that always happens in India. Of course Harry has many bachelor friends too and that makes the discrepancy greater. Miss Mosley is going to wear a white embroidered muslin and the children white spotted muslins all with mauve ribbons alike - they will look very nice, I don't doubt.

People continue to call and make themselves generally agreeable. I will tell you who my friends are when I have made a selection - at present my ideas on the subject are rather chaotic. We are going out to dinner on Christmas Eve - I fancy it will be a party as we are not asked until 7 o'clock - we should go several hours before dinner in any other case. I like late dinners very much as you know - and of course we take nothing after dinner - no tea or supper so it comes to the same thing; here every body takes their servant out to dinner with them to wait. Harry has given me such a delightful little 4"chokra" for my own with a scarlet turban and blue coat - and such a nice little face.

35

[5]Beaumont Pease called the other morning and yesterday he came to dinner. He has been away from the 3 friends for 7 months but is going to rejoin them in Bombay - I am so sorry that I have quite missed them. I suppose they would be in Bombay when I passed through but I had no clue to their whereabouts and no time to seek them as you may imagine.

Have I told you about the parrot here? It is one of the cleverest and noisiest I ever heard - it sits swinging all day long under the trees in front of the verandah, imitating the crows and [6]minas and sparrows, calling the servants in one voice and another, coughing, laughing, chuckling, talking Hindustani and English with equal facility. It has caught my voice exactly and imitates me with a painful exactness. Yesterday I was singing "There is rest for the weary" in the verandah and it began to make such a ridiculous caricature of it that I couldn't go on for laughing. Harry has bought me a guitar - just fancy! and I really mean to learn to play it - it is easy to acquire and it certainly will make my singing more tolerable.

We went to Mr Sheldon's little church yesterday evening. There is no morning service in English, and I have not made my appearance at the big church yet and shall not until after Thursday week [which was to be her wedding day, 31st December]. How I wish I could have you all there my darlings. Harry does not let me feel lonely, and my friends here are very kind but of course I shall want you - especially my mother. How I shall want to hear about the 24th at home and how you all looked and what you did. It is very disappointing not to have our celebration on the same day, but it doesn't seem possible and I can hardly press it, can I? I am so looking forward to your letters next mail - it seems so long since I heard of or from any of you - you are all well, aren't you - and quite reconciled to being without me. I can hardly fancy your going on just in the old way when all is so changed about me, "faces and footsteps and all things strange".

The climate at this time of year is something perfect as long as you keep out of the sun, and that one <u>must</u> do - they tell me - although I am rather apt to be careless in the matter. The view through the door is quite English - a vista of grass and trees, most cool and pretty looking and the constant cawing of crows completes the

36

illusion. The birds are perfectly tame here. The sparrows walk and fly about the drawing room constantly. They are prettier than our English sparrows and most inquisitive impertinent little creatures. The minas are like starlings and like them can be taught to articulate very distinctly.

All the doors and windows are hung with chicks which are transparent reed blinds. The glass is kept open and these closed to admit the air and moderate the light and heat - they are very pretty things and deliciously cool. The verandah has them taken down at this time of year and is open with white pillars like an English portico. It has matting laid down and runs along the front of the house and the two ends. At one end the 7"dhoizi" sits sewing all day long - mending the clothes, making dresses, etc. and doing everything beautifully. The rooms are divided by arched doorways with screens which open and shut like doors - they are light oak frames filled with fluted scarlet stuff and look very pretty.

Dec. 22. I have just been writing all the invitations for our wedding - about 40 altogether, but Harry and I are living in hope that they won't all come. It seems a great pity to make such a fuss and Harry does so dislike it - he is just like Father in that respect.

My luggage all came safely yesterday. The wooden boxes Harry had sent to the house and took out all the things there. The others came up here and I got out my wedding dress and all that I wanted beside - everything is in perfectly good condition, and not the smallest thing is broken - all owing to Father's beautiful packing. Harry is very much pleased with the presents you sent him - I expect he will tell you so himself, although he is very busy just before mail time and has not been at all well these few last days. I tell myself a hundred times a day that there is no occasion to be anxious but you know how fidgetty I am when there is anything the matter with anybody - it is only just the fuss and anxiety and so on, I think, that I have been the cause of his undergoing.

Now haven't I written a good long letter - I feel rather pleased with myself do you know. Give my dear love to everybody who enquires after me - especially Gilbert and Hannah to whom I mean to write next mail, Robert and Emma, the Miss Parrys, Mr & Mrs P. and also remember me kindly to all the young men - the servants, Mary Knowles, Mary Wheatley, Margaret Hudson, etc and tell the latter that the sea is a pretty considerably jolly mode of transit!

My dearest love to you two sisters and the two dear brothers from your loving Elsie

(Dear love to John & Maggie)

Notes:
1. tiffed: had lunch, from the word tiffin
2. fakeers: fakirs, religious mendicants or beggars
3. Parsees: Descendants of Persian Zoroastrians who fled to India from Muslim persecution in the 8th century. Usually wealthy and successful businessmen and chiefly living in western India.
4. chockra: houseboy or servant
5. Joseph Beaumont Pease was a young Quaker businessman who had recently been widowed and arrived in India in 1863 to promote the use of coke as fuel for river steamers. In this connection he would have been especially interested to meet Henry Jacob.
6. minas: mynah birds
7. dhoizi: or derzi, native tailor

Henry Jacob gratefully confirms that Elizabeth has arrived safely in Karachi, and she writes a loving and personal note to her mother, using "thee" and "thou" in the Quaker style of address.

Kurrachee Dec. 18th 1863

My dear Friend Bartholomew Smith

Elisa tells me she wrote to you from Bombay, and as I informed you in my last [letter] I made arrangements for you to receive a telegram as well. I very much fear however that the latter has been neglected, as the gentleman who promised to meet your daughter in Bombay was unfortunately ill and was obliged to depute the office to a friend. Elisa did not I think suffer personally from this arrangement, and seems to have had no difficulty in getting aboard the Kurrachee steamer and proceeding on her voyage. She arrived here last Sunday the 13th after an unusually rapid passage - the Bombay steamers seldom reaching Kurrachee before the 15th. She is in excellent health and spirits, and so far I hope does not regret the very important step she has taken.

Mrs Lidbetter welcomed her to her home most kindly and I am sure spares no pains to make her comfortable - a much more fastidious person than your daughter could not help feeling at home with such kind friends, but Elisa possesses such a happy talent for adapting herself to circumstances that she already seems almost like an old resident.

Had I the slightest doubts about any feelings towards your dear daughter, they would have disappeared upon our becoming personally more closely acquainted. It would be idle to praise her to you who know her so well and love her so dearly - I can only say that the more I see of her, the more difficult I find it to understand how you can ever have borne to part with her. As to expressing a tithe of what I owe you for entrusting her to me, that is quite out of the question. I hope you will not think I write coldly on this subject or that I do not feel very deeply, because I cannot find words sufficiently strong to express my meaning.

Dec 23rd I am sorry it could not be conveniently arranged for our marriage to take place on the 24th as you seemed to wish, but Elisa's things only came to hand from Bombay yesterday. It is now fixed for it to take place on the 31st of this month, and we shall thus begin the new year together. We look hopefully together towards the future although fully sensible that prospects much fairer than ours are not secure against shipwreck. All the happiness that springs from mutual trust and love will at least be ours, and for the rest, we shall I trust meet any difficulties or troubles as they arise as bravely as may be, comforting each other with an affection and confidence which no earthy change or misfortune can alter.

Elisa tells me you all think of me with affection - I seem to have done little to merit either your love or your confidence, but I have had abundant proofs of both. It is a great drawback to my present happiness that I cannot hope to make your personal acquaintance for a long time - perhaps for many years, but with Elisa beside me I shall not find it easy to forget all your goodness, and in the meantime I must trust to her to bring us as closely together as is possible at such a distance, and without the advantage of personal intercourse. Your daughter assures me she is very happy and I really do think she is not deceiving herself - nothing on my part at least shall be wanting to make up to her as far as a husband's love can do for all she has given up for my sake. I will write you again by next mail, and in the meantime with very kind regards to Mrs Smith,

Believe me
yours very truly
Henry Jacob

Please thank Mrs Smith and Pollie very warmly on my behalf for their kind presents. I forgot to mention that Elisa had a balance after paying her expenses from England of £25 odd, which I put in the Bank for her. I thought you would like to know that her funds held out so well. H.J.

My darling Mother

As the other letter will go round [to relatives and friends] I suppose I must just write thee a little assurance that all thy best hopes for me and my happiness with dear Harry are likely to be realized. I wish you could know how entirely worthy he is of the best and deepest love I can give him - and not only worthy of it but just the sort of man whose worthiness is his least attraction, so that what I felt for him at a distance bears no proportion at all to what I feel for him now, he says, and I think that the week we have had already of each other's society would have rewarded a lifetime of waiting - so that I feel quite ashamed to have earned the prospect of lifelong happiness so easily, though it seemed hard at the time.

We will try hard to help each other on the right way - we are neither of us inclined to live carelessly, and I trust that loving each other so much will make us love God more who has given us so much to be thankful for - to me so very much more than I deserve.

Mrs Lidbetter is very kind - it was such a comfort to find her here - I hope thou will write and thank her, Mother dear. I am so sorry we couldn't be married on the 24th as you wished - but it seemed impossible. Harry has not got his clothes and Mrs Lidbetter hasn't got her preparations made and Miss Mosley and the children are going to be Miss Hollis's bridesmaids tomorrow, and it is too much to ask them to be two days in succession. Mr Sleeman is to be Harry's best man as Mr Alsen couldn't make up his mind to the publicity of the situation, so he will be second.

Don't be anxious about my health, dear Mother. I believe with ordinary care I shall do very well indeed. And now goodbye once more with dear dear love and many kisses - one for every night that I have gone to bed without one for Father and thyself. Thy most loving daughter, Elsie.

Note: Extract from *The Friend*: Marriage 12mo 31 1863, at Trinity Church, Kurrachee, HENRY JACOB, jnr, to ELIZA HARRIS, eldest daughter of Isabel and Bartholomew SMITH, Thirsk.

India – January to December 1864

Elizabeth and Henry were married on 31st December 1863 at Trinity Church, Kurrachee, as there was no Friends Meeting House. It was not until 1860 that "marrying before a priest" was no longer a cause for disownment, but a relaxing of the old rigid rule, as long as the Friends concerned were still attached to the Society, was allowed. It was obvious that for Elizabeth and Henry to have a properly registered and legal marriage this was their only choice.

Elizabeth Harris Jacob (née Smith) 1840-1916.
Photo: J. Milner, Ilkley, Yorkshire 1868/9.

Henry Jacob 1836-1905.
Photo: J. Milner, Ilkley, Yorkshire 1868/9.

My dear Father & Mother

It is a great privilege to be able to address you thus at last, but it makes me feel more than ever how much I have to regret in being personally unknown to you. I want to feel towards you as your daughter's husband should do, but it is so difficult to do this when I have never seen or spoken to you.

As I tell Elisa, she has a great advantage over me in this respect as she knows my parents so well, and indeed the only drawback to our present happiness is the fact of your being strangers to me. Perhaps the difficulty I now feel in addressing you may partly wear off in time - at all events it will have the effect of making me the more anxious to see you, and you may be quite sure I shall not feel my happiness complete until my dear wife's family are as well known to me as my own.

Elisa seems to have told you everything there was to be told, and has left nothing for me to add. Many thanks for the kind messages contained in your letters to Elsie - indeed I am very anxious to have you love me but you must necessarily be laboring under the same disadvantages as I am with respect to you. It will indeed be a happy day - when I meet those who loved my darling long before I knew her, and who have given her to me with such entire trustfulness and confidence.

You will not think this note very short or cold will you? I am sure you will see my difficulty, and will not think me wanting in love or respect for you. As I said before, the only way I can show this until I see you is by loving your daughter as she so richly deserves and showing myself as little unworthy of your trust as may be. Give my dear love to my new sisters and brothers who I hope won't think of me quite as a stranger, and with a large portion of the same for yourselves.

Believe me
Your affectionate son
Henry Jacob

The mid 19th century saw a huge increase in reading material to meet the needs of an increasingly literate public. As this letter to Pollie shows, Elizabeth took a lively interest in literature and was keen to read the latest novel or short story. Books by authors such as Dickens, Trollope, and Thackeray were published in part-issue instalments which developed into the weekly or monthly periodical, and included current affairs and other items of general interest. Dickens' All the Year Round at twopence a week at the cheaper end of the market, nevertheless included work by renowned writers and was extremely good value.

Hesse Villa
Kurrachee Jan 25 [1865]

My dearest Pollie

As according to custom I was addressing the envelope to thee before commencing my letter, I couldn't help thinking how queer it was for thee to be "Miss Smith" - the very thing I so recently was myself. How dost thou like the position of eldest daughter, dear? Does it feel very different from being second, or is the difference merely nominal. Of course, when I come home again I shall be less than the least of all, in fact merely a visitor, won't it be funny. I am writing to thee because I have a long delightful letter of thine to answer. I shall make a rule to address mine to those who write to me. I believe Harry means to answer dear Mother's and Father's to him, so I will leave them quite out of the question at present. He is going to be away until 7 o'clock this evening, as Monday is mail day, so I have a long day to write my letters in.

We have quite got into the way of getting up at 6 o'clock and having a good walk before the sun gets hot. This morning we went round by camp, part of the way being across the plain which is covered with sand and enlivened by jungle trees and patches of a shrub very like heath of which I send you a pattern. Then we undress and bathe and dress again and have breakfast as soon after nine as may be, and then hibernating, and then Harry trots off to office. Carlo either goes with him or stays with me. Carlo is a dear affectionate dog, a sort of setter/spaniel, liver and white. He sleeps in our room which is a bachelor habit of his. The other dog, Dick, is a smooth old white terrier, and a great jealousy exists between the two. If Carlo won't eat anything and Harry calls Dick,

Hessie Villa
Kurrachee Jan 25

My dearest Pollie)

As according to custom I was addressing the envelope to thee before commencing my letter. I couldn't help thinking how queer it was for thee to be "Miss Smith". the very thing I so recently was myself. how does thou like the position of eldest daughter - dear? does, it feel very different from being second. or is the difference merely nominal - of course, when I come home again I shall be less than the least of all - in fact merely a visitor, won't it be funny. I am writing to thee because I have

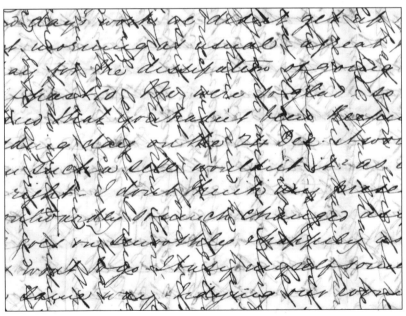

Sample of letter above, showing writing at right angles to save paper.

Carlo looks over his shoulder and gobbles it up as fast as possible. There is a third dog about the house, a brown fat puppy called Moses, but he lives with the servants, indeed he belongs to a recent butler of Harry's and isn't admitted into good society.

I don't think I have described the house to you yet and I don't know how to begin. There are three parlours on the ground floor and a little room opening out of the centre one, which Mr Heslewood calls a boudoir, where we generally sit, as the drawing room is too smallish for ordinary occasions. The said drawing room opens with a glass door out of a little entrance vestibule, and when you enter you have on your right hand four windows in pairs this shape [drawing of two round arched windows] which look towards the next bungalow's compound over a little bit of our own. In front two glass doors leading leading into a verandah matted and closed with [1]chicks, they have tinted or stained glass panes all round and are hung with white curtains edged with pink. On your right hand is a doorway into the centre room hung with similar curtains. These look very pretty against the pale green paper. The walls are hung with several nice photographs of Harry's choosing, and now I must begin again at the entrance door.

Under the four windows is a couch covered with light green chintz and another beside you on the left hand - all the furniture is carved black wood and the chairs match the couches. Between the verandah doors is a bookcase with closets underneath and at each side of the other door is a pier table on each of which stands one of the statuettes, and on one of them two hyacinth bulbs are coming on very well. There is a pretty chandelier in the centre of the room with three lights and plenty of lustres hung with green and white paper leaves and under it the centre table covered with books and in the middle a very pretty ground glass vase set with red and green glass knobs. The table has a very handsome cloth and stands upon a square of bright coloured Brussels carpet which nearly covers the matting of the room. Opposite one of the couches stands a sofa table with books, inkstand, bible, etc. upon it and opposite it another little table with the bookstand full of books. The ceiling is of ribbed wood which is a great improvement upon most of the ceilings here which are of whitewashed canvas. It has just struck me what a grand field for fresco painting this would be!

46

The middle room is quite unfurnished, containing only my easel, a very jolly one indeed that Harry got made for me at Keamaree and I haven't used it yet. The room opens as before mentioned into the drawing room on one side, into this little room with a door and two windows on another, into the dining room on the next and into the little passageway which leads upstairs on the last, also with a door and two windows, so you see every room here is public to every other. The dining room has a table, chiffonier and chairs, two windows looking towards the servants houses in the compound, two glass doors like the drawing room ones leading into the verandah and a door for the servants to bring themselves and dinner in by. This little room which is about 8ft. wide by 14ft. long has six windows and two doors. Those looking towards the sea have venetians but no glass so that we can let the wind in without the glare of the sun. Between us and the sea on this side are the compound, the railway and a long stretch of sand occasionally overflowed by the tide.

Proceeding upstairs, we remark but one principle room - containing 13 windows and two doors, of these one leads into the bathroom and the other into a box room and up onto the roof by a glass door in one of the towers which give our little house such an imposing appearance. The bed stands in the middle of the room and looks very pretty with its net mosquito curtains hanging from the ceiling. There are three wardrobes, two dressing tables and two washstands, and the floor has some pretty strips of carpet over the matting. Altogether our little house is very pretty and satisfactory as I hope you have gathered from my description, everyone remarks upon its Englishness and a gentleman said that it looked like a villa in the suburbs of London. Certainly many much larger bungalows look comfortless in comparison to this dear little home or ours.

We have had a great many callers since last Monday week - some every day except yesterday. The cake is all gone save a little which is cut up in the cake basket awaiting its fate. Today such a strange old gentleman called - a Mr Nuneham who they say has made a vow never to cut his hair or beard until he sees his wife again, at any rate there they are hanging in thick grey masses all round his shoulders and giving him a most weird appearance. The Lidbetters are coming to dine here on Monday. We called there

47

last evening but they were out, however we met them afterwards in camp and asked them to come. They have been very kind in lending me one of their horses, Treasure by name, who I rode before I was married. He is a nice little bay horse and goes nicely beside Harry's chestnut. We are often troubled for want of a ²gharry of our own. There is not one in camp to sell which is fit to use and Harry has to hire them, which is tiresome and expensive, until he meets with one. Treasure has a way of bolting down certain roads unexpectedly which I am not au fait enough to prevent, and which has a very absurd effect, otherwise I manage him as well, and rather better than could be expected.

We ride sometimes to Clifton or Ghizree along a road which runs through a plain of mixed sand and salt sometimes but seldom visited by the tide. From the hills at either place you get close to the shore and have a nice near view of Kurrachee harbour, Manora and the oyster rocks. I have been twice to the government gardens which are beautiful shady tropical looking places, where you can get beautiful vegetables and flowers and walk under palm and banyan trees, to say nothing of banana, guavas, mangoes and pomegranates. The latter are very pretty trees with flowers like a very handsome carnation which look beautiful in bouquets. There also are roses, wallflowers and mignonette and there the band plays sometimes in the evening. We went last Sunday evening and stayed until after the moon had risen - you can hardly imagine the glory of these eastern nights. Everything the moon shines on looks like burnished silver, not grey as in England and the planets and Sirius etc. look like little moons. When the nights get a little warmer we shall take to sitting on the roof after dinner and having coffee there, at present we are glad of a more sheltered situation after sunset and prefer comfort to romance.

Next week we must begin to return the calls which have been paid us, won't it be a nuisance but I expect Harry will go with me whereas I have had to receive all these people alone. He certainly stayed at home one day, having a bad cold, but that day nobody came. You would have laughed to have seen me one day with two of my engineer fellow passengers who came to say goodbye previous to going up-country. They were in a most congratulatory and complimentary vein - both verging on old fogeyism and given to waving of their hands and uttering of set speeches evidently composed beforehand, which was hardly fair considering that I had to make impromptu replies. They drew up their chairs close to the sofa whereon I was sitting and made themselves (dis)agreeable by the space of half an hour. This has been my worst experience, all the other bachelors came singly and I managed them quite easily, particularly as most of them were friends of Harry's and consequently "good fellows".

I intended to fill a great part of this letter with an account of our visit to Sandi and behold I have filled two sheets already. I see I must get another, particularly as I haven't referred to Pollie's letter yet. We went up to Sandi by the quarter past 6am train on Tuesday morning to spend the day with a Mr Donaldson who lives in a bungalow for which Mr Lidbetter is agent and which wants repairing, so Harry's was a visit of inspection as well as pleasure. Sandi is a native village in the jungle through which the Kotree railway passes. Mr Donaldson is about the only European resident and he is living there in order to try an experiment in irrigating the land and trying to make it bear cotton etc. It certainly has a hopeless look at first, a desert of wild cactuses and other prickly trees, the ground a mass of small creepers, but there is the river Mulleer in the wet season and all the year round water to be had for the boring, so Mr Donaldson has made a windmill for raising the water and canals on a small scale to carry it about and hopes to get larger spaces of it cleared and watered year by year. At present he has patches under cultivation and gets good grass and potatoes. The worst of it is that not only he but all his workmen are continually prostrated by Sind fever, caused by the marshiness and consequent malaria.

This is not the flowery season but I never saw anything handsomer than the hedges of castor oil plant which grow out there (after being planted), they have a leaf like an immense "lady's mantle" and spikes of flowers something like horse-chestnut blossoms but with this beautiful peculiarity that hardly any two are the same colour, one white, the next crimson of all shades, then lilac or yellow - with the dense foliage you cannot imagine a handsomer shrub. It grows 12 or 14ft high in a single season. We have some small ones in front of our bungalow which I'm afraid don't get properly watered or they would grow faster, I think. Moses dances about them too much, he smashed a little aloe the other morning only it was Harry's fault for dropping him upon it. We stayed at Mr Donaldson's until 6 o'clock and then went to the station - miserable places these Indian stations are - without any seat or shelter. The native porters, if any, wear no uniform and don't do anything to distinguish themselves as officials, in fact railway planning or executing is yet in its infancy in Sind and performed on the most economical principles.

We had arranged to go at 8 o'clock to see some amateur theatricals by the officers of the 109th - [3]"Kenilworth" was the piece - they burlesqued it very cleverly or rather acted the burlesque. The ladies voices were of the most masculine though and their faces didn't bear a glass being brought to bear upon them. After our hard day's work we didn't get up to walk next morning as usual - a great penalty to pay for the dissipation of going to bed at half past 10.

We were so glad and so relieved to find that you hadn't been keeping our wedding day on the 24th December. As it is, it is alright, I don't think my present life is outwardly so much changed as you think, all goes on smoothly and happily as my life was wont to go. I busy myself something in the same way tidying our room after breakfast, reading or working, mending stockings once a week for my thin ones want mending already, taking the clothes from the [4]dhobie with Ahmed's assistance, putting them away, also once a week. Perhaps the great difference in my day's employment consists in the number of times that I look at my watch - to see how long it wants to Harry's coming home. It is perfectly nice after that, his dear bright face lights the house up. The vignette is something like him minus all the niceness and hands, niceness which the photographers here evidently can't appreciate.

In answer to thy enquiries about my portmanteau and carpet bags, I had endless trouble with them, but the books were much appreciated. Half the old clothes are still on my hands lying deep at the bottom of an ottoman in our room. The creosote bottles and things leaked and made horrid smells and I never used these, and the lump sugar pulverized itself and pervaded everything and there was a nice mess. The white silk umbrella was very useful but the puggree is so heavy I can't wear it, it gives one a headache. Mr Soares has gone back to England already, his stay in India has been of the shortest, people of his colour are sadly looked down upon here and are glad to escape back to the free and equal system.

I like [5]Henry Kingsley's story very much so far, but wish it wasn't going to be such a suicidal affair. [6]Mrs Lirriper hasn't arrived out here yet which is fruitful hot water for all parties, but I have seen the review in the [7]Saturday [Review], I do want to read it. Yes, I think we see all the magazines, [8]Cornhill, [9]Macmillan, [10]All the Year Round once a week, [11]Fraser, [12]Blackwood, [13]Athenaeum, etc., except Good Words and Harry thinks of writing for that. Some of these of course come months after time from the library, but we take the four first per mensum.

I hope you have had a happy Christmas - Tom will have gone back to school before you get this letter. I suppose as usual he has increased in wisdom and stature. Had you any visitors - I think it is time that Maggie thought of coming to see you again. I suppose she won't write to me until I write to her. I did not take [14]Masson's Essays dear, I quite gave up all thoughts of such a thing long ago. I think I packed up very honestly and found nothing yet that doesn't belong to me. I am so glad that Robert is helping Father - he is so capable that if he takes to it he will be a real helpmeet. I am sorry baby May troubles Emma still. I should love to see my pet Nellie walking by her important little self - she mustn't tumble down stairs tell her, or Auntie won't love her. It will be dear Mother's birthday soon [29th January] I remember, and she will be 50 years old, many happy returns Mother darling and don't lose any teeth or get pale or thin or anything before I come back again.

I like thy letters perfectly Pollie darling, every scrap of news in detail especially is like a nugget of gold. I am only sorry I can't write the same and tell you all about Harry, what he says and does, so that you might realize him better. I can only tell you that he is quite the best and dearest husband that ever was, also as clever as he is good, almost, and that is saying a great deal. Don't let Father meddle with the Telegraph wires, Harry says the shock would kill him, and he has been nearly put out cold too once with an electrical machine. I hope the New Year's tea party came off well. I shall expect some report of Father's speeches now that I can't hear them - well, some of you learn shorthand. What are

Gulie and thee going to do with riding skirts, mine has had to be shortened and even now sometimes catches Treasure's feet which is "neither agreeable or salubrious" to quote an engineer friend of mine, by name Mr Brasher, of whom I try to make Harry jealous by quoting him and threatening to fall in love with him if I ever see him again, or something to that effect.

My dear love to you all, my dear Father and Mother, brothers and sisters, believe me as ever your loving sister, Elsie H Jacob.

I hope you are not anxious about my health - it is perfect so far - and I suppose I am gradually getting imperceptibly acclimatized so that the hot weather won't come before I am prepared for it. Harry was never ill, even to begin with, so that I am no exception.

References to place names around Kurrachee (Karachi):
Keamaree: Kiamari, an area of Karachi near the harbour.
Ghizree: Ghizri, part of Karachi leading to Clifton, which was a popular residential area for the English community.
Kotree: Kotri, a village about 90 miles north of Karachi, which at this time could be reached by the railway built in 1861.
Manora: a peninsula at the harbour mouth, which can be seen beyond the Oyster Rocks mentioned by Elizabeth.

Other notes on the text:
1. chicks: split bamboo blinds.
2. gharry: a horse-drawn taxi available for hire.
3. Kenilworth: probably a parody of Sir Walter Scott's novel, published 1821.
4. dhobie: washerman.
5. Henry Kingsley's story: possibly *Ravenshoe* (1862). Henry Kingsley (1830-76) was the younger brother of Charles Kingsley.
6. Mrs Lirriper: a reference to *Mrs Lirriper's Lodgings*, a story by Charles Dickens for the Christmas 1863 issue of of *All the Year Round* , which sold more than 200,000 copies and was the most popular thing he had written since *A Christmas Carol*.
7. *The Saturday Review*: an influential periodical founded in 1855, which ran until 1938.

8. *The Cornhill Magazine* (1860-1975): a literary periodical specialising in the serialisation of novels.
9. *Macmillan's Magazine* (1859-1907) published a wide variety of material, including poetry, serialised fiction and articles on travel and politics.
10. *All the Year Round* was a weekly periodical started by Charles Dickens in 1850 as *Household Words* (until 1859) and which he edited until his death in 1870.
11. *Fraser's Magazine* (1830-82): a general and literary Tory journal of high standing.
12. *Blackwood's Magazine* (1817-1980): a monthly review.
13. *The Athenaeum* (1828-1921) - a monthly review which was eventually purchased by the New Statesman.
14. Masson's Essays: David Masson (1822-1907), biographer, critic and journalist, founded and edited *Macmillan's Magazine*. His *Essays Biographical and Critical* were published in 1856.

From Elizabeth to her mother and younger sister, Gulielma. She confesses to a little homesickness but is determined to make the most of things.

Kurrachee
Feb 8 1864

My dearest Mother and Gulie

I hope you don't object to being both killed with one stone for that is the way I propose to deal with you. The mail that brought your letters was dreadfully late, nearly a week - and at last the boat came in during the night and the letters came unexpectly while we were dressing and breakfast was very late that morning.

You can tell nothing at home of what it is to get letters out here or how lovingly and longingly we think and speak of England as "home" - people here don't speak of their bungalows so - when they say so-and-so is "at home" they always mean in England. The chief amusement of people out here is grumbling at everything Indian and comparing them disadvantageously with home

Gulielma Smith 1846-1909.
Photo taken at Birkenhead 1863.

Isabel Smith. Photo: Sarony,
Leeds 1860s.

things. I have begun upon the principle that this is a mistake and that it is best to take everything as it comes - though indeed I hadn't need complain, for the most powerful magnifying lens brought to bear upon my lot could only find one hardship in it and that is being separated from you, and this is made up for - as far as anything can make up for it - by my dear, ever dearer, husband.

I have got on very badly today with my letters. Two friends of Harry's called - Mr Heslewood and Mr Bolton - and I asked them to have tiffin with me, which is infinitely preferable to having it alone. They sat and talked over it and smoked after it for an indefinite time, and consequently I was greatly hindered, and the mails will be made up tomorrow evening.

Mrs Sheldon, to whom you will remember I had a letter of introduction, has got smallpox and her little boy is staying at Mrs Lidbetter's. It is dreadfully prevalent here and everybody is getting vaccinated. Harry was done the other day with very trifling effects but Miss Mosley had a very sore area something like ours long ago. The disease is a sign of favour from one of their goddesses - Maratha I think - and the consequence is it spreads dreadfully and now the Europeans are suffering from their horrid superstitions.

Harry and I got photographs the other day with Carlo lying in front looking so beautiful, but we look anything but, and are going again - you shall have the first fruits of our success. Carlo has been quite poorly for a day or two with sore ears and Harry has been in low spirits in consequence, at one time he feared he was going mad but he seems getting nicely better. I went, after our being photo-graphed, to Mrs Lidbetter's to spend the day, dined with them at 2 o'clock, then they sent Treasure down to our house and Harry and I had a delightful ride, and then I dined again at 7 at home. Delightful though my ride was, it was rather an unfortunate one. My net came off in cantering and got lost, then all my hairpins came out and my hair descended, so we put into Mr Alsen's bungalow for repairs.

I spent a very pleasant day last week with Mrs Wilson, wife of the Agra bank manager - with whom Henry Hipsley and his friends were so pleased - she is a very young lady of about 18, married some time and very pretty. Harry came in to tiffin as their office is quite near to Mr Wilson's and Mrs Lidbetter and family, Mrs Wilson's papa and a Mr Oliver came to dinner - also the Rev. J Middleton with whom I came up from Bombay and is a very pleasant Scotch clergyman. I was quite amused at dinner time with counting the servants who waited at table, for you must know that here everybody takes their butler out with them. There was our butler, Mrs Wilson's ditto, Mrs Lidbetter's ditto, and the three gentlemen had each a butler, nine in all to wait upon 11 people there. They all looked so picturesque with their dark faces, black moustaches and turbans, no two of which were alike, some scarlet, some white, some dark blue, and all in long clean white linen coats and bare feet. Their dress is always clean and starchy - I think the speciality of the dhobie is for starch. Last time my dresses and skirts came home so stiff that it required some strength to bend them - but they get things beautifully white and all are got up as carefully and elegantly as Mrs Smurthwaite herself could desire.

Along with your letters I had a nice long one from Gilbert and Hannah - I do hope that George Baker is recovered - what a sad thing his illness is. No doubt he reduced himself by overwork into a fit state for catching the fever.

Very often in Tuesday and Saturday evening we drive to the government gardens to hear the band play - here is Harry - au revoir!

Henry Jacob is a devoted and attentive son-in-law.

Kurrachee,
Feby. 9th 1864

My dear Father & Mother

I have certainly not treated you well in not sooner replying to your kind letters received last mail, but Elsie I trust will make excuses for me and tell you how very little time I have for letter writing. The sun rises so late now that our morning walks seem to consume nearly all the time till breakfast, and the remainder of the day is taken up with going to office and dinner - after which in India it is really difficult to help being sleepy and indisposed for exertion.

It was very good of you to write me so kindly and affectionately. If anything could make up for the fact of our being personally unacquainted, such letters as yours would. As I told you before, this is the only tangible drawback to our present great happiness in each other's society. You must not think, as you seem to do, that we are so wrapped up in the present as to be regardless of the future. We have both lived long enough in the world to know by experience how very unsatisfying even the very highest earthly happiness is, and that love is no protection against earthly evils or misfortunes, although it makes them more bearable. For myself, I am always - partly by temperament and partly from other causes - more apt to take too gloomy views of life than the contrary, and I feel already very deeply the responsibilities of married life. So my dear parents, you must not think I write of us as of a pair of butterflies - forgetful of everything in heaven or earth but the enjoyments of the moment.

Elisa's health I am thankful to say, continues excellent. The process of acclimatization has been very easy, and she seems thoroughly well, strong and happy - likes the climate and the country, and helps me to take a cheerful view of everything, even when I feel otherwise disposed, and grumble at our distance from all our friends, and the small chance there seems of our coming together. Surely no-one ever had a more loving trustful wife. But as I said once before, it is needless to praise her to you who knew her and loved her before I did. She bids me tell you that she washes and salts the butter every morning, and is in fact busy with that operation now, kneeling on the floor opposite me and much engrossed with her work. I hope you won't think this a very short letter and Elsie has not improved it by taking it up in her buttery fingers and making a mess of it. She bids me say she is very sorry.

Give my dear love to Pollie and Gulie and my little brother Arty, of whose cleverness Elsie has told me so much - also to Tom, and with a large portion of the same to yourselves, believe me Your affectionate son, Henry Jacob.

We are preparing a little parcel of presents to send home, viz - 2 embroidered cushion covers for mother, 1 silk embroidered Llama shawl for Gulie, 1 sandal-wood work box for Maria Taylor, and a drab cashmere shawl for my mother.

HJ
You dear good people - I wish I knew you all and lived nearer to you.

Kotree
Feby. 22nd 1864

My very dear Father and Mother

I am such a bad hand at describing places that I have asked Harry to tell you about our little trip to this place, the river terminus of the Sind railway. Harry has some friends here whom he wished to see, and so we planned to run up by train, and down again the same day, but Mrs Wood at whose house I (that is Harry) is writing, asked us to stay longer and offered us a bed. We very readily consented, and have been here since Friday. This is Sunday morning and we intend to return to Kurrachee this afternoon.

Kotree is a delightful little place on the banks of the Indus. It consists of a native village which I have not visited, and some twenty or thirty European bungalows, all beautifully embowered in trees. There are no carriages in the place, as there is no place near worth driving to, and the houses are so near each other that people do not require any means of conveyance. The roads in consequence are more like gentleman's avenues than high roads, beautifully shaded with lovely tropical trees, and nicely fenced in with low walls made of mud bricks and whitewashed.

Everything here is built of mud. There is no building stone, and the mud when well mixed with chopped straw is very tenacious, and makes excellent walls, only they have to be very thick. All the houses are flat topped which gives them a charming oriental appearance, and the shade of the trees, the coolness of the climate (at present) and the lovely flowers have kept me in a constant state of pleasurable excitement since we came up.

Mr Wood is the Agent and Superintendent for the flotilla of river steamers which run in connection with the railway, and his house is the largest and best in the place. It is a charming combination of English and Indian ideas of comfort. The rooms look quite English with their papered walls and open fireplaces, but they are surrounded with broad cool verandahs for the warm weather. At present the weather is quite cool, and we have had a blazing wood fire every night since we came.

59

The house stands in a nice garden laid out with walks and beds and plenty of large spreading trees, principally mango trees, which have a very rich foliage, and at this season of the year are covered with a greenish white blossom. There is one particularly fine mango tree at the rear which has a lovely creeper growing up into it like this. [Pen and ink sketch]. I never saw anything so beautiful in its way. The creeper is one mass of magenta colored flowers and it festoons all over the tree with huge pendant wreaths hanging nearly to the ground. Such a glorious feast of colour is worth travelling many miles to see.

Near the tree is a real india rubber tree, I never quite believed before that caoutchouc really came out of trees, but it is a fact after all as the enclosed small piece of india rubber will show you. Harry cut some incisions in the bark and the juice immediately began oozing out just like rich cream. He caught some in his shaving paste pot, and after a few hours it got quite solid. We would have got a larger piece, but the juice oozes very slowly and keeps drying on the bark, and obliging you to make fresh cuts, so that it is rather a slow process.

Another delightful thing is the sweet lime trees, which have the same blossoms as oranges, growing out in the open air and enough to supply wreaths for a 100,000 weddings - only think of that!

25th So far was written on Sunday morning after breakfast and it is now Thursday and we are safe back in our own nice little house. But I must tell you more about Kotree. Harry would have finished this letter at the time it was begun, only I persuaded him to come out in the garden and read [1]"Sartor Resartus" as we sat under the shade of the creeper. Then when Teufelsdrockh was just about leaving the university, it was time to pack up our things, after which came tiffin, and the train, and after four hours' railway journey we got home in time for dinner.

Well, Mr Wood's house as I told you is on the bank of the river, and the two gates of his garden open on to the towing path, or at all events on to a roadway which runs along the bank. The Indus at present is very low, and does not look very significant, but during the inundations it is a rushing mighty stream about twice as broad. When we were at Kotree, the "pulla" fishing season was just commencing and it was very amusing to watch the men at work. The pulla is a most delicious fish, like a salmon, and with similar habits (only its flesh is white) and at this season of the year it seeks the upper rivers in order to spawn.

This rough sketch will show the process. The men lie on their stomachs on large flat earthen pots of this shape and paddle themselves out into the centre of the river, where they turn their heads to the current and allow themselves to float gently down with the stream. They hold their net perpendicularly. It is fixed on a forked pole, and has a string attached to the lower part which the fisherman pulls when he feels a pulla touch the net, and entangles it. He then immediately pulls up the pole and sticks the fish through the gills with an iron pomiard which he carries in his belt so as to kill it, and then pops it into his "chatty" or pot. As soon as he has floated down to the fishing limits he paddles ashore and runs up the bank again with his big pot, pole and net on his head. The river is all dotted over with these pulla fishers and just at present we did pity the poor fellows. Their legs must be so miserably cold.

On Saturday evening when we were walking along the bank of the river just at sunset I did long for father, in order to hear his remarks about the loveliness of the coloring. The mangoes, date palms, bananas and other tropical trees, were cutting clear against the western sky, all ablaze with the most delicately graduated tints of rose and amber, dotted with a few lovely buff colored clouds. But indeed, I often wish for father at times when the sky coloring, always rich in this climate, is more than ordinarily beautiful. One never sees such delicate tints in an English sky.

You cannot think what a charming contrast the tall feathered date palms are to the rounder topped and more English looking mango and babul trees. The top of Mr Wood's house is flat and we used to sit up there of an evening and admire the trees from about the height of their largest branches. But it is of no use trying to describe things which must be seen to be appreciated, and perhaps our appetite was whetted by the bareness of Kurrachee. The garden is full of rose trees, which are in blossom nearly all the year, but unfortunately not in February. The place must look lovely when they are in flower. It is pretty enough even without them.

On Sunday at church (such a nice little church it is too) the clergyman being absent, the service was read by one of the

61

congregation who got into the <u>pulpit</u> for the purpose. He was a little man, and his head only just reached above the pulpit rail. When he knelt down the book was almost over his head, and you cannot think how absurd the little thing looked. He read very badly, too.

I am painting a portrait of Harry to send you, along with some nice presents we have for you. I think I am succeeding very well. When I had laid the first coat on to the face, I put in the background <u>all round</u>, forgetting the body, and my dear husband looked like a whiskered cherub. However, I saw my mistake in time, and after various loud lamentations in my usual manner, wiped off the superfluous paint without difficulty.

Now I am going to write the rest of this letter myself as Harry says he has helped me enough. *[Change of writing at this point as Elizabeth takes up the pen for herself].*

I am sure Harry has done far more justice to Kotree than I could have done, I am such a bad describer, and I have very little left to say. As he has mentioned the little things we have got for you, I may as well tell you what they are, and then you won't expect anything different. We got Mother two embroidered cushion tops; Gulie a white ²chudder as she hadn't one before, only it is a very pretty one with broad white silk embroidery; Pollie a sandalwood card case; Father a pot of preserved ginger; and we are going to get Tom a pair of slippers and Artie a puzzle or something of that kind. We will send them as soon as I get the portrait of Harry finished. I think it is going to be a good likeness and he thinks so himself.

We quite like Mr Glyn - he has just been here to breakfast and has gone with Harry to the office. We were greatly pleased as usual with your dear long letters. What grand times you have had skating. The weather here <u>feels</u> dreadfully cold although I suppose the thermometer varies from 5OF to 7OF morning and evenings, yet one feels it dreadfully by contrast with the middle of the day which is very hot out of doors. As for me, I am <u>never</u> too warm - I get so thoroughly ³starved in the morning that I hardly get warm all day. I can only wear one dress this last day or two and that is my black and white woollen check. Those who have been some time in the country hardly feel the cold while we newcomers are nearly starved to death - it seems as though it ought to be the other way, but Harry says they get so thoroughly heated in the hot season that they never cool properly. We dined at Mrs Lidbetter's last week - Mr Glyn was there also. We had great fun with [4]squails - it is quite a fashionable game here now. Coming home it was so clear and cold in the moonlight that I could almost fancy I saw frost on the ground.

I am very sorry to hear of cousin [5]Pollie Tuke's having had such a bad accident and also about poor Charles Mooler. I am glad you all got safely off the ice. I am very sorry that Emma and the dear children are not well yet. She has a great deal of trouble with them. I wish they would settle down into a healthy state and let her rest at nights. What a sad thing cousin [6]Charles Brown's death is - what will become of poor Emily and all her children, and [7]Ellie Spence too, poor dear child seems to be in a sad state. What a catalogue of misfortunes you had to tell last time.

I hear the bheesti/waterman upstairs in the bathroom which reminds me that I want to tell you how we get our water. It all comes from two or three government wells and is brought in skins on the backs of bullocks. The skins are something the shape of bagpipes, one hanging on each side. There is only one well in our camp fit to drink but the others can be used for bathing, etc. The bullocks here are beautiful creatures with humps on their backs, large brown eyes and hanging ears and some of their horns are nearly a yard long. The larger and handsomer kind which are used for yoking are generally of a pale dove colour and sometimes pure white. I never cease admiring them. You never see a horse or donkey in a cart here, the bullocks draw everything. Natives who can't afford carts carry <u>everything</u> on donkeys - it seems a very slow way. One native who had a contract for raising a railway embankment took the whole of the dirt and rubbish and stones in little bags on donkey back. He found it cheaper than hiring carts. Just fancy the labour of doing it by handfuls in that way, and the trouble of filling and unfilling the bags.

My dear love to everybody, in which Harry unites.
I am, my darling Father and Mother, your loving
Elisa

Notes:
1. *Sartor Resartus*: by Thomas Carlyle (1795-1881) originally published in *Fraser's Magazine* 1833-4.
2. chudder: or chador, large shawl worn by Muslim or Hindu women that covers them from head to foot.
3. starved: meaning "frozen", a bit of north country dialect.
4. squails: game with small wooden discs propelled across a table or board.
5. Cousin Pollie Tuke: the daughter of Bartholomew's Smith's sister Mary Ann who married Daniel Tuke in 1837.
6. Cousin Charles Brown (1816-64) was the son-in-law of Deborah Smith, another of Bartholomew Smith's sisters. He married Emily Spence, Deborah's daughter, in 1852.
7. Ellie Spence, b. 1849, was the daughter of Alfred Henry Spence, the brother of Emily Brown (née Spence).

Elizabeth is enjoying life in India and in spite of the heat has "never been tempted yet to cast my flannel petticoat". English women continued to wear their European clothes, at this time the crinoline, and made no concessions to the weather.

Hesse Villa, Kurrachee
March 24 1864

My dearest Gulie

Every letter I get from home seems more interesting than its predecessors and I don't know to which of you the palm should be awarded for raciness and patience combined. If I had only a tithe of any of your capacities for letter-writing what wonderful epistles I could send home, as remarkable for novelty as for humour and more conspicuous for length than either, but I haven't any power of describing anything, and feel my deficiencies more every time I write. If Harry could only spare time to do duty for me you would be indulged in a constant [1]"feast of reason and flow of soul", instead of being fed, as it were, in a sort of ravenish way in small mouthsful.

I am writing under a cloud too, today, for [2]"my gudeman's awa" for a much longer time than usual. He is going to a funeral at five o'clock when he ought to be at home, and as the cemetery is five miles off, the chances are that he won't be home to dinner at 8 o'clock. It makes the day awfully long although Mr Glyn has good-naturedly promised to come in after office and play croquet with me to keep my spirits up. We find croquet quite a nice amusement, I must acknowledge that, although I scolded Mr J. for his extravagance in buying the game. You must know that I represent the spirit of domestic economy, for Harry can't see a thing that he thinks I would like without wanting to buy it, which is a very bad thing, financially speaking, and I throw all my influence into the opposite scale. The fact is, I have everything I want to begin with, so there is no virtue or self denial in it.

We had Mr & Mrs Wilson and Messrs. Alsen and Riebe to dinner the other evening and enjoyed our game extremely with two drawbacks, one, the absence of grass, or anything except sand to play upon, and other the short twilight, for we can't go out until the sun is quite low about half past 5, and it sets at half past 6, so one game is all we can manage in one evening. Mrs Wilson spent the day with me, coming to tiffin. She is a very sweet looking pleasant girl, only 18, although she looks older and has been married some time. Early marriages are very common here, I know several married ladies who are only about 16 but they look much older here than they would in England.

I was very much pleased with the boys' letters - Artie's was beautifully written, quite a juvenile imitation of copperplate. I must manage to send them at any rate a few lines each. And I must also write a word to [3]Gilbert and Hannah Baker. I was so very glad to hear of their little son's arrival at last, I should think they will quite agree with the proverb "better late than never". You should act that, bring them in in the first scene without the baby and with it in the 2nd, it would require no better illustration.

Before I begin in order to answer thy letter, I must ask you while I remember whether you will do some little commissions for us. I am sending with the picture etc. per next mail (another delay I am sorry to say) my white dress which I want you to get dyed violet and made up again by Miss Metcalf. I suppose it will have to be done the same, so will you ask her to make me a black net or lace [4]berthe to wear over it - it will then be useful to me. I never want anything so grand as white moire and when you are sending it back will you enclose a set of block-tin dish covers, a small set of japanned tea trays (either 4 or 6 of each will do) and a small electro-plated teapot of moderate price. We should also be very much obliged if you would undertake the trouble of bottling us a couple of doz. bottles of rhubarb, green gooseberries, etc. occasionally. We pay a great price for tart fruits here and we thought if we could get them from you at the cost of the fruit and bottles we should save 50% when the carriage is paid. None of the native fruits are fit to cook and one wants fruit in this climate - fresh as well as preserved (not sweet I mean by fresh). The *Ann Buckle* isn't in yet with my boxes but she is daily expected. Will you include all these things in one account and send it by post, please, when you know what they come to. I hope you don't think us exorbitant in our demands upon your time and trouble. If there is anything we can do for you in return you must let us know, and you won't ask in vain.

Since I last wrote to you we have got a pretty little phaeton, not exactly the thing we wanted as it has no hood, and therefore isn't good for going to the office in, but it is a delightful little thing for evening drives. It is made of dark basket work and is quite low and very comfortable. It is like nothing for Harry's horse who looks very handsome in his new harness and goes beautifully considering how seldom he has been driven before. So you may imagine us with our [5]ghora-wallah in his red turban and blue coat perched on a little seat behind, folding his arms a la English footman. There are very few people here who are strong minded enough to acknowledge that they can only afford to drive one horse, nearly everybody has a pair. Thou would be delighted, Gue dear, with the beautiful Arab horses here, they are as common as any other kind and are beautifully handsome and spirited and gentle. Last time I rode Mrs Ross's horse it was dreadfully frisky and ran away with me once or twice, galloping over the plain and prancing about. Fortunately, Harry wasn't there to see, although it was his absence that caused all the mischief, for Maggie Lidbetter was with me on Treasure - and my horse was dreadfully frightened of its strange companion and determined to get away from it. Fortunately the chief point in my horsemanship is my faculty for sticking on, and I didn't feel at all unsafe except in the anticipation that the horse would throw itself down in some of the gullies on the plain; I got a good shaking and that was all.

Last week we went to the Catholic School anniversary, it is the only good one here, and all classes of children go to receive purely secular instruction. It was very like a school treat at home, made more interesting by seeing the mixture of colour from the pink and white English children down through every grade of yellow and bronze, to the blackest little imps you can imagine. The children sang and recited beautifully and we were greatly pleased. I send you The Sindian that you may see the reply I wrote to the editor of a rival paper and the master of a rival school, one or both of whom commented very severely on the children's performance, particularly on their repeating "When taken, to be well shaken" which he said came out of a very wicked book called "broad grins" which contained many improper pieces and must have been put into the hands of the innocent children. As none of us had ever heard of the book, I thought it would be as well to write and say so and inform him what an innocent place the said piece occupied in ordinary school books. The second letter is by Harry, signed Sackree-wallah (woodman) and the other bit marked is the editor's.

I suppose Sarah Ann's wedding will be over long before you get this. I should like my congratulations to be presented to her in a cordial mamer, in my mamer in fact, which is all that can be said! I am glad you like Miss Blakely, I like the list of her attributes decidedly. Some day I hope to make her acquaintance. I am sending the you the rummest photograph of Harry and self. I wish you distinctly to understand that my much-to-be-admired husband has not got a pug nose, or that generally pugnacious look in ordinary life, as you will see when you get my reliable likeness of him, our being taken together is his notion. I still retain my former prejudices in favour of single blessedness. The reason of my fat shaky look in the standing one is that a fly kept hopping on and off my nose all the fifteen seconds and I was shaking with laughter, thereby slurring poor good Harry who couldn't imagine what was the matter and thought I had got the [6]ague. I have got on my native silk dress - made myself - which accounts for its bagginess about the waist. I have been blackening the chair to throw my face off - but I haven't touched it, I think.

Well, dear, I don't seem to have begun answering thy letter yet, although it contains so many noticeable things. I was quite amazed at your temerity in undertaking to sleep with baby Kirton. I don't wonder thou dreamed infanticidal dreams, the wonder is they didn't come true. I heard from Maria Taylor last mail that poor Emmy Spencer woke one night and found her baby dead, wasn't it dreadful. I suppose you have heard of it. What a fine pet Gilbert and Hannah's baby will be for you, I am going to send it a little red frock for when it grows up, if I can get it made by [the time] the box goes to you. What a wonderful success Father's gardening is turning out. I told you of Harry's, didn't I - sowing seeds and every morning digging them up with his stick - and then blaming the crows because they did not grow!

How kind of you to think of sending [7]Woolner's book, just the one that Harry and I have been longing for and for which I was begging in my last letter. It is nearly time Captain L. was turning up, it will be very nice to have him back. We saw or heard nothing of Valentine's Day here. Although Mr Heslewood promised to send me a Valentine from Bombay he never did. I shall not forget you tomorrow (Good Friday). How I shall think of you all and [8]Rievaulx and the beautiful Arden Woods of last year, what a perfect day that was, and you will get dinner on the terrace and run races and very likely go up Slip Ghyll. It makes me awfully homesick to think of it, I mustn't. Harry is to have a holiday, I would rather have him than all my dearly loved moorlands and woodlands, though by setting-to to do it one might easily break one's heart after them. I suppose it would be too much for one woman to have such a husband and home as well, and I have chosen well when all's said and done.

We mean to go to early church tomorrow. We went last Sunday at 7 and found it a great improvement upon mid-day service, a minute of noonday sun just getting in and out of the gharry leaves its effect upon one's head, although it is cool enough indoors generally. At any rate I have never been tempted yet to cast my flannel petticoat, these thick-walled houses with chicks and venetians let in nothing but the wind. If the sun once got in as it does through home windows, I should resign myself to sunstroke and wish it quickly over.

I hope to hear a better account of all the invalids by next mail, remember me very kindly to George Baker. What a long convalescence he is undergoing poor fellow. It must be very trying to an active man like him. We were delighted to hear of your doings on Feb.10. We got precious little fun out of our wedding ourselves amongst an incongruous lot of strangers, and were glad that you managed to enjoy it, although I wish that everybody had been there. Did you remember to send Jennie Lidbetter [probably Jane L, born 1849] some bridecake or Captain L? Mrs Lidbetter said you were sure to send Jennie some, and I'm afraid you forgot. Any attention you can show her they greatly deserve at our hands, and I know they would greatly appreciate. The child will be rather lonely after her Father's departure, I'm afraid.

We much enjoyed poor [9]John Hall's misadventure on the ice - how funny he would look when he came home. Mr Cautly is so thin that I expect he could skate long after stout people of my acquain-

69

tance had given up, which may account for his perseverance. Lest Harry should not have time to answer Father's note this mail, I must tell him that what Lidbetters export is all raw material, cotton wool and seeds. They import manufactured goods such as silk hdkfs, etc., most of which I fancy are made in England. Harry has never seen such a thing as a bandanna since he came. Cashmere shawls even are imported from England and sold as native goods. They can be made so much cheaper by machinery that it pays to send the wool backwards and forwards. Real native things are so awfully dear, that they are only good for curiosities. Although you have it in the wear, my spun silk dress cost a good deal more than people would be willing to pay for the same thing in England. They are worth getting for your own wear but there is no regular market for them here, they only come down by chance.

We are very fortunate here in seeing nearly all the magazines and reviews. Harry takes Cornhill, Macmillan and All the Year Round, etc., once a week. Mr Glyn sends us The Saturday Review regularly and we get [10]Punch, [11]Illustrated London News, Athenaeum, Blackwoods's, etc. etc., from the library. A new periodical comes from there in regular succession every other day, so you may imagine there are a good many about.

I am very sorry to hear of dear old [12]Grandmamma Tuke's death, also of Miss Appleby's. Will you give my dear love to Miss C.... and Miss Marianne and say how sincerely I feel sorry for their great loss in her - she was almost like a mother to them and I am sure they were the best of daughters to her. I am very glad to hear that Mary Ellen Ryott is going to marry Mr J Rhodes - it seems altogether suitable.

I think if thou got to Kurrachee thou would want to stay more than an hour or two, a month or more would be well spent here, I can tell thee. I am beginning to be dreadfully housekeepy and to check our butler's bazaar account. I am taking the items down in a book every evening. I have to shout out every time to Harry to know what he says as his English is even less intelligible than his Hindostanee and he uses both indiscriminately. His first item the other evening was "Mutche" and I thinking he was talking English said "Matches" triumphantly and was making an entry to that effect when he remonstrated "Na, na, Peesh". I thought I had got it this time and was putting down "peaches" - so much, when Harry called out to explain to me that "Fish" was the subject in dispute.

Mr Glyn is coming in so goodbye with dearest love to my Father and Mother, sister and brothers.
I am dear Gulie, ever thy loving sister
Elisa H Jacob

Notes
1. "feast of reason and flow of soul": a quote from *Imitations of Horace* (1733) by Alexander Pope (1688-1744).
2. "my gudeman's awa": from the poem *The Mariner's Wife* (anon).
3. Gilbert and Hannah Baker: an entry in *The Friend* records: To Gilbert and Hannah Baker, the birth of a son Edmund Gilbert on 9th February 1864.
4. lace berthe: a wide collar or cape.
5. ghora-wallah: coachman, or gharry-wallah.
6. the ague: fever or malaria
7. Woolner's book: probably *My Beautiful Lady* (1863) by Thomas Woolner (1828-92) poet and sculptor and one of the original Pre-Raphaelite Brethren, with William Morris and Burne-Jones, etc.
8. Rievaulx: Then as now, the public could enjoy the Rieuvaulx Terraces in North Yorkshire, and the view over Rievaulx Abbey towards Ryedale and the Hambleton hills.
9. John Hall was well-known to the Smith family, and married Elizabeth's sister Mary Ann (Pollie) in 1867.
10. Punch: the famous illustrated weekly comic periodical, founded 1841, at first rather strongly radical, gradually becoming more bland and less political.
11. Illustrated London News: London's first illustrated periodical was founded as a weekly magazine in 1842 by Herbert Ingram and became a monthly in 1971.
12. Grandmamma Tuke (1786-1864): was Mabel, the mother of Daniel Tuke who married Mary Ann Smith, another of Bartholomew 's sisters, in 1837.

Elizabeth's brother Arthur was nine years old at the time of this letter. It was not known in 1864 that the mosquito was the agent for malaria, but they were such a nuisance that people netted their beds at night, unwittingly helping to prevent this terrible disease. Sir Ronald Ross of the Indian Medical Service of the British Army discovered the crucial mosquito-malaria link in August 1897.

Kurrachee, March 24 1864

My very dear Artie

I was greatly pleased to get thy nice letter and to see how very well thou had written it; all the letters were so fat and flourishing, they didn't look as if they were written by a thin little stick of a boy like thee. I advise thee to eat a great many potatoes, for the other day little Amy Lidbetter told her Mamma that she had found out that the more potatoes you eat, the fatter you got, and thy new brother Harry read in a book written by a fat gentleman named [1]Mr Banting that bread, potatoes, sugar, butter etc. make people very fat indeed so he is leaving off eating them, and I should advise thee to eat all the more.

I think thou would be greatly amused to sleep in an Indian bed tucked all round with white net mosquito curtains, just leaving a little hole untucked to creep in at. We creep in as fast as possible, but as sure as can be some mosquitoes get in too. They are small and thin when they first get in but in the morning we see great fat black things sitting on the curtains. The thing is, they have been sucking out of us as much blood as they can hold and when you kill them you get ugly red stains on the curtains and splashes of red on your hands as though you had been murdering somebody or other.

Arthur Smith c1864, aged 10? Photo: John Woodward, Thirsk.

I am thinking today that thou wilt be having a holiday and going in the [2]break to Rievaulx and eating hot cross buns and having dinner on the Temple steps in grand style. There has been a grand Hindoo holiday this week, a very holy time indeed, and in honour of it the natives smear themselves and each other with yellow, crimson and scarlet powder, clothes and all, and this they never wash off until the holy days are over. They also paint stars of all colours on their faces. The old Sindees whose beards are grey have a habit of dyeing them with red and yellow ochre. The old barber, who comes to shave Harry and looks nearly a hundred, has a yellow beard and his brother who came before had a purple moustache and red beard. I only hope they won't persuade Harry to follow the same fashion, for his shows symptoms of greyness already.

With dear love from Harry and myself thy loving sister Elsie

PS. Will thou take the enclosed note to Gilbert Baker's Artie dear for me?

Notes:
1. Mr. Banting: William Banting (1797-1878) was a London under-taker who popularised a slimming diet known as "going Banting", avoiding sugar, starch and fat. It is not clear if he realised the health hazards of being overweight.
2. break (or brake): an open four-wheeled horse-drawn carriage.

Bartholomew Smith was a keen member of the British Temperance League, but Henry Jacob didn't quite share his views. Today temperance seems a quaint outdated philosophy, but drunkeness became a serious problem in the 19th century with industrialisation and the railways, and the need for employees to arrive on time and operate machinery safely. The Quakers were prominent in the temperance movement and were also concerned about the social effect of drink on people's lives and health. In this letter to his father-in-law Harry writes with great tact and diplomacy without compromising his own beliefs.

Kurrachee
April 10th 1864

My dear Father

I cannot allow another mail to go without acknowledging your kind note of the 16th February which I should have replied to by last mail. Elisa is so good in writing letters that my natural indolence is fostered and she finds it difficult to stir me up to attend to the small portion of our correspondence which she thinks ought rightfully to fall to my share. You will have heard before this about the box for Mr Hide, which appears to have been lost through no fault of Elisa's, although it was unfortunate the owner was not more promptly appraised of the disaster. We have had a letter from Mr Hide in Bombay, which Elisa has replied to.

Many thanks for your kind remarks about Teetotalism. The subject is not new to me as I was a total abstainer when a lad, but more mature consideration has led me to different conclusions from yours, probably from the same premises. On sanitary grounds, however, I should not be surprised at myself if I give up eventually the glass of claret and water which forms almost my only indulgence. I don't know why I should call it an indulgence either, any more than if it were a beefsteak, but you good temperance people are so enthusiastic that you almost convince me against reason that there is an eleventh commandment against the moderate use of wines or stimulants. I suppose some of you would go so far as to state this in so many words, but some such opinion seems to crop up in many temperance works, and it is this and the uncharitable tone adopted towards persons who think differently, which more than anything has set me against teetotalism.

The <u>modern</u> doctrine of total abstinence is not treated as a matter on which everyone is entitled to his own opinion, but as a new revelation, with apparently rather more than the authority of scripture, which all must bow down to under pain of a suspicion of heresy. Of course my dear father you will understand I don't write this with reference to anything you have urged. I hear from Elisa and read in the papers a great deal of your noble efforts for the poor around you, and believe that you are engaged in a great and good work of benevolence and reformation which there seems but little scope for here, even if I had strength and faith sufficient for it.

The *Ann Buckle* has arrived and we are anxious to get our boxes, I am especially so to see your pictures. I wish I had had perseverance enough when a lad to have worked as hard in my leisure time as you have done. I wanted much at one time to be an artist but things are perhaps better as they are. I don't suppose I should have risen above mediocrity which would not have satisfied me. Elisa has finished a portrait of me which is a good likeness, but she has rather idealised my heavy features. However, you have a photograph to correct them by. I wish I could paint her in return, but I never did anything in oils, and indeed a pen and Indian ink are my favourite implements.

We are amusing ourselves at present in illustrating a short lyric of Alexander Smith's "Barbara" - each stanza on a separate sheet of white or tinted drawing paper, with illuminated initial letter and a figure etching at the right hand bottom corner. We are rather pleased with our progress, and when the drawings are all completed we intend having it framed for a table book.

I must stop now as the barber is waiting to shave me, and the mail will close in an hour. With dear love to my mother and sisters and little Artie.

Believe me
Your affectionate son
H Jacob

Note: Alexander Smith (c1830-67) was a lace-pattern designer in Glasgow who published several books of poems of a genre satirized by William E Aytoun as the Spasmodic School, verbose, over-blown and sentimental.

A chatty letter from Elizabeth to Pollie relating all the minutiae of daily life.

Kurrachee
April 24 1864

My dearest Pollie

I have done the same very foolish thing of which thou repeats in thy last of having left all the writing to be done on the last day; and I daresay you will be as sorry as I am when you see how poor a production this will be. I had Miss Mosley to spend yesterday with me and that prevented my doing you justice. Thy last was a fine long letter dear, and full of interest to us both as usual. I will dissect it presently.

But first I must tell you that our boxes came per the *Ann Buckle* last week. After a great deal of trouble we got them ashore for the Captain said he didn't think they were on board and Mr Farr (who acts as Lloyds agent while Captain Lidbetter is away) insisted upon going down into the hold to look for them and found them stowed away under a beam. The picture box came without any damage - both pictures and cushions being quite intact. Harry says I must tell you how greatly he appreciates the pictures, both Father's two lake scenes and my head - they are the first oil paintings he says that he ever possessed and he judges of their beauty and value accordingly. They do make our dear little parlour look so gay and are quite a rarity in India.

But the other boxes' fate is much sadder - the books certainly are alright but the juice bottles that were standing upright - not those that were lying on their side - have exploded their corks off and nearly all the juice is lost, flown out among the hay. Perhaps 8 or 10 little bottles are saved whole, none are broken save one that a big plum bottle blew its cork into. The cheese too that Father packed contrary to my judgment amongst the Windsor soap seems to be quite spoiled. The damp from the soap has permeated it and it is quite decayed and soapy, but we are going to try if drying it in the sun will make it any better. The soap too is very damp and cheesy - but we have hopes of it, seeing that it hasn't got to be eaten like the cheese. The hay I think is very much to be blamed for the moist atmosphere. Harry says that cheeses should be packed for exportation in quite dry empty tins. Still, we are so glad that the valuables arrived safe that we don't waste so much regret upon the eatables as they might seem to deserve, and would if they had come alone.

Yesterday morning Harry and I got up soon after five and set off to Keamaree to meet the steamer by which Captain Lidbetter was expected up from Bombay, as we heard the gunfire announcing its arrival. When we got to the wharf we found Mr Farr had gone off in the *Skipjack*, Captain Lidbetter's boat, so we had to take a native boat which went very slowly and when we got to the *Comorin* and Harry went on board, Mr Lidbetter was not there so we had a four miles drive back in the blazing sun for nothing.

The *Skipjack* is a very nice little sailing boat, and the other night Mr Farr, who is a thorough sailor and has made voyages with Captain Lidbetter, took us out in her by moonlight. He and Mr Glyn came to an early dinner at half-past 5 and as soon as it was dark we set off in a hired gharry for Keamaree and found the sailors had gone home to bed, contrary to orders, so they were sent for and blown up. Meanwhile a soaking wet coolie who had been up to his neck in the water carried us aboard in his arms and all the dirt came off him with being so wet and made my clothes horridly brown and dirty. When we were once off we had a delightful sail - sang songs and enjoyed ourselves very much for about 2 hours, then we drove home very sleepy & tired & ready for bed. I didn't envy Mr Farr who had a long ride on horseback after. Mr Glyn lives close by.

Harry and I are going to spend a few days at Clifton with Mr & Mrs Wilson - it is quite close to the sea and very breezy and pleasant now that the weather is so hot. We shall take Ahmed with us, as they have not many servants there and live in a sort of picnic fashion - all the food and water has to be carried up from Kurrachee so I daresay it isn't so much fun for the servants. We are expecting to go on Tuesday morning; I shall enjoy having a nice girl with me all day.

I have been very busy lately beginning some night shirts for Harry - of which I invented the pattern as I don't know how gentlemen's night shirts are generally made. I compounded it of his day shirts and my night dresses! Am I not clever? Also I am making some toilet covers and crotcheting a very pretty fringe for them.

Yesterday Mr Farr sent me by Harry a beautiful canary in a chinese cage - it is such a funny little thing with a tuft of green feathers on its head that spreads in a flat circle over its eyes almost, so that it looks up rather like a little Skye terrier. It is a beautiful singer, but this morning it is so pleased because I gave it a bit of watermelon that it will do nothing but eat.

Totty is so tiresome, she has got a horrid old bone and is trying to hide it in my dress - she is nearly always running after me holding my dress or shawl or something in her mouth. She did such a funny thing the other morning - she has her breakfast of bread and milk while we are having ours and I suppose she thought there wasn't enough for she took the saucer in her little teeth and came running to me with it - but just then came in Ahmed and shouted at her and she let it drop on the floor. I suppose she had seen us hand our plates and thought she would do the same.

Mr Alsen and Mr Riebe have sent us some nice bouquets from their garden lately. The other morning Harry and I were going out when one came and we told the Hamal [servant] to put it into water until we came back - so he plunged the whole thing head first into a deep tin of water with only the stalks sticking out. When I came home I found the delicate flowers, roses and oleanders and jessamine had lost all their scent and nearly all their petals.

Mrs Lidbetter has been buying six dozen bottles of sweetmeats lately for her children, and she brought me three bottles last week consisting of rose, ginger and lemon lozenges. They are very nice - the only fault is I eat too many of them but that evil will correct itself because they will be all the sooner done and then I shall have no further chance of spoiling my appetite.

The other evening Mr Samuel Giles of Bombay dined with us and I discovered that he is the same "Sam Giles" that cousin Willie lived with for so many years and used to talk so much about. He was delighted to hear about Willie all that I could tell him and desired his very kindest regards to him - will you ask Maggie to tell Willie this when she writes, also that Mr Giles is married to his cousin Annie Godfrey whom Willie may possibly know, and has a very fine little boy whom he extols endlessly. Both he and I were very much struck with the coincidence of our meeting, who were familiar with each other's names years ago. He is a rather pleasant man but has been unlucky in business and has just lost an expensive lawsuit. I think this is all I know of him. Mrs Giles was confined at Mrs Lidbetter's and lived there for three months before they went down to Bombay.

I was very much pleased to get Emma's letter, it was good of her to write who must have so little time. We were charmed with Artie's little poem - Harry thinks it as good as the average of magazine productions - certainly it couldn't be worse than some. We were delighted with the "Saturday's" review of Martin Tupper's "Litharo". By the way, I have just remembered that the mail came in late in the evening and we didn't get our letters until midnight, it was about one o'clock when we read them with difficulty by the dim lamplight but that was a better alternative than waiting until morning for we are both of us very impatient people and can't wait for things.

We are so sorry to hear of dear Maria Taylor's illness - we heard from her too by last mail but it must have been written while she was well I think - she said nothing of being ill - but a good deal of going out in the snow etc. You mustn't forget to let us know how she is, for I don't suppose James T will think of writing. I am glad Sarah Ann's wedding went off satisfactorily and that she and the bridegroom thought better of his determination to sit still. I am very glad that George Baker is out again, please remember me most kindly to him. I have not even mentioned my dear "old folks at home". I make up for it by thinking about them - my dearest love to both Father & Mother. You may be sure Harry joins with me in my letter, or rather I join with him, for he quite denies my right to hold property of any kind - he's an awful Turk.

My dear Pollie, Gulie, Tom and Artie, I am your loving sister and brother
H & E H Jacob

Note: *The Saturday Review*: see letter 25th January 1864. Martin Tupper (1810-89) was a prolific and popular writer of verse and prose but his numerous works are now largely forgotten.

An exciting visit to the popular tourist venue of Mugger Peer (or Magar Pir) to see the crocodiles. Elizabeth also describes an earlier visit to a Sindee village to view some old tombs.

Kurrachee
May 19th 1864

My dearest Mother

It did indeed seem a long time since I had seen thy writing when last mail brought thy welcome sight of it. I think that Pollie and Gulie have both written twice since thou wrote. I was almost afraid there was no letter for me this mail, one came for Harry early on the morning of last Monday and none for me, when just as we were starting for an excursion to Mugger Peer (Whit Monday being a holiday here) thy letter was put into my hand. So as we were driving along the road toward Mr Alsen's I began to read and got on swimmingly as far as the end of the first sheet when a great wind came and whirled all the rest away. Of course, I thought it would soon be found again, but it blew across the plain, and apparently into a compound where the man and presently Harry went to seek it, but all to no purpose. It was hopelessly lost. I went into Mr Alsen's and he sent a servant with orders to stay until he found it, and when all was ready and it was fully time for us to start, I still hoped to find it when I came back, but no such good luck was in store for me and I have the vexation of thinking how many interesting bits of home news there must be in the sheet and a half that are gone. It has quite spoilt my pleasure in writing home this time, and besides, I have so little to comment upon I don't know how I shall fill my paper.

I must tell you about Mugger Peer. It is the place you know where there are so unaccountable a number of crocodiles. Our party consisted of Mr Alsen and his partner Mr Riebe, Harry and self, and you may imagine how bad the nine miles of road is when I tell you that it took two carriages each with 3 horses to take the four of us and a butler. It is mostly through a plain of deep uneven sand and beds of rivers, dried up by the heat, with stony sides and sandy bottoms. To improve this the driver kept diverging into the jungle and taking us full speed over sand hills and through small prickly pear bushes, quite "promiscuous", as Pollie says. Many a time I expected to be turned over, for the first horse was a wild half tamed creature and the man who rode it was as bad, so they tore along sending the sand and gravel flying over us in every direction.

Towards the end we turned through an opening in the stony hills which had been alongside of us for some distance and found there a stream of water and a grove of date palms with a travellers bungalow near it, in which we had tiffin consisting partly of an egg and bacon pie which I made to remind us of home picnics, and then went down to the water to see the crocodiles or muggers as they are always called here. They are from 16 to 20 feet long and about fifty often appear at a time but we didn't see so many I think. We had a goat killed to give to them and they came rushing up out of the water in the most fearful manner with their big gaping jaws. They are considered sacred by the natives and are fed on goat by the fakeers who live there on purpose but they don't get nearly enough and occasionally take a native to make up deficiencies. They have eaten two or three since last year. We rested in the bungalow until it got cooler and then set off for a mile's walk over the hot shelterless plain to some hot springs which rise in another grove of palms, the water must be about 90F. Some natives live near and plant a little Indian corn etc. which looks beautifully green. The dates were not ripe and I tasted one which was as bitter as sloes. We were escorted by several natives, one of whom gave me a delicious ripe tamarind, but I didn't see any tamarind trees near.

One of our attendants from Mugger Peer was so especially dirty and disreputable that we ordered him off. It turned out that he was the padri or priest of the place but he certainly didn't raise our idea of the Mahomedan priesthood. He was naked down to his waist from whence hung a pair of ragged dirty baggy trousers, his turban had been white but was rapidly harmonizing in colour with his black hair which stuck through it in all directions. Over one shoulder he carried a red cloth of some kind and his costume was completed by a short butcher's knife in a sheath which hung at his side, and which I suppose he uses in killing goats for the protégés, the muggers. We let him go with us when we found that he was a clerical dignitary, and gave him a half rupee which he appeared to appreciate.

Talking of priests reminds me of a curious colony of them who live in an enclosure near Mrs Lidbetter where they have a holy

81

place - a tomb or something and whom we visited last time we were at Syari about a week ago. Captain Lidbetter took quite a party of us through and I enjoyed the picturesqueness of the thing extremely - they seeming greatly astonished at us in return, but the priest invited us into a new stone temple which they were building and which they had whitened at one end and scrawled all over with pictures exactly like those on old Assyrian slabs in the British Museum and of which they seemed very proud.

The priest in this instance was a dirty Sindee with dabs of red and yellow paint on his face and long black hair tied in knots behind. The yard they live in is sheltered by a fine old banyan tree, striking its roots down everywhere, and under this lived dozens and dozens of men, women, children, dogs, bullocks and donkeys, all belonging more or less remotely to the great fraternity of begging priests or fakeers who infest this country and are the laziest, dirtiest and wickedest of this lazy, dirty and wicked Sindee people. Their houses under the banyan tree were flat topped tents without sides and a pole at each corner where you might see the people sleeping, smoking hemp or eating. I was reminded of gipsies at home - only *they* are so intensely respectable in comparison. Many of these men cannot require more than half a yard of calico to make the whole of their toilet and the children are all quite naked, some of them such pretty little pets with large black eyes and white teeth. There were also some rather nice tombs in the compound and a funny little temple as big as a box standing on end, and a bell hanging outside which the men rung whenever they went in to say their prayers or came out again.

To return to our [1]mutton we came back from Mugger Peer in time for an 8 o'clock dinner which our friends took with us and then we were ready for bed, and I am glad to say didn't feel any the worse for the awful amount of jolting we had undergone.

Harry and I are expecting to go to Tatta tomorrow night to stay over Saturday and Sunday with a Mr Bolton who has asked us to go. Tatta is a wonderful place - a hill covered for miles and miles with tombs of the Ameers and others of less note. Some are very old and beautifully carved but I will tell you a great deal about it next time, if all be well. We shall have a long ride through the jungle on camels, won't it be fun?

I was thinking of you on Whit Tuesday, did you have a fine day and who went. How I should like to have been there and so would dear Harry who is more homesick than I am, poor fellow, and no wonder, for this is his fifth year away from home. Our sister Janie is leaving [2]Mountmellick school next month. She is resigning on account of her views about Baptism and the Eucharist which I fancy are just the same as dear Father's. I wish she could get amongst Friends somewhere where they are not so intolerant as in Ireland.

Beyond getting very hot sometimes, I don't suffer at all from the heat, thank thee, Mother dear, and I am coolness itself compared to those who have been long in the country and whose principal business seems to consist in perspiring profusely. Another season and I shall feel the heat more, most likely.

Poor old Margaret Hudson, what a sad end she has come to. I was hoping the other day only, that all the old people would live until I could see them again, but that was too much to expect with regard to her. How busy you seem with your sewing, Gulie and thee. I have made two out of Harry's six night shirts and they are quite a success in fit and structure altogether.

I am afraid this is not a very interesting letter, but we have done nothing lately besides what I have told. Our dear love to our family circle and mine desires to be extended a little beyond it in the usual direction - to Gilbert and Hannah, the Miss Parrys, Mary Wheatley, etc. and to all our relations who enquire after us. To my darling Father and Mother especially, dear, dear love from their loving daughter, Elsie.

Notes:
1. "To return to our mutton...": an anonymous quote from the French "Revenons a ces moutons", often quoted as "Retournons a nos moutons", meaning, Let us get back to the subject.
2. Mountmellick School, co. Laois, Ireland: A co-educational Quaker school founded in 1786 and known as the Leinster Provincial School until 1855. From that date it was for girls only until its closure in 1921. "Janie" (1830-1918) was Henry's sister, who married George Heather of Dublin as his second wife in 1868; there were no children.

Elizabeth describes most graphically the camel ride by the lakes and woods at Tatta. She was then four and a half months pregnant!

Kurrachee
June 3 1864

My dearest Pollie

After so unfortunately losing dear Mother's letter last mail, you may be sure I was very careful not to have the same accident again, and took care not to read it anywhere but safely indoors. It was as usual a great delight to have so many particulars of home doings. I think the less they are the more we enjoy them.

I am enclosing so long an account of our late trip to Tatta from dear Harry's pen that I shall not add a long letter on my own account - perhaps you will kindly send the lilac sheets and the sketch on to Ballytore [Harry's home in Kildare] and then we needn't do it all over again for them. Isaac Jacob of Stockton [Harry's brother] said in his last letter that he wished you would sometimes send our letters on there - as he never gets one from Ireland. I wish you would whenever you think it suitable, as of course we can't write to all Harry's brothers and sisters every mail, and Stockton is so near Thirsk that you could easily join. I am afraid I write for a pretty extensive circle as it is, I hear of people in all directions having my letters to read.

Harry doesn't tell you that we spent <u>three</u> days at Tatta - going there during Friday night and coming back during Monday night. It was a most enjoyable visit, but we were very tired when we got home, having lost two nights sleep out of four and taken a most unusual amount of exercise at Tatta - including the camel riding which is the most exercising thing you can imagine, a constant vertical jig-jog something like riding on ten donkeys at once if you can imagine such a thing. It would make some people sick but we felt no symptoms of it. I think it did us good.

The heat at Tatta is incomparably greater than it is here - arising I think from the want of the sea breezes and the substitution of a hot dry sirocco like wind which has passed over fifty miles of hot land. We used to undress and lie down in the middle of the day - getting up occasionally for a dip into the tub, the only tolerably cool thing there. It is beautifully wooded about Tatta; and the two lakes, for there is another beside the one Harry describes, lie beautifully amongst the trees and are covered with all kinds of water-fowl, long legged birds like snow-white herons, teal, coots, wild ducks, etc. There is a good deal of game on the hill and one morning when Harry went out shooting with Mr Bolton, they got nearly bitten by a cobra which was lying across their path. They didn't see it until it spread its hood for a spring, and then Mr Bolton fired at it and missed it but fortunately it was frightened and got into a bush.

Near one of the lakes is a Mahomedan monastery, such a queer solitary building with a little place like a hermit's cell near it in the hillside, with just a little door showing that it is a place you can get into. Pilgrims stay at this monastery when they are passing Tatta, which they do constantly, and when we were playing at croquet a number passed, chanting out that sentence, "There is no God but Allah and Mahomed is his prophet," with a startling shriek at the end. It sounded like a shrill hip, hip, hip Hurra. You can have no idea what beautiful tiled work there is inside the tombs, such soft rich patterns, I think [1]Minton's might take a few lessons from them with advantage. The architecture is nearly all saracenic [Islamic], you can get the best idea of it from the colored domes of the Alhambra at the [2]Crystal Palace.

One of Mr Bolton's servants had such a dear little boy with magnificent eyes swimming in light and the sweetest little white teeth. The children's eyes look so lustrous, partly from the parents darkening them all round, although one would have thought them dark enough, and partly from their large size and the long black lashes which overshadow them. This little fellow's name was Maugal (Tuesday). I sent Ahmed to Tatta to get some native sweetmeats for him, but he was very shy and wouldn't take them from me. They said he had never seen a "Ma'am Sahib" before, but his father came with a dish smiling and salaaming, and we gave him the goodies for little Tuesday. There were two kids that would run up the sloping sides of the tents and then down again, like children, such dear little things they were, and amongst the tombs countless green parrots with long tails, and bright blue jays, and green and gold flycatchers, it must be delightful there in the cold season.

It is pretty warm here now - Harry gave me a thermometer the other day and I saw just now it was 91F in a cool corner of our room. I often look to see how hot it is - it was 89F at noon the day before yesterday, 90F yesterday and 91F today, so if it goes on at that rate we shall soon be pretty warm. Today I don't feel it at all uncomfortably - yesterday I sat at the writing table where there was no draught and I was soon bathed in perspiration - so that I went upstairs and undressed. The great thing is to keep between two doors, or anywhere near wind.

The other day Harry and I were at a dinner party at Mr D's, a newly married German gentleman, who has brought from Saxony a charming little wife of about 17 years, but very childish for that age. Her English is a very recent acquirement and one never tires of hearing her pretty broken sentences. We had a good deal of music after dinner and left about 11, dinner lasts from soon after 8 till nearly 10 and the gentlemen smoke some time after that, so the evening is not difficult to dispose of, particularly as we keep pretty early hours in Kurrachee. I think this has been our only dissipation since I last wrote.

Now I must comment upon Pollie's letter, but I forgot to tell you that Miss Mosley is really going to be married in the autumn to Mr Howe of Kotree - a very well-to-do middle aged gentlemen, and as nice as can be. Miss Mosley is nearly 29 so there is not much disparity in age I think. The Lidbetters will be lost without her.

Harry says I must tell thee Pollie dear that the notice thou takes of our commissions is very unbusinesslike - thou mentions nothing particularly and we are wanting the trays, etc. every day and expected at least to hear that you were going to send them off, I hope you have done so before this. I will enclose a note for cousins May and Pollie thanking them for their cartes, and making a distant promise of ours, for our photographer has migrated no-one knows where and our negatives with him. I am glad Pollie so enjoyed thy visit to Bradford dear, thy scraps of news about old friends and relations are delightful. I think memory and patience for detail are thy most valuable qualities! at any rate they are so to us at this distance.

I am very sorry dear Pollie, thy present is so small. I hope you have got the box by this time, perhaps Mother would like thee to join at the cushion or work box - thou must take the will for the deed, seeing Harry and I are not yet able to do as we would in these matters. What a delightful account thou gives of your different spring excursions, it makes my mouth water to hear of Hambleton and the Wensleydale Hills with the young larches overhead and the dear primroses and cowslips for a carpet underfoot. I wonder how long it will be before Harry and I see even a daisy again - I pity us both but especially my dear who has been from home so long when I think of it.

I am naughty enough to hope that you went to Rievaulx and not to Redcar on Whit Tuesday, I think the former would do you more good mentally and bodily. What a pity dear Father will go to such horrid places in pursuance of his philanthropy, I suppose on the principle that the path of duty is always an inodorous [arduous?] one. I wonder if Father thinks we forget him because my letters are generally addressed to Mother or the girls. He must not think so - they are all for him and Harry is so nearly a teetotaller now that he got a headache with drinking a little champagne at Mr D's. I don't think we shall attempt anything in the way of taking up matting or general cleaning this year, as we are pretty sure to have to leave this house in September, and we shall try to get a bungalow at Clifton for a while.

I have written Gilbert and Hannah so short a letter that perhaps you will show them these sheets of mine and Harry's. I hope you never feel anxious about my health - it is quite as good as it was in England - I never have anything the matter with me, and a most capital appetite. The air is so damp here too, that the heat seldom makes one thirsty which is a great comfort - England is a far thirstier place in summer.

My dear, dear love to you all and don't forget my love to Emma and Robert and my dear children Nellie and May.
Thy very loving Elsie.

Notes:
1. Minton's: English ceramics manufacturers of Stoke-on-Trent, who were famous for their tiles.
2. Crystal Palace: The huge glass building of the Great Exhibition of 1851 was removed in 1854 from Hyde Park to Sydenham in south London, where it became a favourite place for Victorian family outings, with its gardens, fountains and exhibitions of art and natural history.

A terrible fire has destroyed the home and business of the Baker family back in Thirsk. Elizabeth and Henry are troubled by ants which get everywhere and eat everything. The young couple value their exercise and get up at 4.15am to have a walk before it gets too hot.

Kurrachee

June 19 1864

My dearest Gulie

For a long time after I had read thy letter I could think of nothing else but poor [1]Gilbert and Hannah Baker, and they have been preying upon my mind more or less ever since. I was shocked too to see by the paper that they were not properly insured - how did that happen, I wonder. But the worst of all and what one cannot but feel the most sorry about, is the loss of all Gilbert's books and plants, a loss that can never be replaced, and which I think must have discouraged him sadly. Have they any idea how the fire originated? The old house must have burnt down very quickly and no wonder, doesn't it make dear Father doubly anxious about fire. I can just imagine him prowling about last thing in the shop and cellars, to make sure. Poor George Baker seems to have nothing but hindrances, first his illness and then this fire. It is very fortunate that John Baker is both able and willing to help his sons so effectually - and that people are so willing to be good-natured generally.

Harry and I will soon be turned out of our house too, by a devouring element in the shape of an extortionate old Jew landlord. Our time is up in September but we are thinking of leaving on the 20th of next month as we have been able to secure a bungalow at Clifton at that time, and they are very difficult to get, and besides, I had much rather have the trouble of moving now than then. We don't expect to be so comfortable at Clifton as we are here, but it is a fine healthy place with plenty of sea breezes (and snakes). The worst of it is that Harry will have four miles dusty drive to office, and that is hardly a desideratum in warm weather. Mr Alsen and Mr Riebe think of going out if they can get a house - so we shall be able to make up a croquet party, there are some fine hard places on the sand where we played when up there with the Wilsons.

Mr Glyn is going down to Bombay today to stay for a month or so. He gets dreadfully bored by the quietness of this place after a London life, so Harry will be somewhat busier at the office. We are going to drive down to Mr Alsen's garden some evening soon, to try and get a chameleon to tame. I want to see if it will clear the house of ants, and he has numbers amongst his trees. I have great hopes of succeeding as they are very easily tamed, and I know they are insectivorous.

We are nearly in despair about the ants, they cover everything, and get into all our food. The sideboard which stands with its feet in water tins is the only thing they can't get into, and if so much as a piece of paper or a hair blows into the tins they cross upon it and fill the sugar bowl etc. directly. These are not large ants at all, and fortunately we are not troubled with those, either black or white, but a small spidery kind, very rapid in their movements. At Mrs Lidbetter's the ants are just as tiresome but they are as big or bigger than this [picture of an ant about an inch long] which Harry has drawn, and when they come running across the white dinner cloth they look dreadful. They bite too, Harry got his feet bitten at Tatta where they were in the bedroom. They carry off food by wholesale and in one night they will carry away a very large heap of horses corn, or grain as it is called here.

The piece of lilac thou sent me was quite sweet when it came and reminded me very strongly of the dear old tree over the garden door, and of "Edwin's bower", and all the dear old places. I fear Father's gardening enthusiasm will have reduced them all to ruin as untidy relics of the past.

Harry and I are getting up in the morning now at a quarter past four and taking a brisk walk before sunrise which is most enjoyable. Yesterday morning we saw a great number of locusts and the dogs had fine fun chasing them. They are a much larger insect than I had fancied - some are four inches long. This morning when I was dressing one flew out of my clothes, and Totty, who with Carlo generally stays upstairs while we dress, caught it and ate it up, shell, wings and all, making a most horrid crunching noise that would have upset Mother completely. I suppose the unlucky insect had come in at the window. We are rather afraid of a general visitation, and I am sure vegetables and fruit etc. are dear enough now without losing all this season's crops.

I had two presents of Bombay mangoes yesterday. They are a great improvement upon those grown in Sind, and are most delicious. Mr Barns sent quite a large tray full which will last us several days. They are greenish and smooth outside but the pulp is of a bright orange and stains hands, face, tablecloths etc. in a very unpleasant manner. They are about the only fruit I like here - grapes are as plentiful as gooseberries at home but smaller and less sweet than those which grow indoors in England. The gardeners never thin the bunches or prune the vine leaves to let the sun in, or I don't doubt the fruit might be as fine as any they grow just as wild as brambles or hop vines.

We are troubled just as you are by the mail constantly going out on a Monday - but as church is either early in the morning or late in the evening, and we are fast in the house during the middle of the day, we have more time than you have, especially as reading continuously makes one very drowsy when it is so hot.

We were very much amused at the idea of Pollie and thee handing pails of water - but it was very good of you to help. (The account of thy doings at the fire has just attracted us again.)

I want to hear all about Whit Tuesday and whether you went by Arden Valley as we did that nice last time. The other night Harry and I took a gharry and went out about 9 in the evening to see what we could of the Mussulman [Muslim] festival, [2]"Hobson, Jobson" as it is called here, but which singular name is a corruption of the names of two of their martyrs Hoossein and Joosein whose death it is kept to celebrate. The principal feature of the affair is the carrying about of representations of their tombs, gilt and tinselled, and at night illuminated. About fifty of these "taboots" [tazias] as they are called, were made in camp by different classes of Mahomedans, and carried about preceded by tom-toms and dancing devils of different kinds. We were very unfortunate in missing the processions and saw but little, we didn't go quite late enough. The last day they are carried in great state and thrown into the sea. There was a report that the [3]Mohurram was to be inaugurated by murdering all the

Europeans, but fortunately (for themselves especially) they thought better of it and we slept undisturbed.

Mr Alsen came to breakfast this morning as he does often on Sunday, and brought his bullpup Leo with him. He says he caught me a chameleon before he came but Leo killed it. My dog Totty had fine fun with him for a playfellow and they knocked about without ceasing all the morning. Totty has come off, I see, with a swollen eye. They certainly were dreadfully rough. Carlo and Dick were not so well pleased with the intruder, the latter especially was most inhospitable and unfriendly, showing his teeth and growling constantly.

I am painting at present a copy of that fruit piece of Lance's which Father gave me, for a wedding present for Miss Mosley. I don't know whether it's the effect of the climate but the Antwerp blue which I mixed with crimson lake for the purple grapes has cracked already although they are not finished. I don't know whether I can hide it with glazing. I don't remember ever being warned against the mixture I used - I used a little megilp [linseed oil and varnish] but not much. I daresay dear Father can tell me the reason.

I have never received "Pet Marjorie". You haven't mentioned it again - will you always tell us exactly when you send things off, please, and then we shall know what measures to take for getting them at this end. I suppose my dear Mother will write to me next time; my dear, dear love to her and Father and Pollie, Tom Artie and thyself. I think I must find time to send a note to the Bakers, a propos of their calamity. My dear Harry joins me in this message of love - I mustn't ask him to add a word this time as he has been so good - actually writing to his own home!

Ever your loving Elsie.

Notes:
1. Gilbert and Hannah Baker: John Gilbert Baker was a keen botanist and in 1863 published *North Yorkshire: Studies of its Botany, Geology, Climate and Physical Geography*. His "books and plants" which Elizabeth refers to, probably contained drawings and dried flower specimens for future publication. It seems that the fire was a defining moment for him, as by the time their second child, Katherine Unthank, was born on 4

February 1869, Gilbert and Hannah were living at 25 Sidney Villas, Richmond, Surrey, near the Royal Botanic Gardens at Kew. He was described as one of the founders of ecological botany, became a Fellow of the Royal Society and was Keeper of the Herbarium at Kew from 1890-99.

2. *Collins Dictionary* describes *hobson-jobson* as a 19th century Anglo-Indian folk-etymological variant of the Arabic "O Hasan! O Husain!" - a ritual lament for the grandsons of Mohammed.

3. Mohurram: "properly the name of the 1st month of the Mahommedan lunar year. But in India the term is applied to the period of fasting and public mourning observed during that month in commemoration of the death of Hasan and of his brother Husain (AD 669 and 680)." This is a quote from *Hobson-Jobson: being a Glossary of Anglo-Indian Colloquial Words and Phrases, and of Kindred Terms,* by H Yule and A C Burnell (London, John Murray, 1886).

Two personal letters from Elizabeth to her parents, no date but probably written June/July 1864. These would have been for family reading only. As before, she reassures her parents that she is very well and that the heat is no problem. Except for smallpox vaccination there were no other immunisations and everybody knew how dangerous the Indian climate was for Europeans. Now that a baby was on the way Elizabeth's family must have been even more concerned for her health.

Dearest Father and Mother

I must send a special little note of thanks from Harry and myself for your most generous present - which I hope will get here safely some time next month. I will thank you then for everything specially. At present I will only say that it is welcome to us not only as a proof of your kindness but as a reduction of the expenses of what will be here, I expect especially, a very costly occasion - nurses etc. being very scarce and expensive, and it was all the more pleasant that it was so entirely unexpected.

I keep quite well and hearty, thank you. The heat is much less than I expected and it suits me much better than an English winter ever did. I am really bored by nothing but the wind - one's hair is always blown about and one loses things constantly. I find the first sheet of dear Father's letter has disappeared - which is a great nuisance as I wanted to thank him for his nice account of the York Meeting. I have just been thanking Silvanus Thompson for sending the minute which I think most kind and liberal. Mr Bagnell the clergyman called the morning it came and I showed it to him as a proof of the liberality of sentiment amongst Friends, and he was greatly pleased with it - particularly when he saw James Backhouse's name at the end - for he knew some of the Darlington [1]Backhouses and Peases.

Captain Lidbetter has said nothing about thy note - so I don't know what he means to do. We would manage to go in spite of the distance if he settled anything, but Harry does not like to say anything about it because he didn't enter into some attempt of the kind which the Lidbetters made before. I will tell you what happens.

Pollie will think she is cheated of her lawful rights if I don't say the rest of my say to her, so good bye in dearest love from your grateful and loving children -
H & E H Jacob.

Note:
1. Backhouses and Peases: well-known Quaker families.

Elizabeth considers it very important to get some regular exercise.

My dearest Mother

I was very much relieved to hear that you were going to send most of the little clothes ready made - as I am sure I shouldn't have had time to make half after they got here. Why, it will be some time in August before I see them even if you send them off as you expect, for parcels are detained at least a mail in Bombay. I should be very badly off if it happened to me as it did last week to the lady next door whose baby came two months before it was expected. She fortunately had things mostly ready - but I shouldn't have a thing of any kind, for I cannot make even the flannels without a pattern.

Don't be at all afraid of my forsaking my teetotal principles - here if anywhere one can appreciate them and they stand me in good stead - nobody feels the heat less than I do. I am very little troubled with lassitude or weariness, if I am tired I can always go to sleep, though that isn't considered very good in India. The one thing I want is exercise and that is almost impossible to get without feeling the worse for it. The only time we can walk to advantage is before sunrise - and that involves getting up about four o'clock and being at home again before half-past-five. Sometimes we manage it, but not regularly, as we oversleep ourselves as often as not, and the gun firing which is our signal for both getting up and going to bed often fails to wake us, particularly when the wind is high, and I am sorry to say that sometimes even when Harry does awake he is difficult to move.

So taking exercise in India is a most problematical thing, and I seldom get any, except going up and down stairs, unless you call a drive in the evening exercise. However, I feel quite well in spite of it, so don't be at all anxious my dear Mother - only don't be at all surprised if in a few years I am as stout as Aunt Mary Ann. Harry says he believes I shall be and I can hardly get my rings on at all which were quite large enough six months ago. Everybody gets fat at Kurrachee, I suppose it is being so hungry and walking so little.

Thanking thee, dear Mother, for all the trouble about the little things. I am thy most loving Elsie.

PS. You may send us word of any partialities you have in the way of <u>names</u> - I warn you that Harry is very difficult to suit!

Elizabeth has some advice on how to send parcels from England and is pestered by locusts.

Kurrachee, July 4 1864

My dearest Father and Mother

It was so delightful to get a letter from each of you at the same time, particularly as they were so entirely different that no-one could have guessed they were comtemporaneous productions. I don't know which was the nicest - I feel like the little boy who said "he liked both best" but I will answer Mother's first because "place aux dames" is a rule one mustn't violate.

I wish dear Mother thou had had thy own way in this instance about sending our parcel overland, as they are things we want daily. If sent by sea, it is better to ship direct for Kurrachee, as plenty of ships come straight here, and there is often a delay in sending things on from Bombay if there is no interested party to look after them - this is a hint for next time. Don't be discouraged by the failure of our last packing of preserves - they will come all

Bartholomew Smith.
Photo: Sarony, Leeds 1860s.

Isabel Smith.
Photo: Sarony, Leeds 1860s.

right if properly packed. Those we buy here are in stone jars, the corks fastened on with shellac, and carefully covered with tinfoil fastened round the neck of the jar, and they are always quite tight and safe. These are placed in sawdust, never in hay which is the dampest and worst thing possible, and ferments itself before it gets here. I think these are all the precautions necessary, and they are none of them very troublesome ones. I suppose by this time you will have got our box - I hope it was all right and the Hyderabad work not very much tarnished.

How I should like to see Emma's little darlings now that they can run about. How charming Nellie must look - does she still wear her comb? but you seem to be transferring your admiration to May. I don't think I should be so disloyal. They must wish for a boy next time I think. I am very glad poor Mrs Tangye has a baby at last and that she has given it such a pretty name. I did love thee, dear Mother, for telling me so much about Whit Tuesday - it was the next best thing to being there, and I can just imagine the smell of Pollie's and Gulie's splendid handfuls of lilies. I should never get over my longing for English flowers and trees and fields and showers if I stayed in India all my life - which God forbid.

The rain I miss especially. There has been none here since last July except one shower when I was at Mrs Lidbetter's and one since - nothing to speak of and over directly, and you may imagine how badly it is wanted. Meat is thin and dear for want of fodder, and vegetables and food for horses are very scarce. The tanks are nearly dry - but the wells seem to hold out wonderfully. It astonishes me to see our perennial supply of good water, filtered and iced as we drink it, it is as good as can be. I can't think what we should do without ice, everybody in Kurrachee uses it, and it is sent up country, and there is no danger is its running short. Another American ship load came in lately - nobody will eat the machine made ice that can get American, it is so much denser and purer. Harry and I use three pounds a day for which we pay 4½ annas - sixpence three farthings. The coinage here is the most cumbersome thing in the world. You hardly ever see any silver piece but a rupee and there is no gold coinage - so for a pound you have ten heavy silver pieces, much heavier than our florins I'm sure. In a rupee there are sixteen annas, and in an anna 12 pies. This is a very extravagant system, I find, for no European carries anything but rupees and they stand for sixpences in giving away or spending. The copper one never sees used except by natives, although I suppose it must be given as change in business.

We didn't get the newspaper which Father said he had sent with an account of the Rievaulx Temperance trip - so I suppose you forgot to post it. I send you some native poetry, the first I ever heard or saw of, and an absurd letter which purports to be written by an ill-used butler, but it is a skit most likely by an Englishman upon the dreadful way they treat us - you can't imagine I daresay how natural all the Anglo-Indian slang which it is written in, is to us here, or how true to nature the butler is. However, I send it, and a translation, merely premising that the sentence in parenthesis is supposed to be introduced by the professional bazaar writer, whom every native who can't write English employs to do it for him. The bazaar list is very similar to the one I take down from Ahmed every day after breakfast, only fortunately mine is only half as large including meat. I do believe our butler is an honest little man in his way, you will see that servants are in the habit of getting these Baboos [English-writing Indian clerk - a rather derogatory term] to write them out good characters at a rupee each, just fancy, and how dreadfully taken-in their masters get - but things are much worse in Bengal, they say, than they are here.

We haven't long to stay now in our present bungalow - our destination when we leave it is again undecided. We do not know whether we shall go to Clifton because there is another house vacant not far from us, and we may have to take it at once if we mean to get it at all. In that case we shall give up Clifton altogether. It is not nearly so nice as this, of course, it is older and dirty and smells of muskrats, but we must not expect another house so nice as this. Harry has bought a piece of land just beyond the railway very cheap, 7000 square yards for £2O and he thinks of trying to get some Parsee to build for him, but that is uncertain at present. It is only a sandy plain now but the Municipality is marking out roads there and Harry means to make a continual stir at the Board until it is done. It will make the land much more valuable, particularly as they talking of building the new station in that neighbourhood.

I am very glad that Pollie and Gulie are riding a little, there is nothing so nice - it is a long time since I was on horseback. I was quite grieved when thou told me that Gulie had given her dog back - she would feel it greatly I'm sure. Sometimes we think we shall have to send Totty away, but I should be very sorry, for though not always good, she is a dear affectionate little thing and most useful for eating locusts which the other dogs won't touch. We are dreadfully troubled by the locusts coming into our bedroom - Harry says it is owing to the flat roofs at each side, where they stop to rest for they are dreadfully torpid, having come too soon and encountering the cold sea wind. They are huge blundering loathsome creatures, and start up with a great flop - unexpectedly - from amongst ones clothes or wherever they have settled. They cling very fast too, and yesterday I was running away from one that was jumping after me, and got into bed and was covering myself up when I found it was sticking to my nightgown! I believe I shall have a fit one day with getting up so suddenly horrified. Last night I was undressing when I suddenly fancied the cork of one of the bottles on the dressing table was turning round and making faces at me. It was a big red locust, turning as I moved so as to keep its ugly head and shoulders opposite me, just like something uncanny with its great eyes. Totty was in bed so Harry had to kill it, much against his will, after chasing it up and down for five minutes.

We have been enjoying the mango season for the last month or two. Those we get in Sind are not very good, but when as often happens, we get some from Bombay they are a real treat, and smell when ripe just like a bunch of cowslips. A big one is as large as a man's fist but a flattish oval in shape, outside a greenish yellow but inside a splendid orange. The pulp is very solid and can be taken out with a spoon - it stains dreadfully to eat them with one's fingers - Harry says the corners of my mouth are permanently jaundiced as it is. The Sind mangoes, which are part of my daily fare when I can't get the others but which Harry despises, are lemon colored inside and out, and very poor in comparison to the others. The mango tree is a huge forest tree not a bit like a fruit tree, but must look splendid with its dark masses of leaves when the golden fruit is hanging all over it. Mr Glyn who is at present in Bombay sent us some up by the last steamer which were the best I have tasted.

I have often regretted that I didn't send home to Pollie and Gulie in the box, a quantity of very nice stuff that we use here as a headwash - it is called "sikikia" and is the bark of some tree or shrub and as cheap as dirt almost. It is boiled in water until it is as dark as coffee then the water is strained off and used when cold, preceded by lemon juice. It only requires you to be careful not to swallow it - as it is poisonous - and to wash it well off with cold water, and it leaves the head beautifully white and clean, and the hair very soft and glossy so that it requires but little oil. Harry and I use it once a week, indeed I believe it is a usual practice here - it is the safest and least troublesome hair wash I ever saw. I have quite forgotten what it is to have my head at all scurfy, I have quite left off my elaborate way of frizzing and plaiting my hair - it was always in my eyes. Now I wear it brushed back and put into a net, old fashioned way, so as to expose the least area to the wind, and though not beautiful it is very tidy and convenient.

What a lark it is for old Mr Taggitt to think of getting married. They are going to break up the family circle with a vengeance, are any of the Miss Parrys going to be married, I wonder! I am sure now that Mr T has set them the example that they are not a bit more unlikely than he. I do hope that our sister Janie will come to see you, she is fond of hill walking and would pedestrianize with you. I think, dear Father, thou must have forgotten that I told thee that Harry began to try Mr Banting's system soon after we were married, when it was first talked about. He began to get thinner but soon relapsed, and eats potatoes with a vengeance now to make up for lost time. I am glad to hear that it suits Uncle Dan. Aunt had better try too - and some day I mean to, if I see any prospect of having to walk downstairs backwards!

We send dear Mother, some hair [as a keepsake - sometimes put into jewellery or a locket] with dear love to you all. Harry's hair is no more than an inch long anywhere. Ever your most loving - Elsie.

Another personal letter from Elizabeth to her Mother, about July/August 1864

My dearest Mother

This to thank thee for thy kind letter accompanying Gulie's. We are very glad that you got the box safely - but much disappointed that for some unexplained reason thou sent the workbox on to Maria Taylor - instead of keeping it thyself, as we bought and intended it specially for thee - and had quite given up the idea of sending a present to Maria this time. We didn't even know that we had ever mentioned our intention of doing so to you. Of course, if she has got it or if you have said anything about it to her, it is no use saying a word more about it - and if thou had had a nice present as well nobody would be more welcome to the box, but we are quite grieved [that] thou should have comparatively nothing. Such mischances will happen. Was the mistake ours or yours?

Thank thee a hundred times, dear Mother, for all thy trouble about the little things. Please thank Gulie greatly for making the robe, I suppose I mustn't do so in the big letter - I will say more about it when it comes which I hope will be before next mail goes out - also Pollie and thyself for the shoes and pinafores. I have made myself quite unhappy thinking of you sitting indoors this fine summer weather sewing for me when you ought to be enjoying yourselves out of doors, and I who have so much time have done nothing for myself yet but make <u>one</u> bib and begun to work a head flannel. It was very kind of Miss Parry to think of making silk shoes. I will try to write to her after they come.

I have the prospect of a very good monthly nurse named Mrs Forbes who is much recommended - she is a nice homely looking Scotch woman. Dr Mackenzie Skues who is the surgeon of the 109th Regiment, is the doctor I like best here - he is also a Scotchman and a very pleasant man, about as great a gossip as Dr Ryott, but I haven't spoken either to him or the nurse yet. I mean to very soon, as you must engage a nurse here some time before - or you may lose your chance.

I am pretty regular now in walking out early - as the mornings are cloudy and cool until 7 or half-past.

Ever thy loving daughter,
Elsie.

Harry and Elizabeth live for the mail and boxes of goods from England, although sometimes things arrive in less than perfect condition!

Kurrachee, Aug 19 1864

My dearest Mother and Father

I quite hoped to have been able to announce the receipt of the box which I am anxiously expecting as I have no doubt it has been sometime in Bombay, and would have been forwarded had dear Father sent the bill of lading to Doshabhai Merwangee's. As it is, they have had to wait for it. I dare say say he didn't know that the post from here to Bombay takes six days by land; as it has to go by horse dak, that is, by mounted postmen, whenever there is no steamer going down, so that the bill of lading will just about have got to Bombay now and we quite hope to see the box by next steamer from Bombay. I tell you this that you may know next time you send anything overland to direct the bill of lading as well as the box to the agents. Your two letters were the only ones we had last mail, not one from any of Harry's people so they were doubly welcome, even Gilbert's did not arrive although thou mentions his writing. Will you tell him not to address his letters in future "North West Hindostan" as there is a part of India called the North West Provinces and I fear his last letter has travelled up there, many hundred miles away from here. As for Kurrachee, it is not in the north of India at all, but very near the middle - Kurrachee is enough by itself, but you can put "Sind" if you like to be specific.

I am writing this in our new house, which we like extremely now that we are settled in it, the rooms are so spacious compared to those in the other house, and here we have a bedroom and bathroom downstairs, in addition to the upstairs one, which is a delightfully large airy room, and we find the verandahs a great improvement. The front one runs along the whole front, 62 feet long by 8 wide, the back one the same. In the latter the servants do some of their work, washing dishes etc., cleaning shoes, for there are no kitchens here. The cook house is in the compound adjoining the other servants' houses and is the funniest little place about 9 feet square without fireplace or chimney, for the former are substituted little square 12inch pigeon holes built in a row and mortared; with bits of iron projecting for the pots to stand on. They

102

have to make a wood or charcoal fire for everything they cook, and they bake or boil alike in covered tins set over the fire. In consequence I suppose of having a separate fire for each thing our food is always perfectly cooked - "done to a turn" - and what is more wonderful they very seldom smoke anything. I suppose the smoke makes the best of its opportunities by escaping through the roof and windows.

At present, there is no regular road to this house, and we have been amused, once or twice, at people's attempts at driving across the plain from the Ghizree road, and turning back in despair at the impassibility of the nullah [a stream or drain]. However, there is a way, if they only knew it, although it can't be called a road, the latter we are to have presently as a sum of money has been sanctioned for the formation of that much-needed luxury.

We are very sorry, dear Mother, that you have taken so much trouble about the bottled fruit. We can get it here, and not very extravagant in price, and consequently I think you had much better not try to send them to us, considering the trouble and risk it involves, whereas those we get are generally in very good condition. I suppose the importers know exactly how to fulfil the required conditions for making both bottles and fruit keep, which certainly is a very difficult thing for those who haven't had so much experience. The large stone bottles of plum jam that came with the apricot where quite empty when they got here. The jam had fermented and blown the tops off, and mixed itself with the hay in the most unpleasant manner.

While I remember, I want to ask you to send me one pair of medium coloured kid gloves - yellow, or any colour but the new browns which won't keep, lilac or lavender will, I believe - every other mail - that is, once a month, and Harry a pair once every two months. It is no use having more at once, and I believe that is the only way to have decent coloured gloves here. They should be folded in something thin and waterproof, I should think tinfoil, and I believe will come for very little by post. Of course you must add the postage to the price of the gloves and we will pay for them once in a while. My size is 7½ and Harry's 8 ladies or 7¾ gentlemen's, but I think he likes ladies gloves best. Perhaps you had better tell us how much a year it will be. We have got no bill

103

for the trays etc. yet, and we can pay both at the same time. I haven't a single pair of ladies coloured gloves left. Those I laid by mildewed hopelessly at once, and half a dozen pair that I saved by wearing, and so keeping them always out, are just done. It was very grevious to throw a dozen pair of nice gloves away, and taught me a lesson not to lay any more by. Ladies here I think mostly get them by post in the way I have mentioned, and I hope you won't find it very tiresome to keep us supplied.

This letter seems to be getting full of business, and I fear won't be very interesting - yours were both delightfully so, and we _were_ so relieved to hear that dear Mother had kept the workbox. We could't imagine what she meant by sending it away. Will thou tell Pollie that I have had my chudder [chador] washed and that it looks as good as new. I was rather doubtful about giving it to the dhobi as they have the reputation of spoiling things, but he has not only done that well, but my black grenadine shawl which would mildew in spite of my efforts to keep it dry, and now looks very nice indeed again.

Harry says he will sketch me onto a canvas for you, but he has no practice in handling oil colours and I think it doubtful when I shall paint again after I finish the two I have on hand, the Greek head and the fruit for Miss Mosley. The latter I don't enjoy doing at all, although it looks pretty well. The former we are going to hang up. I think I have coloured it quite as well as usual, and it is a beautiful subject. There is a Greek lady here and most charming she is.

How nice for Tom to have a little visiting and see his friends, it will do him good to go about a little, although he isn't as gauche as most boys of his age [15], and knows how to speak to people. The Lidbetters don't live at Clifton although they stayed there a long time last year. They live about three miles inland exactly in the opposite direction. At present they are staying at Kearmari, which is the shipping part of the town and divided from Kurrachee by a mole about two miles long, being itself an island which forms one side of the harbour. I will ask Harry to make you a little plan on a piece of paper, and then you can see whereabouts we all live.

I am glad to hear that Sydney is married, and should like my love and congratulations to be given to him if you should see or have any communication with him. I should like a carte of Mrs Syd if you could get me one, indeed I am very greedy of cartes so if you have any superfluous ones you may ship them over to me. We rarely see new ones here and I haven't one of [1]Alexandra of any kind, whereas I dare say you have a dozen and perhaps could spare me one with her baby. I'm glad thou had resolutions to refuse cousin Bessie's self invitation - you couldn't do worse than have her. I was afraid she would be pawning herself upon you for ever now that I have gone - the only one who didn't encourage or at least tolerate her intolerableness, you were all too civil. She is the only person in the world towards whom I should advocate inhospitality, which I hold to be the most inviolate duty, so you mustn't think me altogether a heathen for talking so.

Harry and I are trying to walk regularly in the morning, but don't succeed very well. Yesterday morning we found quite a number of flowers of different kinds in consequence of the rain last week, and small patches of grass already gone to seed. I think the monsoon is breaking and the hot season coming again. There is quite blue sky today, the first for months except just after rain of which there has been three falls this season, although no great depth has fallen, not so much as comes in a few hours sometimes. Potatoes are getting wretchedly bad and there is no present prospect of getting new ones. I can't imagine why they shouldn't plant them so as to come when the others are done. Agriculture is certainly most primitive here and nobody seems to care to suggest improvements.

I suppose Pollie and Gulie and all are at home again now, <u>mind you go to Ireland</u>. We are in love to all of you as if married, Your most loving son and daughter.

[Written across page]
Harry told me to tell Father that tigers seldom come down so far from the hills as to Tatta, and that there is not the slightest danger of meeting one "promiscuous" [meaning here - by accident] as it is always a matter of the public notoriety where a tiger is frequenting a district, and nobody goes out without plenty of preparation. There is generally a paragraph in the papers stating that a tiger has been seen or is supposed to be in such and such a neighbourhood, so you mustn't again imagine us in danger from such

causes. I forgot to put "via Marseilles" on my last letter. I am afraid you would be disappointed at its not arriving at the proper time. How does Artie like the prospect of giving up his favourite Ackworth scheme? I am very glad you have decided for him to go at once to York [probably to Bootham school, with his brother Tom].

Note:
1. Alexandra: This was Alexandra of Denmark who married the future Edward VII in 1863. The baby was their eldest son, Albert Victor, Duke of Clarence, who died in 1892, so that their second son inherited the throne as George V in 1910.

Elizabeth is getting very excited about the forthcoming birth of her baby. At the same time she is rather worried about the misunderstanding with Captain Lidbetter which means that Harry will be out of a job by the end of the year. Once again, she pleads with her parents to visit Ireland to meet Harry's family at Ballitore.

Kurrachee, Sept 3rd 1864

My dearest Mother

Pollie must excuse my not addressing this letter to her, because I want to tell thee how delighted I am with my box and its contents. It came quite safely at the beginning of the week with everything inside it in perfectly good condition, and all as beautiful as can be. I did so enjoy unpacking it, and seeing all the dear little things come out, one by one. I can hardly believe that it is <u>all</u> a present, is it really? The little robe Gulie made is absolutely perfect, and the pinafores and shoes are so too - did you not have a sewing machine for the pinafores? and did you make anything beside, except the little binders?

I have had a lady to look at the things and tell me if all's right for India and she says that I need do nothing but open the things behind as here the ayahs have large quilted things to nurse upon, made of cotton, which are removed when necessary and the spoiling of dresses, skirts, etc. saved. It is too hot to wrap children up much round their waists so I have already begun upon the night-dresses, monthly gowns and long dresses (except the robes) - this and the making of muslin binders instead of flannel, and a couple more long skirts and a common hood and shawl of some kind are all that your kindness has left for my share of the work. This with trimming the basket and bassinette and making sheets etc. for it, will just keep me nicely doing for a month. Mrs McNeill tells me I shall want 3 dozen goodries, the quilted things I spoke of, but I will get a dhirzie to make them for me.

I was delighted with the cloak and hood, they were exactly as I should have chosen, as thou knows dear Mother, in fact it is so with regard to all the things, they are <u>perfectly</u> nice and pretty. I was especially delighted with thy kindness in sending me so much muslin diaper trimmings etc., materials for short things would be very difficult to buy here and as bad as they are dear. Miss Parry must excuse my writing this time to thank her for the dear little blue silk boots - I feel so busy I can only just spare time to write you a short letter, I am afraid, and a short one to Ballytore. The veil I haven't mentioned - it is as beautiful as everything else. I don't think, dear Mother, that thou need complain of the quality of any of the things - they are good enough for anything and so beautifully made - surely nobody ever had so little trouble as I have had and so nice and complete a provision. The waterproof articles will be most useful and my dressing gown is just to my taste. I have made myself a lace cap for sitting up - like a grand nightcap, that and making a head flannel and <u>one</u> bib is all I had done when the box came, as of course I didn't know what to do. Now I know exactly and shall be busy accordingly.

The violet powder is the only thing I didn't need (I have a tin case of it that I bought for myself when I had a little prickly heat) and it spilled out in coming but of course it didn't spoil anything. I think you will be glad that you have been so kind to us when I tell you that we are likely to be presently reduced to a state of comparative mendicancy - in fact, that Harry has no prospects whatever beyond the beginning of the year - having suddenly heard from Mr Lidbetter that a relative of his own is coming to be with him instead. You may imagine how astonished we were and how anxious we are as to what is to become of us. Harry will explain how this has happened. It appears that Mr Lidbetter was displeased with Harry for looking after a chance of getting an agency in England in May last for another firm, although he had Captain Lidbetter's leave to do so. It came to nothing and we supposed that all was just as usual, then Mr Lidbetter writes a letter to Harry saying that as he doesn't appreciate the chances of a partnership with him, he wrote out 3 months ago for his cousin Charles Lidbetter to join him and has no further need for his services beyond January! Why couldn't he have told us then, and then Harry would have had a little more time to look about him. He is going to write to my Father also, I believe, and Uncle John Davies and cousin James Taylor, as he is au fait both in cotton dealing and shipping and has the advantage of a five years' Indian experience. Surely he ought to be able to find something to do either here or in England, <u>the latter if possible</u>, for five years out here is enough for anyone's health at one time, and to think of being at home again - I hardly dare to think of it, particularly as getting our expected little one away so young might prevent its ever being the worse for the climate which is so bad for children, though less so here than elsewhere in India, I believe. You must try not to feel disturbed about us - surely as Harry has done nothing wrong it will be all right for him and very likely better in the long run than being joined to a very extravagant and not very business-like partner.

Thursday 4th. Harry has read so far and says that I mustn't say anything depreciatory about Captain Lidbetter, but as it is true I will let it stand and not talk any more about business.

I don't feel to have said half enough about my box and its contents. I am sure you will never half know how much obliged to you I am. I can only hope that you will see some of the things being worn, wouldn't that be delightful. I have got an ayah recently, I didn't want one until next month but this one seemed too good to let slip for the sake of a month's wages, so I have taken her now. We are going to part with one of our house servants so as to get accommodation for her in the compound, and not increase our expenses. We have fixed upon the Mussal [Muslim] to go, although he is a really nice man and we are sorry to part with him, so Ahmed will have to do with no assistant but a coolie for washing dishes, etc. I seem to have nothing for the Ayah to do at present. She can't sew properly so she plaits my hair and helps me a little in the morning, and then seems quite at a loose end for the rest of the day. She has a turquoise stud through one nostril, I suppose in lieu of a nosering which is still more objectionable.

Did I tell you what immense rings some of the women here wear in their noses? Three or four inches in circumference and so heavy with jewels that they have to bring down a lock of hair over their foreheads and tie them up, others wear gold discs and one caste of women all have a thing exactly like a padlock fastened through their nostril, only made of some valuable metal. The poor people here spend <u>all</u> their money on ornaments except the few farthings a day they need for food, so that even the poorest have silver rings and bangles, if they can't afford gold and jewels, and murders are often committed to get these, especially upon children. A woman was found dead near our other house on the shore just before we left, with her ears, feet and hands cut off, evidently for the sake of her valuables.

It is quite time to thank Tom and Pollie for their delightful letters - we enjoyed them thoroughly especially as they came on Sunday when Harry was at home. I quite meant to have answered Tom's at once, but he must excuse me just at present, I am so very busy. What a pleasant time he seems to have had amongst his friends. I wish Pollie and Gulie had sent us a carte of those taken by Sarony. I admired May's and Pollie Tuke's so greatly and it is very tantalising to hear of new cartes and not see them. Pollie's descriptions of Derbyshire were most graphic and delightful - how you must have enjoyed your few days there amongst "fresh hills and pastures new" - if Milton will excuse my altering his nouns.

I hope by the time this letter reaches Thirsk you will have been to Ireland, Mother dear - Father and thyself, and besides Maggie, seen as many of <u>our</u> friends as possible. I should like both our families to be like one, if possible, only you live so far away from each other, and are all rather stay-at-home people. Please thank Mr Howard most warmly for his very kind letter - it shall not remain unanswered a mail longer than I can help. It was very kind of him to think of writing to me. In dearest love to all of our parents, sisters and brothers from Harry and myself, I am your very loving Elsie.

[From Harry on the last page] Pollie's account of your visit to Derbyshire is perfectly delightful. I wish we could join in some of your excursions. H. J.

[On a scrap of paper from Elizabeth]

PS. I forgot to tell you that I have been busy making a long dress of the beautiful muslin you sent. It is only trimmed round the bottom and I am making another, also trimmed round the bottom in points which I offer as a suggestion to Gulie [sketch of trim] - tree stitch on dress with tucks above, insertion made pointed, work sewed on with tree stitch, very quick and easy trimming - but most of the muslin I am keeping for shorter dresses.

Did I ever tell you what a dear little blue and white hood I made - a round one like Maggie had for the first - and a blue and white flannel shawl for going out into the compound with, you know I couldn't use your lovely white hood and cloak for common [every day].

Henry Jacob asks his father-in-law for help and advice.

Kurrachee Sept 4th 1864

My dear Father

Elisa has given you a rough outline of the circumstances which have led to a little rupture between myself and Captain Lidbetter, and seems to think that you ought to be more fully informed as to the details - I hardly think myself that this is necessary.

The gist of the matter seems to be that Captain L set a somewhat higher value than I did upon the connection which he offered me next year in the shape of a partnership. Anyhow, he appears to have taken offence at my looking a little around me before finally closing with him, and rather unhandsomely as I think sent to England without saying anything about it to me, and entered into arrangements with a cousin of his to come out and join him - not mentioning the circumstance to me when the whole affair was concluded. In the meantime, I had, after a good deal of consideration, pretty well decided upon availing myself of the Captain's offer, as the safest if not the most brilliant course open to me, and was of course somewhat taken aback by finding the ground thus taken from under me.

However there is now no help for it, and after all I do not think I have lost a great deal in the matter. I doubt very much if he and I would long have pulled on together, as I have not the very highest opinion of his business talents, and as senior partner he would probably commit me to a good deal I did not quite approve of. I have at all events now five or six months to look about me in, and have little fear of [not] meeting with some means of earning a livelihood.

The only point Elisa and myself are doubtful about, and on which we would like your advice, is whether it would be wiser to look to a permanent residence in India or in England. You must remember that it takes more than twice (some say three times) the income to make one comfortable in India that would suffice in England. This with my present income of over £500, I do not consider myself much better than with £200 or £300 at home. Health too is an important consideration, and although I have great cause to be thankful on this point so far, yet as I have been five years from home without a change, I have no right to expect that good health will always be my portion, any more than my neighbour's.

Some of our friends here recommend my going to Liverpool or London and endeavouring to meet with some employment there. I should feel much obliged if you would consult a little with Uncle John Davies and give me his opinion on the point. My qualifications are a fair knowledge of Indian agency business, and a knowledge of the language sufficient to enable me to accept a post in Bombay or Kurrachee. I have some years experience and believe I have a good standing here amongst mercantile men and others. I have been 3 years secretary to the Chamber of Commerce. Of course I am <u>au fait</u> in accounts, book keeping etc. You might tell Uncle that the Kurrachee Price Current and Market report which he receives every mail from T Lidbetter & Co. has been drawn up by me for years past.

If I receive any encouragement we shall certainly come home. It would be worth making some sacrifice and running some risk for, and I hope you will write me on this point. Cousin James Taylor's advice [Isabel Smith's nephew] would also be useful but I mean to write him myself. You said something recently about the profits to be derived from illustrating books - is there anything worth looking after in that line?

Elsie and I are more grateful than we can easily tell you for the beautiful presents you have sent us. You would be rewarded could you see the dear thing turning over, re-arranging and admiring all the little articles - she is as busy and important as possible.

With tenderest love to all, Believe me,
Your very affectionate son
H Jacob

[Footnote written across the left hand side of the last page]
Is there a newspaper in Liverpool which wants editing? I am up to all that sort of work, having edited an Indian paper for two years and written six columns of leading matter weekly during that period.

A chatty and loving letter to her youngest sister, Gulielma, with ideas of possible names for the baby. Still no news of a post for Harry but Elizabeth seems to have complete confidence in him. She is not past making an affectionate dig at him as master and head of the family.

Kurrachee
Sep 23 1864

My dearest Gulie

Almost every day since last time I wrote I have been thinking that I omitted all mention of the most beautiful robe thou sent me, or at all events said very little about it. I remember that I determined to send thee a separate note, which was the reason that the big letter contained so little of its praises, indeed, I'm afraid you would think my criticisms about everything lukewarm, whereas I was more delighted that you can imagine. Very often ladies come in and ask to look at my little things from England, and it is generally admitted that such a robe and hood and cloak never made their appearance in this land of heathen darkness before, and everything else comes in for its meed [merited portion] of praise, but the beauty and amount of work in the robe is something uncontemplateable [beyond contemplation!].

I think I have hardly done so much since I was married, although I have been very busy indeed since the precious box came. I wish you could see the berceaunette now that it is finished. I got a native to make the basket work and trimmed it with the pink calico and white spotted muslin of a thicker nature, keeping the other for the basket. The frills I edged with Valenciennes [lace] I brought out with me, headed with waved braid, and very charming it looks, particularly since I fastened my wedding veil onto it for mosquito

Gulielma Smith in her early 20s c1867.

113

curtains, suspending it from the hood with pink and white rosettes. Mother guessed the amount of spotted muslin exactly, without measuring beforehand I hadn't an inch to spare literally. I found the ayah very useful in doing the unpleasant parts, she can manage coarse strong sewing very well. The basket isn't finished yet, I shall do it exactly to match the other. I have made all the little bedclothes too, including frilled pillowcases etc., it does look so jolly. I am very busy still making bibs, binders of calico, crocheted shoes for common and lots of other little things. You mustn't show this letter to anybody - I think it is of so very domestic a nature.

Last time I wrote my pleasure in all these little preparations was quite spoiled by the bad news I had to tell you about Harry and the sudden falling away of all his business prospects at Mr Lidbetter's. Things are no better now except that we have got more used to looking upon ourselves as homeless outcasts. I have only one consolation, that it happened through no fault of Harry's. He has not made much move yet towards securing another berth in India, waiting to see what the tone of feeling is at home as to his comparative chance in England, but he wrote answering an advertisement offering a thousand rupees a month for an Editor for an up-country newspaper. However, Harry thinks from the high salary that it must be at some dreadfully hot and unhealthy place, probably at Meerut where the Mofussillite was edited by the late John Lang, and he says he should not think of going there, much less taking me, for any amount of money, indeed I think it wouldn't be right to do so.

When we hear from Father etc Harry will know what to do, and if home prospects of business in cotton etc are not encouraging, he will most likely go down to Bombay and see what he can get there. At any rate, we must make up our minds to leave Kurrachee and be knocked about the world a little. I have had very easy times of it so far in my life and I don't grudge roughing it a little, as poor folks must, but it is very hard upon Harry, who thought he had us both comfortably provided for, for the term of our natural lives, particularly just now when he was anxious enough to begin with about me, although that is quite gratuitous on his part, nobody gave anybody less reason to be anxious than I have done so far. I go out every morning (nearly) for a walk, sometimes about three miles, getting home by seven. Sometimes Harry goes with me but more frequently I meet a nice girl - Miss Wilkinson - on the Clifton road and walk with her.

Harry has so many committees etc to attend, and the Municipality is in a very excited state just now. The Governor of Sind - or Chief Commissioner - has been coming down upon them for misusing the public money etc during the past year, and wants the present secretary, Dr Cary, and surveyor, Mr Barnes, sent about their business as the root of all evil. Harry's was one of the three names he proposed as being any of them fit to fill the double office, at a handsome salary, but the municipal commissioners, of whom you know Harry is one, are very angry and won't have anything to do with his suggestion, and the ratepayers are dissatisfied both with the administration of the Municipality and the Chief Commissioner for finding fault with them, and are having indignation meetings and great fun. Harry has been put upon a special Committee for reconstituting the Municipal Board and settling who they will have for Secretary etc. I don't myself think they will make any changes in the latter respect, out of sheer opposition, and I don't think there is the smallest chance of Harry's being put in, but that is just the thing I should like for him, although it would be very far from a bed of roses and he doesn't much think as I do about its desirability. I think it is a place where cleverness and talent would go for something, and at any rate business habits would be appreciated after poor old Dr Cary's muddles.

Now after this lucid description of our civic battles, I must tell you about Miss Mosley's wedding which took place yesterday. It was an evening ceremony, a thing just legalized in India, and rather nice for a change. At first I thought I wouldn't go at all, but then I did go to church with Harry at five o'clock dressed in my best, and found about fifty wedding guests there, also dressed in their best. It was a pretty sight, all the officers in full dress with their cocked hats etc and I should think half the company were military. Maggie and Amy were the bridesmaids in pink and white. We waited an immense while for the bride, I should think John Howe had been in church three-quarters of an hour when she came with Mr Lidbetter as papa. She was dressed in a cloud of tarlatan over silk with a Limerick lace veil and looked very nice indeed. After the ceremony everybody went home to dress for the evening - supper at eight o'clock in a tent. The rest I take from Harry's description as I didn't go. There were about sixty guests to dinner (or supper) and the tents were beautifully decorated with evergreens, devices and flags. The tables were beautifully laid out and splendidly supplied, and they got home before twelve. That is about all I gleaned from Harry's account as told into my sleepy ears first thing this morning. The tangible result of the wedding, as far as I am concerned, is a big piece of bride-cake which Harry would like to have taken away again when he found how affectionately disposed I was towards it. However, I didn't <u>insist</u> upon eating any until morning and when I woke and asked for it at five I was told to wait until seven, so you see what strict order I am kept in by my Bluebeard of a husband.

We only had your one letter again last mail, really our friends don't treat us well, especially James and Maria who very seldom write, indeed - Gilbert and Hannah we haven't heard from for an age. Harry says I am to tell you that whenever you are in doubt about sending photographs always to decide in the affirmative, you can never get wrong that way and last time we were greatly tantalized by your mention of photographs in passé that never developed themselves into actualities.

Thank you for your suggestions upon the subject of nomenclature. Harry and I only can agree upon two or three names at all and that not definitely - Lewis Arthur after our two little brothers is a favourite with us, or Esmond Henry. The latter is my choice - I think it perfectly jolly, but you'll see the weaker vessel (me) will go to the wall, and the other (Harry) will be in the ascendant. Honora is the only girl's name we both like except Beatrix which is rather too grand, and the other is simple and Irish enough for anything so <u>that</u> I expect it may be, if required, with Nora for short, or Honor, the latter prettiest, and now you know what to expect.

I was very much interested in all thy details about Thirsk people, Gulie dear, weddings etc. quite a little "annals of the poor". Here there are no poor people scarcely, natives who are allowed 3/4 a day (six pies) by the hospital or other sick fund are well off, unless married and with families in which case they <u>are</u> a little hard up, and they don't linger on as invalids here as poor people do in

England. They are so slenderly constructed that they die almost directly anything ails them, such as a bad cold. The fact is their vegetable diet makes them good for nothing, they haven't a particle of stamina and can't endure a tenth part of the hardships of a meat eating European. I want dear Father to know this for certain, as he used to preach certain strange doctrines about the desirability of rice in India. A little is good, being easy of digestion, but much is very bad indeed.

This is a shocking place for suicides - soldiers especially, not having enough to do, succumb to the depressing climate, but the other day a very sad one took place caused by overwork. It was a Mr M. a young judge here, who did it - his wife had just come out to him from England and he was staying at Clifton for his health. He was a very good pious man but suffering from fever, and though not actually delirious, evidently affected by it to some extent. He cut his throat after deliberately calling his wife who came in a moment too late to stop him, but saw him do it - could anything be more dreadful. It made everyone feel very sad here, he was so well-known and liked.

I hope thou wilt often wear thy cashmere shawl, Gulie dear, it will only spoil with lying by, and it is meant to wear, not to look at. Our dearest love to Father, Mother, Pollie and the boys. I must write soon to Tom, this time or next, I think. Tell Artie to write to me.

In dear love to thyself and kind remembrances to everyone who remembers me.

I am thy loving sister, Elsie.

A special message of love my dear Gulie from your loving "big brother" whom you have never seen. E. keeps almost perfectly well, I am happy and thankful to say.

Love to you all, H.J.

Harry has been offered a job in Zanzibar with the trading firm of Fleming & Co. Elizabeth reassures her mother that the climate though hot, is not too bad. India under British rule had good communications, roads, railways and regular boats from England but Zanzibar was altogether a different place, as they were to discover.

Kurrachee, Oct 8 1864

My dearest Mother

Thou wilt be glad to see that I am still quite well and able to write my usual letter home, even though it is rather shorter than usual,which is quite possible, for writing is rather a tiring occupation, and always makes me very hot; I think this room where the writing table is - is not so cool as the large centre room, where I sit to work. I shall not try to answer all the letters we got by last mail, which is my usual practice - we had such a rare number - besides thine and Father's and Emma's. There was one from Gilbert and one from Hannah, one from Harry's Mother, one from Isaac J [Harry's eldest brother], one from Charlie, one from Maria Taylor and one from Jane Riccalton, and Harry had one from Mr Kimpton and Mr Glyn, both of whom have lately gone home; twelve altogether. It was most delightful - only after the home ones we never can agree which to read first, and they are taken out of their envelopes and put back again many, many times. I am always astonished that you can send me such interesting letters, but you have more chance than I have because you don't know any of the people here.

I have been out to dinner since I last wrote, and although I told Mrs McNeill over and over again that I had decided not to go out again at present, she persuaded me to go. Their bungalow is quite near ours, and we walked over after dark, I without any hat on for the sake of my hair, but nobody saw me. We found quite a large party and enjoyed ourselves much, although dinner takes up all the evening. The gentlemen didn't leave the dining room until nearly eleven and then we went home. You mustn't think they are drinking wine all the time, they spend it in smoking and talking. I persuaded Harry to go to Sandi last Saturday, there was a large volunteer picnic and about a thousand people went. He joined a nice party of Lidbetters, Wilsons, McNeills &c, and seemed to enjoy himself greatly. They had croquet, blind man's buff &c, as the day got cool. I went to spend the day with Mrs

West, a lady incapacitated like myself and we watched the train set off with our husbands &c, it was decorated with flags, evergreens and palm branches and consisted of about 30 carriages. The 23rd Regiment lent its band and all together it was quite a grand affair - the first of the kind in Sinde.

Sandi is the place I told you once of our visiting, where Mr Donaldson has built a windmill, and is trying to irrigate the land with water from the river Mulleer, but he cannot get enough as the river is nearly always dry, and even by digging very deep he gets precious little, only enough for about 45 acres of land after all his trouble; you see, every yard of the land must be watered daily to make anything grow. We have just got new potatoes from Bombay - that reminds me, just think of their not being in season until October, and here in Sinde they are only just sowing them I believe. They are not half so good as home new potatoes but they are waxy and stiff and a great improvement upon the horrid old things we have been eating for three months past.

The Mrs West I mentioned just now has engaged the same nurse that I have - Mrs Forbes - and I calculated upon her having done with her before now, whereas the tiresome creature doesn't want her yet, so I am beginning to be afraid that I shall miss her. I have heard of another but Mrs Forbes is the best in the station, an experienced Scotch woman, both in England and in India, and as good as anyone at home could be, I hear. I have finished all necessary preparations I think, except making this downstairs room ready. It doesn't look like a bedroom at present, being littered with all sorts of things - easel - maps - writing table - papers &c. I must get Harry to find some other place for all his belongings, and then there will be little left to do.

You will be anxious to hear whether we have heard of anything in the way of business which Harry thinks likely - the most eligible thing yet is a proposal of Fleming & Co., a large and very wealthy and important firm, that he should take charge of their branch at Zanzibar on the African coast. It isn't very far from here and though hot, the climate isn't bad, on account of its being a small island, so I think if they offer anything like a reasonable compensation for living in such a savage place, Harry will think seriously of taking it, but not decide until we hear from home, although I don't suppose you can have anything definite to propose. There is a small settlement of English there and a British Consul so we should not be altogether away from civilization, or in any danger of being eaten up by the blacks. I only hope we shouldn't have to keep slaves there, but that the blacks could be made to understand the receiving of wages and other mutual obligations.

Harry called on the Commissioner the other day and he was very affable, although H. belongs to such a rebellious and refractory body. I expect Harry will resign his seat on the Municipality in a day or two, as the Independent members can no longer hold their own against the Government majority and it appears very likely that the vote of censure upon the Commissioner's letter will be rescinded - in which case the only dignified way will be for those who passed the vote to retire and leave the Commissioner to his own obstinate devices. The man has more absolute power than our own Sovereign and over a larger territory, which he uses in the most arbitrary manner, for instance, the Mr Bolton that we went to see at Tatta, has just been presented by him to an appointment, which he had no right to expect, worth a thousand rupees (£100) a month, with horse allowance and a house rent free and very little work to do! That is something for a young man of 28, isn't it? He came in the other evening in great glee, and said he thought himself one of the luckiest fellows in Sinde.

I have had great fun this week in watching the races from our upstairs window, this I believe is the last evening. I told you the grand stand is very close to us and with a telescope one can see the horses nearly all round the course - of course there are no racehorses here - gentlemen run their own riding horses - and some of them are their own jockeys, while some get jockeys up from Bombay. The greatest fun I think is in watching the people come and go - everybody seems to be there from Camp and lots of natives, hundreds upon hundreds; they make a very gay crowd and come in the funniest vehicles, bullock carts and dummies and buggies of all kinds, some on camels with scarlet saddles and others on lovely little long tailed Arabs, prancing along with their flowing robes and monstrous turbans just like a picture.

Maggie and Amy Lidbetter came on Thursday to spend the day and see the races, and seemed greatly to enjoy it - it was such fun to see my dog Totty playing with Amy, they never stopped all day.

What Totty liked best was for Amy to lie on her face on the floor and let him worry her and run away with her net, then when he wanted her to get up he would push his little nose under her face and pat her head with his paw, and do all sorts of queer things; I thought I should never be tired of watching them.

If we leave here Harry says we can't take any dog but Carlo, but I shall be very sorry to lose poor Totty, and even old Dick deserves some consideration. You would be amused if you heard how regularly they rush upstairs at five or six o'clock a.m. when the Hamal opens the outer door, and come bouncing in wild with delight, but Totty has a little private way of getting in through a hole in the verandah and often comes quietly in during the night and sleeps beside us on the carpet, or rather, beside Carlo, for that is his regular place. He precedes us upstairs with the utmost regularity and lies down always in a certain place by the bed and is asleep in a minute.

I forgot to tell thee Mother dear, that Mrs Lidbetter has very kindly offered to come and stay with me when I need her. They live about four miles away so it is a long way to send - however I will avail myself of her kindness if possible. I shouldn't like to disturb her at any unreasonable hour as she is a delicate ailing body and not good for much exertion, but if it happened conveniently I shall be glad to have her, so that the nurse may not feel altogether responsible. Indeed, Mother darling, nobody can take thy place - and I feel that I shall virtually have nobody with me as thou art not here. Thank Pollie for sending the names - we still don't agree - I think it will end in our shaking some up in a bag and seeing what turns up. We like Sydney Harris, Harold Smith, Lewis Arthur or Esmond Henry about equally, and of girls names we have thought of Isabel Lucy (after our Mothers), Honora, Gulielma Mary, and a few others that I can't remember. Kathleen is very pretty too, but it is a very difficult matter to settle, the fact is, we have settled it a dozen times and next time always forget what the last decision was! Now do go to Ireland, there's a dear good Father and Mother, we do so want you to see our relations there, you will be putting it off until too late in the season if you don't take care. I heard of cousin [1]Pollie Tuke's intended marriage from you and Maria T and Jane Riccalton. I know Alfred Priestman a little, he is very nice indeed and Pollie will make him a dear little wife, will you congratulate her from us both at the earliest opportunity.

We were very much struck with Gulie's carte's likeness to me, I thought it was one of me at first sight - but on examination it proves to be very like Gulie - better even than Kitchen's, but why does she wear her hair over her ears, it makes her look so old. Pollie ought to have sent us hers I think - why didn't she? I began some time ago to paint my own likeness, and Harry too began to go on with it, but really I am so ugly we don't like doing it and we have no canvasses the right size - and can't get them even in Bombay. I send you a pattern of paper the colour of my complexion, I have just been matching it at the glass and I have no colour in my cheeks and this in spite of always being quite well and never having indigestion or anything. I suppose the climate does it but I am more and more surprised that Harry is as rosy and fresh looking as ever, just healthily tanned as he might be after a month at the Lakes; he is delightful to look at in this land of sallow faces, as indeed he would be in any land.

Dear Father mustn't think I have neglected his letter because I haven't replied to any of his items of news. How I do long sometimes for a taste of English fruit, a bon Chrétien pear especially, and how cordially I do dislike the water melons, custard apples &c that we get here, and that don't taste of anything in particular. Now that figs are out of season I cannot like any fruit at all and yet one almost needs to eat some daily. Was it the Blenheim Pippins the boys took again this year, they really are too bad. I am afraid I left dear Father a very troublesome legacy in Joseph Barber, he seems to be constantly getting into and giving trouble. I think he is one of the few cases that one may fairly say are quite hopeless - in fact as Caleb Williams would say - he is a "moral idiot". Will you remember me kindly to Thomas Thompson, I hope his wife will keep him steady. Here's a long letter after all, with it comes the dear <u>love</u> of your truly loving daughter Elsie and Harry's too.

Perhaps you may get some news by next mail, but don't expect it till it comes, or get at all fidgetty.

Note:
1. Pollie Tuke: Pollie Tuke (1842-79) married Alfred Priestman (1831-1910) in 1865. She was the daughter of Daniel Tuke and Bartholomew's sister, Mary Ann Smith.

Elizabeth asks Pollie if she would send news of her baby's birth to the relatives. The ramification of family connections was enormous as Bartholomew Smith was the youngest of eleven children, all but three of whom married and had even more children and grandchildren. The Oddies are from her mother's side, and there were many relatives from Henry's family too.

Kurrachee
Oct 17 1864

My dearest Pollie

The mail only came in yesterday - bringing thine as the only home letter for Harry and myself, so we didn't fail to appreciate it, especially as our man came back without one, and until the postman came we feared ourselves entirely forgotten - well, hardly that - but altogether neglected.

I am writing now, dear, to ask thee whether thou wilt undertake to write a notification of the little event we are expecting, as soon as you receive notice of it from Harry, to our different relatives - and so save the heavy postage. I will give thee the names I think of and then thou can say I wished them to be written to and nobody will feel neglected. We are thinking of sending cards here but it will be a nicer way to write to home friends, if thou doesn't think it too much trouble - Aunt Esther, Aunt Mary Ann, Aunt Elizabeth, Uncle John Spence, Uncle William, Aunt Hannah Peirson, Maggie, Aunt Lydia - Sam and Isy, Cousin John O [Oddie] & Rachel, Lizzie Taylor & Aunt Betsy, Cousin John and Sue Taylor, Mariana and Gulie Spence, old Aunt Mary, Mrs Henry Brown, Lizzie Wilson, Uncle James Hills. Please add any to the list that I may have forgotten - and don't be alarmed at the array of names - a line will suffice. Harry will write to his friends and to Maria Taylor as well as to you. I am glad you saw dear Aunt Jane Jacob at York, she is a sweet old lady I know, although I have only seen her once.

I wish that Father and Mother wouldn't let any little thing prevent their going to Ireland. Harry says, and I partly agree with him, that their seeing our other father and mother and getting to know and love them, is of more immediate importance than Bible Meetings, which after all might be held by somebody else. I think they <u>might</u> go, that is all I can say.

Nothing more has transpired yet with regard to our Zanzibar prospects but Harry seems to think it very likely to come to something. You mustn't mind our going to such a savage place - it is said to be quite healthy that is - the island - which is twenty miles from the coast of Zanzibar and where Europeans live. I fancy there are from half a dozen to a dozen white people there - but no ladies, so one of you girls will have to make up your minds to come out to me some day when I have tried what it is like. Though 6 degrees south only from the equator - the climate is about the same as this, varying from 78 to 89 degrees or so all the year round and of course plenty of breeze from the sea. It is in the possession of the Imaum or Sultan of Muscat and all the blacks there are slaves - I suppose we should get over the difficulty by hiring them. I think this is all I know of the place - some say it is very fruitful, and some rocky, so we will suppose it to be a judicious combination. Of course, Harry won't go unless he can get a very good salary, or a good percentage - £1000 a year or so - it wouldn't be worth while for much less, he says, for most things we wanted except food, would have to come from England. It would be quite like being a merchant in the Arabian Nights - shipping ivory and gold dust and spices &c wouldn't it, and importing cloths of different kinds for native clothing. I think I should like to help hunt the elephants sometimes in order to get the tusks, only that the mainland is so unhealthy. It is the place that poor [1]Captain Speke started from. We were so sorry to hear of his having been killed by his own gun while out shooting - it seems doubly sad for him to die by an accident after surviving so many dangers by flood and field.

I am sure you would enjoy staying at Gilling [about 10 miles east of Thirsk] - farmhouses are always delightful even when inhabited by barbarians - how much more when nice well-educated people are combined with the other luxuries thou mentions - though I don't suppose anyone there can make cheesecakes like Mrs Frank Taylor - it would be impossible both to have a cultivated mind and such a capacity as that.

I dare say you will all be surprised at my being able to write to you on this date - not more so than I am, I'm sure. I am as well and strong as ever and took a three mile walk with Harry this morning without feeling the least fatigue. Harry is beginning to believe my prospects quite legendary and refuses to listen to any more of my prognostications. I am taking advantage of my well-ness to get this letter written and I think I will try to answer Gilbert's and Hannah's too - although it will be quite old by mail time, perhaps they would rather have it than nothing.

Harry has resigned his seat on the Management Committee which I am very glad of - so now he is out of many of the rows. The Committee, in consequence of all the independent members leaving, is now entirely in Government hands, which is altogether illegal so they must make some change. Is the [2]American War coming to an end for certain, or why has cotton gone down so suddenly. We can't make it out here, for certainly peace prospects don't seem on the improve. Did Uncle John make or lose anything in the panic for it must have been a tremendous time in L'pool. Robert never writes, and if he did, I dare say he wouldn't descend so low as cotton.

Our dearest love to you all. I am glad Tom is growing such a fine big fellow. I think you will do well to get rid of Ernest, for Tom's sake, he never was nice or "fit for society". Tell dearest Father and Mother not to be anxious about me.

I am dear, Thy loving Elsie.

PS. I am writing to thank Fanny and Lucy for their beautiful cartes.

Note:
1. John Hanning Speke (1827-1864), one of the great British explorers of the 19th century, was a member of Sir Richard Burton's expedition to find the great lake in the heart of Africa, which was said to be the source of the Nile. They travelled inland from Dar-es-Salaam, on the coast of what is now Tanzania, and in February 1858 were the first Europeans to reach Lake Tanganyika. Speke then journeyed on alone northwards and found "the great lake" which he named Victoria in honour of the Queen. In 1862, on a second expedition with James Grant, Speke discovered that Lake Victoria was indeed a source of the Nile but Burton challenged his conclusion as not providing enough evidence. On 15th September 1864, the day that he was to have had a public debate with Burton on the subject, Speke was killed by his own gun in a hunting accident, perhaps suicide, in Wiltshire. As Elizabeth says, it was

terrible for him to have endured all those hardships to die in such an ignominious way.

2. "The American War .." the Civil War, 1861-5, was fought on the issues of separation and slavery, and blocked the supply of raw cotton from the southern states to European markets. This opened up a marketing niche for Indian cotton, which Thomas Lidbetter took advantage of, but when the war ended and the lower-priced American supply resumed, the demand for Indian cotton dropped back.

One can imagine Elizabeth sitting up in bed two days after the birth of her baby writing a little note in pencil to her Mother. She was probably wise not to have a doctor in attendance as they were mostly employed for the Indian Army and not experienced in obstetrics, as well as being an extra expense.

October 23rd [1864]

My dearest Mother

I am so glad to be strong enough today to write a few lines myself to announce our dear baby's arrival. She made her appearance on Friday the 21st inst. at half-past four o'clock in the afternoon and is now sleeping quietly beside me, for a wonder, for she has been quite naughty ever since she was born and will be nursed or else cry. I had no doctor with me, as I had foredetermined, and I did perfectly well with Nurse Forbes and the ayah. Harry was away at office and came home just in time to find all nicely over, and very thankful he was to find all well and a dear little daughter to kiss him when he came back.

She is not very pretty yet but I daresay she will be - Harry is sending you a picture of her which is very like her indeed. She has large features, and large well-opened eyes, that she hardly ever shuts. They are dark slate colour at present and may be either blue or brown, her little bit of hair and eyebrows and eyelashes are all very dark indeed and she has nice red cheeks like Harry's. Her funniest part is a large pug-nose sharp at the end but she is a bonny sensible looking child for her age.

We are going to call her Honora, as we can't choose among family names. I hope you will like it. I forgot to tell you that Mrs Lidbetter wrote the day before to ask me whether she should go to Kotree for a few days and I was so perfectly well that I told her she need not stay on my account - however it happened a few hours only after she had gone - and I did quite well without her and didn't miss any comfort or attention I could have had if a dozen people had been there. I have already begun to feed baby a little and in another day or so hope to be able to do it altogether.

My dearest love to you all, especially to my dear baby's grand-papa and grandmama and uncles and aunts, I think she is more like Artie than anybody.

Your loving daughter,
Elsie

A delightful letter from Henry, the new and doting father, to his Mother-in-law, Isabel Smith

Kurrachee

Oct. 23rd 1864

My very dear Mother

Elisa's little pencil note, which you will be relieved to find she is already strong enough to write, will tell you that we have got a dear little daughter at last, not on my birthday as we had been hoping, but only 11 days afterwards, so that I can still look upon it as a birthday present - the most precious I ever had in my life. I think we long more than anything to have some of you here to see our little pet. We seem to have no-one to show her to, at least no-one who will acknowledge as fully as you would the undoubted fact that she is the canniest little girl in the whole world.

Everything went off as well as possible. E. was so well on the 20th that we took our usual morning walk of a couple of miles, and continued just as usual all day, in fact so well that she allowed Mrs Lidbetter to go off to Kotree, although the latter would have remained at the slightest hint. My pet was however a little tired and poorly at bedtime, and passed a bad night. She was in pain when I woke, and so we sent for the nurse who arrived about 9 o'clock, but did not think at first that anything was going to happen. I went to office as usual, leaving E. in Nurse Forbes' care and when I came home about 5pm. my little daughter had been born about half an hour, and her mother quite comfortable and free from pain. She has been wonderfully well since, and so far as appearances go might, one would think, be up and about.

But we are going to be very careful, and she must be a good girl and remain in bed for a long while yet. She has a capital nurse who saved us the worry and expense of a doctor and has managed things admirably, but I fear she will have to go away very soon, as another lady who lives near is expecting to be confined immediately.

E. bids me tell you that she has been able to feed baby a good deal today and the little thing is much happier since her natural food has been ready for her, and is sleeping most persistently. At first she did hardly anything but scream. I hardly know what else to tell you. The sketch I made yesterday was <u>very</u> like her then but she seems to me much prettier today, and I never tire of looking at her dear little mouth, but can't tell you what color her eyes are going to be yet. It is certain they will have dark brows and lashes and her little modicum of hair is also dark. She is a beautiful healthy color, her forehead pale and cheeks beautifully tinted and is very mature in her appearance, in fact nurse says she would have done to be born a few days ago.

I am writing at E's bedside, who is looking very pretty, especially since she has closed her eyes to take a nap. This is a nice cheerful room opening out of the sitting room, and close to the bathroom, etc. which is very convenient for washing purposes. We have a pretty light American bedstead in it, a couch for nurse, wardrobe, washstand and toilet table, and a small table and a few chairs. The berceaunette [bassinette or cradle], which is a most magnificent thing to look at, stands on an ottoman opposite me, but nurse does not believe in berceanettes, and won't put baby in, saying she would lose it - I suppose E. will have her own way in a day or two.

With regard to our prospects I think I have pretty much decided to go to Zanzibar, and shall probably run down to Bombay in the course of a fortnight in order to see the head of the firm, Mr John Fleming, who is expected in Bombay by the mail [steamer] after next. We like the idea of going to Zanzibar very well, and I hope to be able to secure good terms from W. Nicol & Co. The post will be a pleasant one, as I shall have everything my own way, and will have no one over me nearer than London. The business too is one that I know I shall be up to, as it is much what I am used to here. From all we can hear the climate is good and equable, and there is a small colony of Europeans who will I hope be sociable and pleasant.

E. bids me ask father to send the announcement of little Honora's birth to 'The Friend' and 'British Friend'. You might send us the number it appears in - she was born on the 21st inst. at about 4pm. I am also to tell you that she is above the average size but not very large, not as big as Maggie's baby, Elisa says, but then as I tell her, Maggie's baby was a boy. The little pet has been sleeping beautifully for an hour past, since she got a drink from her mother this morning, and I do so wish you could see the canny wee darling.

24th Oct - I must finish this letter tonight as I shall not have time to add to it tomorrow. Elsie has been very nicely all day and is now we hope safely thro' her troubles. Baby likes her new diet amazingly and will do nothing but feed and sleep as she ought to do. She has been asleep nearly all day they tell me and the difficulty is to get her awake in order to come to her mother.

I am afraid you will think this a short letter and I know I have not told you half all you will want to know. Next mail however you will perhaps have a long letter from E. herself who will supply all deficiencies.

With dear love from us both
I am Your loving son
Henry Jacob

Elizabeth is managing her new baby very well, and breastfeeding rather than putting her out to a wet-nurse which was a common practice among Europeans. In spite of the fact that Harry's relations with Captain Lidbetter have cooled somewhat, Mrs Lidbetter is being most helpful and supportive to the new mother. Bartholomew and Isabel Smith still haven't managed a trip to Ireland to visit Harry's parents, much to Elizabeth's dismay.

Kurrachee
Nov 8 1864

My dearest Mother

Many thanks for all that came by last mail - thy dear little note and Gulie's letter and the opportune gloves, which I was glad to have last Sunday, for I went to church for the first time for some weeks. Both Harry's and mine fit perfectly and his will come in very conveniently too, to wear in Bombay, where he goes tomorrow by the mail steamer that carries these letters. Unless there is an intermediate steamer, he will have to be away for a fortnight, although a day or two would do for his business which is only to see Mr Fleming and make arrangements about Zanzibar.

It seems very possible that we shall leave here before the end of the year, so Harry said I had better ask you not to send off the other little parcel of things which thou speaks of until you hear something definite of our movements, or we may miss them altogether. I am quite puzzled to think what more you can have to send me, after the complete supply I got before - how kind you are to the dear little pet. I only wish she knew who to thank for her trousseau. All her things fit very well indeed so far. I have put her into the short sleeved gowns, with a robe for state occasions, as she was a fortnight old last Friday.

But I suppose you will want to hear all about us. I got on very well I am thankful to say. Nurse Forbes was obliged to leave me on the sixth day as Mrs West sent for her, and at first I was rather lost with only the ayah to do for us both, but I got up on the 9th day (Nurse thinking it was the 10th and you may be sure I didn't undeceive her). She came for a day or two more just for half an hour in the morning to wash baby and then I could do it myself. I went to church last Sunday, as I said, and yesterday and today took nearly my usual walk on the Clifton Road. We are so thankful that all has gone so well. Harry seems quite astounded to find how little anxiety it has cost him. He was prepared to be in a heart-broken state over an invalid wife, but found me not half so "interesting" as he expected, only a little hungrier than usual, and no wonder, if you could see what an appetite baby has. She sleeps pretty well at night but during the last few days requires nursing nearly the whole day.

I am very fortunate in having a really nice ayah, who has had plenty of experience in babies, for clever as I thought myself I find I am very ignorant, and I have generally nobody to consult. The Hamal too is a capital nurse, and often gets baby to sleep when nobody else can. He always goes out walking with it and the ayah, as the custom is here. The natives are passionately fond of children especially white ones, and I think the men are even better nurses than the women. We have quite settled to call baby Honora. She is growing such a sweet plump little darling, how many times a day do I wish that her grandpapa and grandmamma and aunts and uncles could see her. Her eyes seem quite inclined to be a dark grey with very dark eyelashes. We thought at first they were turning brown, but they have left off doing so. She is getting more and more like Harry, she has the same smooth broad forehead and such a large beautifully shaped head covered with very short thick dark-coloured down and small pretty ears. Her mouth is like Pollie's I think with a long upper lip and small under one, and her nose is greatly improved, so that she is quite a bonnie baby and not large featured now that her face is getting so fat. I am greatly hoping to get the ayah to go with us to Africa when it is finally settled for us to go. I shall ask her to do so and Harry has great hankerings after the butler's company so it is quite possible that we may migrate like the patriarchs of old - "servants and children and cattle", Carlo representing the latter.

We have very pleasant accounts of Zanzibar and think we shall like it a great deal better than Kurrachee. We are sending you a letter about it in reply to one which Mr Nicol wrote on our behalf to a friend of his. Besides this we have read of its being a coral island rich in all manner of ferns and plants and producing pineapples and oranges <u>wild</u>, besides groves of spices, and it must be the very country for artists as it abounds in the copal tree. The climate is very well-spoken of - milder than Bombay and drier;

the temperature moderated by a constant sea breeze so that its being close to the equator doesn't signify. I never thought when cousin Robert and I used to joke about having a house built across the line, for warmth, how nearly it would come true in my case.

The weather here is horrible just now, dreadfully cold in the morning and evening and as hot as can be in the middle of the day, 88F yesterday in this cool house in the shade, then a nasty unhealthy land wind blows all day, which we are obliged to shut out carefully, and which brings in clouds of dust. In fact it is as disagreeable as the cold season always is, judging by last winter's experience here, so that we shan't be very sorry to leave it for a more equable climate.

I forgot to tell you that the *Zillah* is in at last, with our box on board I suppose, although she has not unloaded yet. She has been more than five months on the way and we had nearly given her up. The things will be very acceptable as I am rather tired of our little black earthenware native tea-pot with a broken spout and the lid tied on with a string!

I have very little pleasure in writing letters this mail because I keep thinking that the same steamer that takes these is to take Harry away from me and I have yet to learn how I can manage without him. He has never been a whole day away before and it does seem very hard lines for him to stay a whole fortnight. You will be glad to hear that I am not going to stay in this deserted house meanwhile. Mrs Lidbetter has kindly asked me to go there, and although I have had many scruples about taking baby to trouble them, Harry has persuaded me to avail myself of their kindness, and certainly it will be much pleasanter in many ways.

Mrs Lidbetter has been very kind since she came from Kotree. She has spent part of two days here herself and several times sent to enquire after us. She seems very sorry that baby isn't a boy: she is so fond of boys and so greatly disappointed that all hers died young and left her only the three girls. I can't say that I am a bit sorry that our pet isn't a boy, she is so delightful as she is. It is so pretty to see Harry nursing her; she seems to appreciate him so much and he is so fond of her and holds her quite cleverly now, squaring his elbows after the fashion of novices in the art of nursing. We were so grieved to hear of poor [1]Isaac's loss in his dear little boy. I think one cannot tell what it must be to lose a child until one becomes a parent and feels what a precious charge it is. I think too it fills us with new love to our own parents when we get to understand a little how tenderly they have been caring for us all these years. I am sure it it so with me.

We are so disappointed that you have put off your Irish visit. We do so want you to know our other parents, but I feel sure you will go as soon as you possibly can. Don't forget to send us your new likenesses, it is so delightful getting photographs from home. We were very much pleased with Artie's, the face is capital, but he looks rather afraid of his new clothes which are to be sure, rather alarming things and look like school and lessons and not like the home pet who has got into them. I think considering that he is "Uncle Artie" now, they are very suitable. I will show the picture to baby some day and tell her who it is; nobody ever heard of an uncle in a tunic I should think.

How you must have enjoyed the walk home from Gilling or I should say, from Hovingham. I have often seen the road you came along from the top of the Gilling coach, the driver told us it was the Malton road and I have often thought what a splendid view there must be from the top. I find I am talking to Gulie now, or rather alluding to her letter, and Mount Suever [?], how dearly I should like to see that [2]"Chateau-en-Espagne" again. Wouldn't it be nice if Harry and I lived in it with baby and you came always to see us, and slept on dried ferns and heather as we planned to do. I wonder shall I ever show Harry all the old familiar places he knows so well by name, for I am never tired of talking of them. How good Tom is to get on so well at [3]York. I think nobody could have a more satisfactory son at school, he has done nothing but give you pleasure since he went, by being both good and clever. I hope dear little Artie will be equally successful.

Now goodbye dear, dear Father and Mother. Next mail I hope to tell you some definite news about our future prospects, as Harry will telegraph to me directly he has seen the head of the firm in Bombay. I am very glad Aunt Ann is comforted by my proximity, but as I am going westward again so shortly she won't have much benefit of me I'm afraid. I shall feel nearer to you in Zanzibar because it is west from here.

Again farewell, your loving Elsie

Dear love to Pollie, Gulie, Artie and please tell Emma I will try to write to her next mail. I was very glad fo her letter. Will you kindly send the enclosed letter to Ballytore when you have read and digested it?

Notes:
1. Isaac's loss: his son Tom, born 1859, died 1864. Isaac Jacob was Henry's eldest brother.
2. Chateaux en Espagne: Castles in the air; something that exists only in the imagination, literally, castles in Spain, where there are no chateaux.
3. Tom at York: The Quaker school for boys at Bootham, founded 1823.

There is a note of despair in this letter. No position has been found in England for Harry. Reading between the lines, Elizabeth's parents are happy to give them a home while Harry finds work, but the Jacobs don't want to be a burden. In order to be registered baby Nora had to be baptised according to the rites of the Anglican church, but the chaplain was very sympathetic to the conscience of Friends and made the ceremony as simple as possible.

Kurrachee
Nov. 23 1864

My own dearest Mother

Last mail brought us the letters which speak so hopefully of our returning to England soon, and you may imagine how painful they were to me both on our own account and on yours. On our own - because we have long ago given up the idea of returning to England without any definite prospect, and on yours because I know you will be so disappointed and I can't bear to think of dear Father looking out as anxiously as I know he will for some opening for Harry at home.

Harry has not yet seen your letters - he has been in Bombay for nearly a fortnight making final arrangements for going to Zanzibar. He has made pretty satisfactory terms with Nicol's, he tells me in a letter I had from him this morning - he has engaged himself for 3 years (three years longer banishment for us who long so for home) and they are to pay him £960 the first year (800 Rupees a month) and to increase it the second if the business there answers their expectations. This will be a very good salary there as the place is much cheaper than Kurrachee, here we have had to live quite up to our income - £600 a year - and to deny ourselves every extra such as a carriage or giving dinners to our friends. We have had nothing but the office buggy for months now and been as economical as possible and yet effected no saving - in fact provisions and other things are getting so dear now that I don't think we could have lived upon it another year - I should think the Lidbetters spend twice that.

We shall be going to Zanzibar almost as soon as Harry gets home I expect, and I am very busy selling our furniture by sending round to our friends a list with the prices attached - the usual way here, and I expect we shall go back to a half empty house. I quite dread your next letters coming - dear ones - with their hopeful expectation of seeing us. I had no idea you would recommend our coming home - Harry soon decided that he would only do so in case of our not being able to find a living out here as he didn't like the idea of going back to England as poor as he came out, and still less of taking advantage of your kindness "to sponge upon you" as he calls it, which would feel very different to staying with you for the same length of time if we were pretty well-off, as I hope we may be by the time we come home - may God spare us all to see each other before many years have passed.

I was so pleased with the likenesses you sent us - they are quite the best I ever saw of you, and I am quite anxious to show them to Harry when he comes back. The Lidbetters are extremely kind but I am weary of being without him and hope we may never be parted again as long as we live. Dear baby is my great consolation - she is growing such a fat bouncing girl and looks about her at everything in the most knowing way, even the tiny speck of a night light attracts her and nearly makes her break her neck in twisting her head to look at it. You never saw a more vivacious baby of a month old - when I am going to feed her she smacks her lips and bobs her head against me and clutches hold of my dress in the most impatient way, and hinders me so that she has a long time to wait. She is going to be very pretty after all - I see - she has long dark eyelashes and beautiful dark blue eyes - almost black - and a very sweet little mouth - but Harry thinks she is spoilt by her long top lip - and says he doesn't thank our family for it. You will be glad to hear that she isn't the least bit like me - but is a combination of her papa and her Aunt Polly so far. Won't Harry be pleased when he comes back, he hasn't seen her since she was a fortnight old. I only wish she wasn't so bitten by mosquitoes - there are so many at this end of camp and both Norrie [Nora] and I are greatly disfigured by red spots from their bites - I have, I think, three on my nose!

I asked my Ayah today whether she will go with me to Africa, but I told her not to answer me until she had thought about it. I don't know whether Harry means to take Ahmed or not.

I don't know what you will say, but we were obliged to get baby christened - by obliged I mean that they won't give any certificate of birth except a baptismal certificate and there is no registrar in Sind except the chaplains - so that she couldn't be named without. However, the Revd. Mr Bagnell is a very nice man who knows Friends and he said he would do it privately without any sponsors or making us say anything, as it was against our conscience, so he offered a short prayer and baptised her "Honora" and that was all. So we saved our consciences as well as we could, for infant baptism is quite a mockery we both think and we told Mr Bagnell so. You see there is no legal recognition of dissenters here, or any provision for their scruples. I hope we haven't disqualified our dear little girl for Friends' schools if she lives to grow up - at any rate they would take her in at [1]Polam!

I am reading at present Victor Hugo's last book *Les Misérables* and I must recommend Pollie and Gulie to do the same - it is the best and cleverest novel I ever read, as much superior to the ordinary run of novels as you can imagine. Every sentence is worth remembering nearly, it is full of original thoughts, and reveals the goodness there is in the worst classes of people. The hero is a convict, and a more noble man never commanded admiration. I must give you one sentence that I think is equal to any of Henry Kingsley's child's talk in *Ravenshoe*. Two little French girls are dressing their kitten up in dolls' clothes - and have thrown the doll away on the floor - and one says, "This doll, sister, is more amusing than the other, you see, for it moves, it cries, and is warm, so we will play with it. It is my little daughter and I am a lady; you will call upon me and look at it. <u>By degrees you will see its whiskers</u>, and that will surprise you, and then you will see its ears and its tail, and that will surprise you too, and you will say to me, Oh, my goodness! and I shall answer, Yes, Madame, it is a little child I have like that, <u>little children are so at present</u>." Isn't it deliciously childish, especially what I have underlined.

You must excuse a short letter this time, my dear Mother and Father, as I am so unsettled. We shall always thank you in our hearts for the kindness of both your letters - nothing could exceed it. It is indeed delightful to us to feel that we have a home in England and such loving friends to welcome us to it. Dear baby sends her grandpapa and grandmama each a kiss. I couldn't get any more as she began to make faces at me for kissing her so often.

With dear love to Pollie, Gulie, Tom, Artie and most of all yourselves I am your ever loving daughter, Elsie.

Note:
1. Polam Hall, Darlington, Co Durham is a private Quaker school
   for girls founded in 1854, where presumably infant baptism
   was no bar for entry to the school even in those days.

Elizabeth is resigned to living in Zanzibar, and knows she will miss the regular letters from home. The mail was very erratic to and from Zanzibar and could take several months.

Victoria Hotel, Bombay

Dec 13 1864

My dearest Mother

There were so many letters inside the last home envelope that I hardly know which to answer but I think I can't get wrong if I address this to thee, although it must needs be a very short one as we are now en route for Zanzibar, and our time for writing and everything else is limited. It is grievous to think that we shall get no more letters from you regularly and you none from us every fortnight, but only when there happens to be communication with our out of the way home. Harry thinks that the best way for you to address us is - H Jacob, H.A. Fraser & Co. Zanzibar (via Marseilles). H.A. Fraser is the name of Nicol's branch firm there and the (via Marseilles) may be useful to prevent them from going round the Cape, though goodness knows how they will be sent. I suppose however we shall fare no worse than the other Europeans there, but we shall sadly miss your dear regular letters full of news of yourselves and all friends. You may however be sure that we will write by <u>every</u> opportunity.

We left Kurrachee on the 10th Dec - the anniversary of the day on which I arrived in India - wasn't it queer that I should spend exactly a year in India, not reckoning these few days in Bombay. We expect to sail next Monday in the *Naval Brigade* a barque of about 600 tons in which Harry says the accommodation is very comfortable, and the captain has promised us his stateroom in consideration of there being a lady and baby in the case. We have been in such a hurry since I wrote to you last - Harry didn't get up from Bombay until the 2nd and between that and the 10th we had our affairs to arrange, things to sell, &c. However we managed by leaving many of our things in the hands of an auctioneer for sale.

Dear little baby is very cross today - she was vaccinated just before we left Kurrachee and the places are just beginning to be inflamed. I felt quite sick the first day on board the steamer and had to leave baby's washing and dressing to the ayah and to Ahmed, both of

140

whom are going with us to Zanzibar. I had to get a new ayah as the old one would not come, at least her husband would not let her. We are quite a large family altogether - Harry, baby, myself, Ahmed, the ayah, Carlo and a black Persian cat called Satan which was given me on board the *Governor Higginson*. It is quite a young one and looks lost in its long fur - it is already quite good friends with Carlo who generally chevies [chivies] cats.

The principal thing I wanted to write about I haven't yet mentioned which is that we got the things from off the *Zillah* just the day before we left Kurrachee, and were very much pleased indeed with them. You may imagine how delighted I was with the unexpected shawl which I imagine is a present from Mother? also with the cocoa, biscuits, teapot stand, cocoa jug, photograph &c. But why do you not send us a bill of the things we ordered - we have not paid for a single thing since we left home and Harry says that we shall want so many things sending to Zanzibar that we cannot possibly feel easy to send for them unless you give us some chance of paying our debts regularly. We have no objection to presents now and then, but when we <u>send</u> for things we do hope you will allow us to pay for them.

[Harry writes] E has been called away by baby, so I am finishing her letter for her. We arrived in Bombay this morning about 2am and came ashore as soon as it was light. We had considerable difficulty in finding a hotel which would take us in as they were nearly all full with the passengers just arrived by the English mail. However, at last we hit on this place the *Victoria Gardens Hotel* and like our quarters very well. Most Bombay hotels are execrable, but this one being new is nice and clean, which is a great point.

[Elizabeth takes up the pen again] I was going to thank you very much for your trouble in sending us the things, and most especially for such as are presents - the shawl I admire extremely, it will be the very thing for Zanzibar, how very kind of you to think of sending it to me. We are going to indulge ourselves with some cocoa and biscuits on board ship - they have come in most conveniently for the voyage. We had such a nice party of people on board ship as we came down from Kurrachee - Mr & Mrs Wilson and several others that we knew, including Mr Alsen, who I hope will dine with us this evening. It is time for us to go out so I must cut shorter this very short letter.

Many thanks to Pollie for her nice long letter and to Father for short one. I am so glad that he has changed his mind partly about our coming home, as we really could not have felt easy to do so, and hope that this is the right thing for us. Dear Artie wrote a famous letter - pray thank him for taking so much pains with it. Everybody takes dear baby for three months old though she is only 7 weeks and I am greatly proud of her fat hard cheeks and so indeed is her dear papa.

In dear love I am your most loving daughter and sister
Elisa H Jacob.

As ever, Elizabeth makes the best of things and is anxious to be in Zanzibar and get on with her life. Nora's smallpox vaccination has "taken" successfully and the mosquito bites haven't infected her with malaria. Mrs Lidbetter cautions Elizabeth not to over stimulate the baby in case her intellect is harmed!

Victoria Gardens Hotel, Bombay

December 18th 1864

My very dearest Father & Mother

I am writing to you again although it is not nearly mail time, because it may be a long time before I have another chance of sending a letter direct to you, and I want you to have the last news of us before we sail. It is now Sunday and the vessells sailing is deferred until Wednesday, so that we are having a long wait here. We missed your last letters as they went up to Kurrachee, and Harry forgot to leave the post office people our address, or they might have been sent down by dak [post by a relay of men or horses] - I wonder when we shall get them.

We are having a very pleasant stay in Bombay, the weather is delightful, and we go out morning and evening into the lovely Victoria Gardens. I wish often that you could see them with the sun rising and setting amongst the "feathery palm trees" and the walks bordered by such glorious colored flowers, to say nothing of the creepers which climb about everywhere and cover the tree stems and hang their blossoms from the branches.

Yesterday Sorabjee (Mr Lidbetter's Parsee broker) asked us to go out to their country house at Parell where they have very large disorderly gardens but they are still pretty and have plenty of date trees in them, and pomelows [grapefruit] and oranges. Pomelow trees are exactly like orange trees but larger and the fruit looks lovely when growing - it is like a large pale yellow orange as big as your head quite, but I do not much like the flavour of the pulp which is pink or red and grows in divisions like oranges.

Sorabjee introduced us to a lot of Parsee ladies of his family, his wife, her mother, grandmother, etc. and his children, two of whom are married although the eldest can't be sixteen. We saw his wife and family before in the fort where they generally live, but the rest were strangers to us. I admired their dress extremely and they wear a great deal of jewellery. Yesterday Mrs Sorabjee wore a sort of lace chemise with short sleeves and a low jacket of purple velvet fastened with a diamond brooch and over all a splendid crimson sari or scarf of rich silk which folds round the waist and hangs down like a petticoat, and the edge of which comes up over one shoulder and covers the head. The other day I took baby into the fort to see her and she gave her a little silk parsee dress and a cap made of gold and silver thread such as their children wear. I mean to put Nora into it as soon as she is big enough.

December 20th. We are constantly disappointed as to the date of our vessel's sailing for Zanzibar. It gets put off from one day to another, and we are weary of staying at this hotel besides its being very expensive. The Captain promises that he will go on Thursday morning, but we still feel doubtful about it. We went to be photographed last Saturday, and will send you the result - they are considered the best photographers who have yet come out to India and I hope the result may be successful. Harry has gone to the port now to see about them. I tried to get baby taken, but she was awake and consequently as merry and restless as possible, so I gave up the attempt at once. I must wait until she gets a little older.

She is such a fat laughing baby by this time, and is two months old tomorrow. I wish you could see her when we play with her, she laughs out loud sometimes and tries so hard to talk. She looks dreadful at present with mosquito bites, her face is almost covered with little red burns. We got her vaccinated just before we left Kurrachee and "it took" beautifully and the places are now getting well, so that is one trouble well over. Everyone says that she is a splendid baby for her age, and indeed the other day when she was beside Mrs Sam Giles baby who is a year old, her face looked nearly as large, and it is small in proportion to her head which is splendidly developed and the most beautifully shaped you ever saw. Mrs Lidbetter said that the only fear was that her intellect would come too early and that we must try and not excite her mind, already she delights in red things when you dangle them in the air. You will think I am like Maggie in writing about baby, but indeed it is a most tempting subject.

To turn to a more everyday one, I must tell you that we think the people here cook our food in poisonous vessels (they always use copper ones) and we think don't get them regularly tinned as they should do, for I had a most obstinate and violent attack of sickness and diarrhoea the other night with great pain, which we could not attribute to any other cause. After trying "Dalby" brandy etc. and finding that nothing would stay in my stomach, Harry got frightened and called up an old doctor who fortunately lives upstairs and he gave me an opiate which relieved me and next day I was quite cured by a dose of chalk medicine [kaolin]. The old doctor says that mine is the third case which has occurred in this hotel lately and he has no doubt it is caused by the stingyness of the Parsee proprietor who grudges the two rupees a month which one has always to pay for lining cooking vessels. So we are going to insist upon our butler seeing my broth etc cooked himself and that it is done in a proper pan.

I am writing principally, I remember, to ask you to send out some things, addressed to "Smith, Fleming & Co" City London (the firm for which Harry is going to Zanzibar) with directions to forward them by the <u>first</u> ship for Zanzibar. There is direct and pretty frequent communication between London and Z. and I hope often to have the chance of sending you some coral, shells, and perhaps pineapples! As Harry will have all the responsibility of loading the ships, we shall easily be able to put things on board. I should like dresses principally, to the amount of about £10, for which Harry will presently send you a draft; something very light and thin - [1]grenadines and muslins, <u>at least one</u> silk grenadine, a nice one, and perhaps a very pale colored silk alpaca, Mother knows the kind I like. I should like one or two white muslins with colored spots if you can get them, and the rest small patterned colored muslins either chintz or any other kind that are going, and a few kid shoes and boots for baby. If you see any nice white [2]garibaldis, ready-made, I should like some thin ones. I have seen some pretty braided ones worn here, I suppose English made. I think that is all, and if I have suggested more than the price I mentioned, we can make it up.

My <u>dear</u> love to you all, in which Harry will write when he comes. When we get settled in our new home you shall have some nice long letters, we have been so dreadfully unsettled lately, and then Artie may expect a reply to his nice long fairy tale of a letter. I hope that all our dear ones are well and will keep so. We shall often feel anxious now that we have longer to wait for letters and so will you, I fear.

Ever, my darling Mother and Grandmamma,
Thy loving daughter, Elsie.

Notes:
1. Grenadine: a light thin grained fabric made of silk or wool.
2. Garibaldi: a woman's loose blouse with long sleeves, popular in the 1860s, copied from the red flannel shirt worn by Garibaldi's soldiers.

At last the family is going to Zanzibar. Harry is determined to prove to his father-in-law that the place is completely healthy and safe to live in.

Bombay, December 22 1864

My dear Father

Yours and Gulie's letters reached me this morning as I came ashore from the ship to make final arrangements before joining Elisa on board. We shall sail in a few hours and I scribble a few hasty lines to endeavour to reassure you about the unhealthiness of Zanzibar. I have conversed with several people who have been there themselves or knew others that had been, and all the reliable testimony I can obtain is to the same effect, that although the mainland is healthy, the climate of the island where we shall reside is good.

It is swept by sea breezes which keep it cool, and we do not at all anticipate ill health there. I have no apprehensions on this point, evidence being so unanimously to the contrary. I wish I could have met with some employment in India but the opening I have availed myself of was the only one I could hear of, and I am much pleased at having been able to connect myself in a confidential and responsible situation with the leading house in Bombay. I do not think I should have been wise to have missed the chance. I may mention that the Life Insurance people have no objection to my going to Zanzibar.

Please thank Gulie for her long letter, I have not had time to read either hers or yours properly yet. Elisa and baby are both well and the latter thrives wonderfully.

Dear love to you all
from Your affectionate son
Harry

Zanzibar – January to September 1865

The beautiful coral island of Zanzibar, in the Indian Ocean off the east coast of Africa (now Tanzania), is still an exotic, clove-scented and mysterious place. The first immigrants were Africans, then it was settled by the Persians; in the 16th century by the Portuguese, and later by the Arabs under the Sultanate of Muscat and Oman. During the late 18th and early 19th century it was a flourishing trading centre for slaves and ivory, as well as cloves, spices, palm oil and coconuts. Sir Richard Burton on his way to explore the African interior came this way in 1856 and described Zanzibar as "all seemed wrapped in a soft and sensuous repose, in the tranquil life of the Lotus Eaters, in the swoonlike slumbers of the Seven Sleepers". An Arabic form of the African Swahili is the most widely spoken language, the religion is Muslim, and the additional influence of Indian and European cultures has made it a truly cosmopolitan place. On the dark side were the terrible diseases: cholera was estimated to have killed 20,000 people in the epidemics of 1859 and 69, malaria and smallpox were endemic, and there was violence, slavery and piracy.

On board the *Naval Brigade*
January 6th 1865

My dearest Mother

We have just this minute cast anchor in Zanzibar harbour after a beautiful passage of 15 days, and find the mail just leaving here, so must send you a line which I want you to forward to Ireland as I have not time for two letters.

We like the appearance of the island extremely - it is very finely wooded and smells deliciously of spices as we sail along. Harry is going on shore this evening to see about our house. We do not yet know where we are going to live, whether over the office or not, but Harry will see about it. We are all so much better for the voyage and burned of a rich red brown colour. Baby is the most

Henry and Elizabeth Jacob.
Photographed in Zanzibar
1865.

charming colour - rosy and brown, and so dreadfully fat, her cheeks are as hard as apples. I do wish you could see her, she is the best child in the world and invariably sleeps all the evening and night without without once waking. She laughs out loud when you play with her, and will lie in her cradle and laugh at you for an hour together.

They are stopping me so I must say goodbye at once, with dearest love and remembrances to all. You see what instruments I am working with and must excuse me, your ever loving son, daughter and grand-daughter
Harry, Elsie and Nora.

In spite of Britain's anti-slavery agreements with the Sultan of Oman the practice still continued. Elizabeth writes more fully, and very indignantly, of the row between Harry and Captain Lidbetter.

Malindy Quarter, Zanzibar
Jan 22 1865

My dearest Father and Mother

It seems late to wish you all a Happy New Year but as this is the first chance I have had of doing so, you must accept it from both of us. We are beginning to feel settled in our new home, having been here nearly 3 weeks. We had a most pleasant passage from Bombay in the *Naval Brigade*, a barque of about 600 tons. We ran down before the North East monsoon wind, and were only 15 days on the passage, beating *The Wasp*, one of Hill's steamers, by several days. The *Naval Brigade* is loading here with cloves, ivory, etc. and we see a good deal of the Captain (Moon) who brought us down.

Dear baby improved very much during the voyage and got finely sunburnt, but I find myself unable, I suppose partly from change of climate and partly from her getting so big, to give her as much nourishment as she needs and my perseverance in avoiding any other sort of food has made her a little thinner than she was (although Captain Fraser says she is still as fat as a pig) and yesterday I began to give her water arrowroot with a little sugar in it, which she greatly disliked at first, shuddering and making horrible faces when she tasted it, but today she has drunk quite a good deal and I hope it may do her good. Of course, I shall go on feeding her about 3 times a day, which is as much as I can manage. Nobody is able to feed a baby altogether in a hot climate and I was often warned in India that I should not be able to manage it, but I wouldn't believe it. One thing is, one can't eat as much as in England, and here there is no bread that I can fancy, which is a great drawback. It is as dark and tough as bad flour and bad cookery can make it. I essayed to make some the other day, but it was like solid lumps of baked clay, and could neither be cut nor bitten, so I daren't say a word more about it.

We are beginning to be reconciled to our way of life here, that is to the impossibility of walking out, or doing anything but ride donkeys out of doors. The larger houses are so closely surrounded by mat huts and the streets between are so narrow and filthy and full of nearly naked Arab soldiers with spears and yataghans, etc. [a curved Turkish sword] that it is impossible for a crinoline to get along. None of the streets are more than 6 or 8 feet wide and some less than that so that one's skirts not only sweep the ground, which is never otherwise swept, but the houses at both sides. Captain Fraser has sent out to Kokotony to his sugar plantation for two nice white riding donkeys, so that Harry and I can trot out merrily at 6 o'clock every morning and come back before it is hot.

About a mile from here the country begins and is lovelier than you can imagine. I am hopeless at being able to convey to you any idea of the delicious grass there is, and the mass of coconut palms and mangoes and orange trees which shade the paths, all laden with their respective fruits, growing wild, of course. Then in the hedges and under the shady trees pineapples grow and ripen. I saw lots the other day when we went out for a picnic with most of the Europeans here to a shamba or Arab country house about two miles off, and which had but one room and a large arched verandah room where we sat. Baby and ayah were with me of course, and as I sat in the inner room and fed baby I looked out of the windows (there is no glass in windows here) and saw the loveliest tiny birds about as big as wasps, crimson and blue and green, flying about amongst the trees and grass. I did so wish you could have seen us and all the beauties around. They make me nearly wild after Kurrachee's barreness.

The loveliest thing I saw that day was the blue water lily which grows in abundance in the ponds in the woods. It is the same as we saw in the tropical room at Sydenham [the Crystal Palace] but about twice as fine and smelling most delicious. I never saw such an intense purple blue as it is. I think it is as handsome as any flower I ever saw. The thumbergia too, that yellow creeping flower with the black centre that grows in hothouses, I saw wild here, looking lovely amongst the grass. Captain Fraser says that he believes this to be the most fertile soil and climate in the world, and so it is easy to imagine. The blacks are lazy in proportion [consequence], they are mostly slaves, but they have two days every week to themselves and they grow manioc root [tapioca] for their food by merely breaking it into short bits and sticking it into the ground, and it comes up plentifully.

Our servants here are mostly Bombay Portuguese but the under ones are slaves hired from their masters who allow them to keep part of their wages. The worst part of this island is that the Sultan carries on the slave trade enormously in spite of treaties with the English who keep two men-of-war here whose boats are always capturing slavers, but he still persists in exporting them - stealing them sometimes from their very doors. The slaves are sold in the market each day from sunrise to sunset. I have not been there yet, but I have seen many poor runaway slaves fastened in gangs, men, women and children together, with rings sometimes round their necks and chains connecting them.

On the picnic day we took our croquet out to the shamba and there was played the first game of croquet that ever was played in Zanzibar. Baby got a good deal tired that day with being so much out in the open air. She got a great fright while she was sleeping in the shamba - two dreadful looking negroes peeped in at the low window close to which she was sleeping and grinned at her, and although she sees many such faces every day, she awoke suddenly and began to give short terrified screams which frightened me greatly until I saw what was the matter. I was afraid it was a snake or something.

One evening on shipboard while the ayah was carrying her about the deck, she suddenly threw herself far back and began looking up and laughing and crowing and holding up her little hands to try to catch something. The ayah couldn't think what she wanted but I came and saw that it was the moon that excited her cupidity - for a long time she would look at nothing else, she appeared quite enraptured. The moon here is a much more brilliant object than it is in England, it glitters so beautifully. We lost sight of the North star the very day we crossed the line [equator] and now we see the Southern Cross every night but Orion is still visible here. We found it very cool at sea even when we were on the line and here the temperature is very similar to India. This is the hottest season of the year too and yet it isn't a bit too hot. In March the rains begin and then it is much cooler.

These houses are not nearly so well built as those in India. They look like big white-washed factories with numerous small windows generally destitute of glass, and shutting with Venetian blinds. I am writing now in our little parlour which adjoins our bedroom, and where we have all our little belongings, pictures, etc. Our meals we take with Captain Fraser who is Nicol's partner here, and Mr Peebles who is the book-keeper. Harry finds things very much behindhand and is very busy. The drawing room is very well furnished and is a fine long room, full of English things. This house is built in the Arab style with the doors round a square court, the roof supported on ugly square topped pillars which are walled in between to make rooms.

Jan 23: Since I began this the ayah has got a little fever, as newcomers often do here, especially natives, so I shall have the entire responsibility of baby as she often won't go to Ahmed and must cut my letter short in consequence. I didn't get to church yesterday for the same reason. We have a Bishop here and a chaplain. The Bishop (Tozer) is quite a young man and rather shy with ladies. He came here to go up the Zambesi or somewhere but the natives won't hear of being Christianized at present, in spite of all Livingstone's glowing accounts, so he stays here. We also have a very rich German Baron named Von der Decken who is going up the Juba to explore the interior, a German artist and other notabilities.

There are two ladies here, both nice, Mrs Colonel Playfair and Mrs Seward, the doctor's wife, and each have a little girl here about 2½ years old. Mrs Playfair's is called Nora! We dined at the Playfair's the other evening but I came away directly after dinner as I was anxious about baby. Captain Fraser and Harry have been setting a [1]sewing machine to rights for me and I am going to try it some day soon as baby wants some short clothes making. Children however, require to be very lightly dressed here - she has half a dozen short flannel petticoats, some red and some white. These she wears with a pinafore over them tied at the shoulder and that is all, no shirt or dress or anything but shoes. Will you send me some cornflour if you haven't sent the box off, a good deal of it will keep for baby, and some socks as well as shoes, and some trimming for my dresses. I think I should like a whole piece of black lace insertion, it is so useful for trimming anything and everything, and I should like a black lace shawl or mantle if you have one by you. We send you £10 but can forward anything further when the bill comes to hand. I hope you will send it off as soon as the things are ready.

I must tell you what a shabby trick Captain Lidbetter played Harry just before we came away, though I know dear old Harry thinks I had better not be so vindictive, and I am sure you will think as I do, that we are better away from him. The case is this. Harry asked him for permission to go down to Bombay in the middle of November to see Nicol & Co. about coming to Zanzibar which he readily granted and Harry went, coming back on 2nd December and going occasionally to office until the 10th December when we finally came away. Harry, you know, had the sole charge of the books at Capt. Lidbetter's as Mr L knows nothing of book-keeping, but when he closed our account there, drawing his salary up to the end of November, he just showed him the book and asked if all was right between them. Mr L said it was, so you may judge of our astonishment at receiving the very night before we sailed a very rude letter from Captain Lidbetter saying that Harry "had overdrawn his salary 200 rupees!" - that being the half month when he was away in Bombay, although he had never had a holiday for two years, except 3 days when he was married and had been going occasionally to office in December!

Captain Lidbetter isn't a man who cares about money either, so it was pure revenge upon Harry for getting a good berth when he had turned him off. Of course, Harry was dreadfully hurt and vexed and sent the money back saying that in spite of all Captain Lidbetter had done to injure him, he had hoped to go away feeling friendly to him, but that it was now no longer possible and that the money was fairly his own. In reply to which Harry received another very unpleasant note saying that it was "just like his impudence" or something of that kind. So that was the end of the Lidbetter partnership and I hope we shall never see .... [next line crossed out by Harry]. I am sure Harry worked hard enough for every farthing he got, besides taking entire care of the business while Mr L was in England, for which he got no acknowledgment of even a verbal kind, and the worst of it all was that we wanted the money to pay our passage. If Nicol's hadn't behaved in the handsomest manner paying my passage as well as Harry's,

154

we should have been embarrassed in our circumstances from having to live so long in a Bombay hotel and not being able to sell our furniture, but having to leave it behind at a broker's to sell for us. However we are all right now, and mustn't look back upon our little pecuniary troubles which are now at an end I hope.

This seems a very nice climate indeed, and being able to get out every day into the lovely country is such a treat that we feel inclined to be very happy and contented. We like Captain Fraser greatly: he is a very clever, pleasant man, with a queer amusing sarcastic vein of ill temper that I like and so does Harry. He is always making fun of poor Mr Peebles, although he likes him and is kind to him in his own way.

[Now Harry writes] I don't think Elsie has written a very nice account of my little squabble with Capt. L. I did not tell him he had done anything to injure me and I don't exactly consider him a swindler. However, E was very indignant about the affair and has exaggerated a little in her wrath. Pray read her account 'cum grano salis' [with a pinch of salt]. Please send this letter to Ireland as we have been only able to write very briefly to our friends there.

Your very loving children
H & E H Jacob.

Note:
1. The Singer sewing machine with a vertical needle motion was patented in 1852, the first of its kind.

This is a series of four letters, written on 5th February, 27th February, 5th March and 27th March, so infrequent were the mail boats to England. The British Consul, writing from Zanzibar in 1859, remarked that during the northern monsoon in January and February the town was full of piratical Arabs from the Persian Gulf who come, "solely for the purpose of kidnapping slaves and children, which they convey for sale to the coasts of Arabia and Persia." Elizabeth is aware of this and keeps a close watch on her baby. In 1824 Seyyid bin Sa'id (1791-1856) Sultan of Oman, transferred his capital from Muscat on the Arabian Peninsula to Zanzibar, where he built a great palace at Mtoni. This is Sultan Seyd mentioned in Elisa's letter. His son Majid bin Sa'id (Seyd Majid in the letter) inherited the Sultanate of Zanzibar on his father's death. Elizabeth gives a fantastic description of her visit to the Sultan's sister, Bibi Suliman.

Malindy, Zanzibar

Feb 5 1865

My dearest Pollie

I don't in the least know to whom I ought to write this time. I have got my head into such a muddle in this out of the way place that I cannot even remember the date of my last letter home, and as to the last one from home, it is nearly two months since we heard a word from you. The last was Gulie's letter in Bombay with dear Father's enclosure warning us too late not to go to Zanzibar. Not getting letters from home regularly is about the only real deprivation we have here that we had not in India, and the climate seems equally healthy with that of Kurrachee, about the same percentage of fever among the Europeans and that generally caused by exposure.

Mr Jablonski the French consul says that during the eight years he has been here he has been quite well and is a most healthy little man still. Mr Mill ditto and he has been here ten years and is going home soon to fetch his wife which will make another lady here, so you see, you need not fear for us; in the natural course of things we shall be as well here as can be, and there is the same Providence here to take care of us poor lonely people, as there is to mind the favored ones at home. Captain Fraser was saying the other day that he has been out two years now and means to go and look after Zanzibar interests at home for a while as soon as the sugar plantation at ¹Kokotony [Mkokotoni] is in working order, leaving Harry meanwhile to manage here, and then changing places and letting Harry go home for a year or two.

That is a distant prospect, but I am hoping that by the time baby is two years old or so, and wants to leave tropical climates, it may come to pass. Everyone says that a hot climate is better than England for very young children, but that they soon need the bracing cold when they get older, so if all be well with us and we are obliged to stay here for some years longer, we shall most likely bring you a little charge, if you will undertake her for us. At present I am not able to send you anything so precious, so I have asked Captain Moon to take charge of a black-faced monkey for you. It is one of the little Zanzibar native monkeys, and I hope it will get to England safely and be quite tame by the time it reaches you.

I am greatly disappointed not to be able to send you anything better, but I find great difficulty in getting any shells and coral. Perhaps when we have been here longer we may find something to send. Mr Peebles is sending home lots of grass mats, but I am sure you would think them rubbish and they are very bulky and very cheap, so we will leave sending them until some other time.

I told you in may last letter that I had begun to give baby water and arrowroot as she was evidently half-starved upon what I had for her. Well, the experiment didn't answer at all, she got diarrhoea and was a little thinner every day I fancied, and at last came out all over with prickly heat so that I asked Dr Seward to come and see her. He said she required good cow's milk without water two or three times a day and no arrowroot on any account, so we get some milk fresh for her every day and are going to try to buy a cow for her, and you would be astonished to see how she flourishes upon it, and how jolly and fat she is getting again. She is the most entertaining little pet you can imagine, and smiles so prettily whenever she sees her papa or me. She pulls his whiskers and gives him wet kisses, and he is _so_ delighted. How I wish you could see her. She can play at bo-peep as well as I can and greatly she enjoys it. The ayah is quite well again by this time, which makes my day's work a very different affair, especially as baby and she were both poorly at the same time.

Yesterday evening Harry and I gave a dinner to all of the Europeans who had called upon us, comprehending most of the people here - 18 were at dinner altogether but the servants didn't give us such a good dinner as we used to get in India on similar occasions, and what makes it more provoking is that one can do nothing to help. The kitchen here is on the roof and a horrid dirty smoky place it is, judging from outside. I did what I could to make the table look nice by arranging vases, three tiers of crimson tea roses and greenery of different kinds, but I didn't like the turnout altogether.

Most of the people here are French and Germans and Americans, only two families of English besides ourselves. In England some of the people would be thought quite swells, but they all seem alike here. There was Baron Von Der Decken, the African traveller, who has forty thousand a year, and Bishop Tozer, a stupid, bulky red-haired youth in a white cassock of some kind; but you mustn't tell anybody I said so, because he is a great dignitary - and his satellite, the [2]Rev Dr Steer; and two navy captains, Captain Fraser being one, great swells they think themselves, besides the three consuls who are nobody particular; the two doctors, French and English; and other merchants. Only one lady besides myself - Mrs Seward; Mrs Playfair did not come. They are not friendly with Captain Fraser, for some official reason or other. Some of us played squails [a game with small wooded discs propelled across a table or board] and some, billiards - we have a small billiard table in the drawing rom. Some of us sang a little, in hopes of choruses which failed, and at nine o'clock everybody goes to bed. I ought to tell you that we dine earlier here than in India, half-past four or five.

What I enjoy most here are the morning rides that Harry and I get on the two [3]white donkeys from Kokotony. We go about half a mile through the streets and then over the bridge across the creek and straight into the woods along the beautiful paths, through green grassy plots between the stems of the tall coconut palms and under the heavy foliage of the mango trees with pineapples and shrubs amongst the grass, or else along the narrowest lanes with thorn hedges very like English ones - hanging full of creepers of every kind, but only one that I have seen yet with beautiful flowers, scarlet like a flame, beside the cream colored thumbergia I told you of with a maroon colored centre. Many of these creepers have beautiful berries, scarlet and green, and there are a great many fruit like potato apples, in fact they are on a sort of wild potato plant but they grow very tall.

Poor baby cannot go out into these woods - it is not safe for her to go out into the streets with the ayah or even better protected, the northern Arabs would soon steal her and sell her to Muscat. They say she would be worth two or three hundred dollars there and besides, we live far away from the other Europeans, which makes it more unsafe. They all reside at the Shangany end of the town, while we are the only ones who live at Malindy. However, it seems very desirable that we should be near the others and Captain Fraser is talking of our going there, when we can get a house. These people hate us on account of our men-of-war being here to intercept their slavers. I send baby and ayah up onto the roof before sunrise and in the evening which is the best substitute we can command. When she gets big enough we mean her to have a little donkey and a pannier and go with us.

Gulie's letter brought the news of uncle William's death - which I was partly prepared for by Mother's letter preceding it. I hope that we all may meet again even the most unworthy of us.

February 27: It is more than three weeks since I began this letter and yet there is no sign of the mail getting to Seychelles on its way home. We are waiting for the [4]Lyra to come up from Johanna and she is stuck upon some coral reefs or other this long time. We find the only variety in the society here is caused by the presence of the Queen's ships. The naval officers are often very nice men. Captain Garforth of the *Penguin* who is here at present and comes here a good deal is a jolly little creature and took us a nice sail in his boat the other evening. It was such a treat to be in a boat with a crew of fine handsome man-of war's men, after being always used to nasty dirty incompetent native sailors such as took us to church yesterday morning.

You know the church is held in the Bishop's house at Shangany and as it is impossible to walk through the streets in the heat (and indeed it is hardly safe or suitable for an English woman to walk in them at all, however well-protected), we went in the boat, and a dreadful time we had of it. First I had to be carried at least a hundred yards in a chair over the wet sands at low water by four coolies, with another holding an umbrella over my head. After being emptied into the boat out of the chair I had the fun of watching Harry and Mr Peebles being carried in the dirty sailors' arms and presently they too were deposited beside me, and Carlo who insisted upon frisking beside them also jumped in, dripping wet, regardless of my go-to-meeting clothes. Poor Mr Peebles complained sadly of his white trousers and waistcoat which had suffered from contact with the dirty sailors arms and back. Then we set off and found it very rough and the sailors wouldn't pull properly and consequently the boat wouldn't steer and got into the trough of the sea. We had to find our way amongst the native shipping in the harbour in constant danger of getting foul of the cables, and worst of all, we had to land in a heavy surf at Shangany, and got to church tired and cross to find ourselves too soon by ten minutes. However, the Bishop took us upstairs to to his room where we amused ourselves until church time. This is our first attempt at going to church in the morning and a very discouraging one it was.

Apropos of Harry's going to church in a velvet coat I must tell you how busy I am, sewing. I have to do everything myself as I can't get a dhurzie (tailor) and baby wants lots of things. The other day I made a bargain with Harry that if he would get for me a piece of black patent velvet that was going to be sold by auction, I would make him a coat of part of it. I cut it out by one of his and made it up, it is a great success, and Captain Fraser and Mr Peebles wish they too had wives that could make velvet coats. The former's wife is at home in Scotland, the latter is a bachelor.

March 5: This will be a very disjointed letter I'm afraid, and I see that I have not told you yet that between the first and second times of writing we received a delightful batch of home letters - the only ones we have had since we came here nearly two months ago, although there must be two or three mails waiting for us in Bombay. They were the ones you wrote after hearing of our dear baby's arrival, and most delightfully affectionate pleasant letters they were to have. I wish you could see dear baby now, wouldn't Mother devour her with kisses if she kissed her likeness so much, and wouldn't Nora give her lots of wet ones in return with her mouth and eyes both wide open to get the full benefit. She is the liveliest merriest little darling you ever saw, always playing some prank or other, hiding her face in her frock, or driving her feet by her shoe string, or shamming to go to sleep by turning away from you suddenly, and then when you say "baby has gone to sleep" she throws herself back towards you and bursts out laughing.

I wish you could have seen her yesterday when Saburi, our little negro servant, was taking care of her. She likes him so much and yesterday he had tied a red handkerchief over his cap, which with his other attractions made him quite irresistible, and I heard her in the other room laughing so much that I went to see what was the matter. I found her sitting in a big arm-chair and Saburi kneeling down in front of her fanning her and bobbing his head and showing his teeth. Every time he spoke and every time he moved his head or his lips she burst out laughing at him and tried to catch his teeth or his big thick lips or his handkerchief. Her general amusement is catching our hair or her papa's whiskers but Saburi's hair is just little tiny hard knots (at intervals) as big as a pea, like all the negroes have here. The women's is a little more plentiful and about an inch long, and they are obliged to shave seams out of it, as they can't part it. Many of the women have partings made all over, like the divisions of an orange.

We have missed our morning rides lately as the donkeys legs are greasy or mangey or something, from not being properly dried and so we get no exercise at all generally. The last time we were out, my donkey fell suddenly in the midst of a quick canter and I flew over his head a long way, and Harry's did the same a few days before, but was not going quite so quick, so he fell more gently. This was before we knew their legs were weak. They will be well again soon I hope. Last time we were out we saw such a number of oriole's nests - pendant between the fronds of the palm leaves just like the pictures in children's books, and the lovely brilliant blue orioles flying about in dozens. They build in company like rooks.

This morning some gentleman here, evidently a German, sent me an anonymous letter and a present of a milch goat for baby, saying in the letter that "he hoped he might be the means indirectly of my being seen in a society(?) where I was invited as well as himself", alluding to a dinner party at the Baron's last week to which

I refused to go because we haven't yet got the cow we are expecting, so that of course I am obliged to stay at home with baby in the evening. I certainly had been to Dr Seward's a few evenings before, but I took baby with me and she got so excited with seeing little Nora Playfair and Minnie Seward that she wouldn't go to sleep when she got home. Baby gets fresh milk every morning from a rich old Hindoo, Khorjee, who makes us a present of it, so that I couldn't ask for it in the evening as well, and the difficulty is that Hindoos hold cows sacred and won't sell either them or their milk, so we have sent a letter to an Arab near Kokotony to ask for a cow as a present! Of course, we shall send him an equivalent, also as a present, that is the way we do business here.

This week we are going out to Colonel [5]Playfair's country house or shamba, as they are called here, to spend a few days. If we like the house we shall very likely rent it when the Playfairs leave Zanzibar. It is beautifully situated on the opposite curve of the bay, so that we can see it from our windows. It stands just back from the shore surrounded by orange groves and a nice garden with the woods close by, which is what I long for. Here, only half a mile away from the loveliest country in the world, we are (at present hopelessly) entangled in a labyrinth of filthy eastern streets - I feel quite like [6]Tantalus when I go on the roof and see round me woods, creeks, islands and all inaccessible. We have a boat certainly but the menfolk are generally too tired to go out in the evening. Harry works from half-past six in the morning until four in the afternoon, and Capt. Fraser if anything, more than that.

Buying and weighing ivory for shipment is the principal thing just now, and Harry is learning to know the difference between a good and a bad tusk which requires very nice discrimination. The lower storey of the house now contains more than 12 tons of ivory in tusks and serivellas (baby tusks), some of enormous size, and all of it worth from 10-12 shillings a pound. Besides ivory they export ebony, [7]gum copal, coconut oil, cloves, and orchella weed, a seaweed which is greatly used in England for red and purple dye. I was watching the men yesterday spreading coconuts on the roof of the warehouse to dry, previous to being put into the oil presses.

162

March 27: I wish you could see the lovely little sparrows here, though indeed you have seen many like them in cages under the name of Java sparrows. Their principal features are scarlet beaks and legs, the former being large, exactly like an English sparrow. They are soberly colored but have a very beautifully jet black head and tail, with white cheeks and a black ring round their necks, bright blue grey backs and pinkish underneath. They are as plentiful as house sparrows and as quarrelsome.

The other day Harry went with the Consul and the other English gentlemen here, to pay his respects to the Sultan who received them in great state with Persian and Arab soldiers in the courtyard, and who came outside his door to meet them. I can tell you better about my visit a day or two afterwards, which was merely a private one which Mrs Playfair and I paid, ostensibly to his sister, but in reality it was to him, for he received us in a long plain marble paved room which had two crimson chairs at one end on which we were seated. He sat on one side and his four brothers at the other, his womenfolk being banished to a distance of about fifty feet so that we could not possibly speak to them, and found it very stupid as the Sultan can't even speak Hindostani, so we had to speak in that language to the interpreter who translated into Arabic. Presently came a tray of sweetmeats placed on two chairs close to our knees, then large glasses of some sweet stuff, apparently coconut milk with pounded almonds and sugar in it, then a cup of black coffee. Then a quantity of attar of roses poured on our handkerchiefs, and then we were at liberty to go, the Sultan accompanying us to the door of his palace.

We then set off to see his other sisters who have houses of their own. The first is called Bibi Aysher (Bibi means Lady) and lives in the dirtiest house you ever saw, indeed the houses are all alike. First a dirty courtyard with ducks gobbling in pools of dirty water, and dirty slaves cooking omelettes etc. for the royal table, then a staircase so narrow and dark and dirty that one's shoulders and head get the benefit as well as our dress skirts and I lamented greatly over my white lace shawl (Mrs Playfair, having experience, put on a black one), then you get to the women's rooms with the eunuchs outside the door - for they are most carefully guarded. Bibi Aysher we found squatting on a mat couch chewing betel nut and spitting out of the window. With her was her Mother, one of the late Sultan's wives (Seyd-Seyd was a great man and Imam of Muscat as well as Sultan of Zanzibar, but his sons divided his kingdom and Seyd Majid got this share of it) - he actually stole European women for his harem. This one is said to be a Frenchwoman and indeed she is quite white and has been very beautiful. She was kidnapped when a child, they say, so you will understand why we take such care of our babies. Bibi Aysher was very quiet and the principal amusement was sweetmeats, sherbet, coffee, [8]attar of roses etc [9]"da capo".

By the way, I have had presents of some small bottles of attar of roses which I mean to send you as soon as I have an opportunity, as it almost impossible to get in England and it is very expensive even here - greatly as the Arabs lavish it, I suppose to show their luxury. You will find a drop sufficient at once, indeed a few drops put onto cottonwool in a drawer will scent everything in it like musk. I have put about a dozen drops into a scent bottle full of spirits of wine and find it makes a very nice scent.

But I must tell you about our other visit to Bibi Suliman which was by far the most interesting. She came clattering down stairs to meet us, being very young and lively, saying "How are you?" in English and then bursting out laughing at our surprise. She then took hold of my hand and began dragging me upstairs, saying "stairs - come" and laughing afresh at every proof of her learning. She could also speak a little Hindostani so we got on very well with her. She was a most picturesque figure as she stood there, I wish you could have seen her, she must be very pretty indeed if one could see her without her mask, which hides all but eyes, mouth and chin, but she wouldn't remove it, although we asked her, no Arab lady will. She was dressed in a crimson silk and silver striped tunic with trousers, but you could hardly see her dress for gold and jewels. Her nose, ears, arms, hands, legs, neck and head were literally laden with, I should think, as many as she could carry, for I took up one of her neck ornaments which was hanging on the bedpost and it must have weighed a pound, all solid gold, and she had about six of these of different kinds hanging round her neck, besides most magnificent rings, bracelets, earrings and leg rings. You cannot imagine the massiveness of them - each earring was about a foot long and she had six in each ear poor thing. She said it hurt her very much but that she was never allowed to take them out, and she showed us a little velvet pillow, made so that her temples only could rest on it, as of course she could not have laid upon these great jewelled earrings. She had the most beautiful emeralds and pearls hanging from her necklaces, and precious stones set all over them. The room she was in was thoroughly eastern and luxurious. The matting was covered with Persian carpets at the head of each of which was a large and small velvet pillow with red silk ends standing against the wall. There were also leopard-skin rugs and some European carved chairs and bedsteads - the latter she said she never used. This was the only place in any of these royal residences that looked fresh and clean even. She also gave us English coffee - or what she called "English" in great glee - that is, coffee with milk and sugar and also in English cups, so you see she is a highly civilized specimen of an Arab princess.

Now I must turn to your dear home letters after all this selfish gossip, but I know you like to hear me tell new things. I must not forget to tell you that Captain Ben Raschid, the Arab from whom Captain Fraser asked for a cow, has sent us one which is now on its way from Kokotony, which I am very glad of.

March 27: After many disappointments, we hear that the French man-of-war *Loiret* is going to Seychelles on the 31st to take our homeward bound letters, but I fear you must be very anxious, after our being so long silent. You must remember that "no news is good news" generally, bad news travels fast enough. We are as badly off as you are for letters. The last home letters that came for us from Bombay are dated December 2nd, and we are longing for later dates. I think you must have missed writing, as we have letters from Ballitore of a month later. Dear Father's as usual contains good accounts of his missionary labour, which it is good to hear, and at the same time discouraging in this place, where we know no more of the language than is necessary for our daily wants, and two or three years training of a servant does not often result in so much as teaching him to distinguish truth from falsehood. I really believe that many of them don't know the difference, and as for the Christian virtues - gratitude, love temperance, etc. etc. there are no words in their language to express them at all, so I don't know how you could set about teaching them except by good example.

I am glad that the gardening has been so successful last year. We are hoping to go into that branch of industry ourselves shortly, for I am most happy to tell you that we have secured Col. Playfair's country house from the first of next month, for as long as we stay in Zanzibar. We went out to visit Col. and Mrs Playfair there last week to see if we liked the place and we were so delighted with it that Col.P. got the lease transferred to us, as Mrs Playfair is going to England by the *Loiret*. I can't describe it properly, but Harry will send you a sketch when we get there. It stands on the other side of the bay and I can see it from these windows about 4 miles off. It is built on the very edge of the low rocky shore about 12 feet above where the sea washes the coral foundations at high water, so that the windows seaward look straight over the bay, but behind the house the woods come close up, only separated from the house by a grove of oranges and a hedge of tea roses. Under the orange trees is the dining table, and when the branches are full of fruit they hang so low that the oranges are within reach, just fancy what it will be when they are in full blossom. There is a nice little garden on one side of the house with lovely creepers running over trelliswork and a water course full of ferns running through it to the sea. The garden paths go off imperceptibly into the woods and we have a few acres of land, all wooded nearly, where the cow can feed, and where we can help ourselves to coconuts, by climbing 60 or 70 feet, all the year round.

The house itself is large and very commodious, with a high thatched roof, which I believe is not very watertight at present. I wish you could see the paradise it is, with humming birds amongst the trees and butterflies a great deal bigger among the flowers, and the air full of fireflies after sunset, in the shadow of the trees especially, through which baby and ayah and I will walk to meet Harry in the evening when he rides in. When he sails in the boat we will sit at the top of the flight of steps leading from the garden into the sea at high water, and watch him coming, like princesses in an enchanted castle, but at low water, alas, our knight will have to be carried over the wet shore in a chair by four negroes in the most unpoetical manner.

I wish I could tell you half of the beauties of our woods, that I found out during the day or two we were there. Can you imagine an underwood of wild orange, almond and clove trees, overtopped by mangoes and these again by the tall graceful palms? Then you plunge suddenly into a wilderness of sugar cane and papyrus and emerge into a grassy glen with low thatched palm leaf huts of the negroes, surrounded by little patches of pumpkin and manioc. I daresay I shall find out new beauties every day - what would I give to have Pollie or Gulie to live with me in this beautiful but lonely place, while Harry is away all day at office. Could you spare one for a year or two, not more, for baby must go home by that time. If you can, write to Smith, Fleming & Co. to ask when the next ship is coming round the cape, put the young lady into it, under the Captain's care. In three months she will find herself, if all be well, watching the humming birds like big green bees, popping in and out of their nest at "St Patrick's-by-the-Sea", and the moon rising amongst the palm tree tops turning them all to silver, out of a bedroom window with no glass in it, as Harry and I watched it the other night, and I thought that in all the world there couldn't be a lovelier place.

I do think that to have been here for a short time is a thing to be glad of for all one's life after. Of course one gets home-sick if there is a chance of having to stay too long and I would go home tomorrow with Harry if he had any business there.

And now for dear Mother's letter with its rejoicings over darling baby. I think it is almost a blessing she is not at home to be so dreadfully spoilt. I am making arrangements with the ayah and her papa to have her very strictly brought up so that if she has to go home to Thirsk she may not be very troublesome. She is just the child for you to spoil - so lovable and and bonnie and fat and fond of being petted, and yet so full of wild spirits, always pretending different things, and as the ayah says "apua dil me hasanta" - "laughing in her heart". She is five months old now, and full of tricks. The last day or two she spent most of her leisure time in holding one of her hands up and twisting it round and round, moving all her fingers, as if to admire its pinkness inside and universal fatness, and then trying to slap it with the other hand, pretending to be vexed with it, and making noises at it. She generally misses it and slaps her face or her tomach which makes her laugh. Harry says that he believes her thoughts are constantly employed in making up reasons for laughing. She doesn't wear any shoes this hot weather and when not otherwise employed she sucks one of her great toes as diligently as other children suck their thumbs. I have seen her put both great toes into her mouth together, which I think is quite an acrobatic feat. Both Harry and I feel that such a bright quick-tempered child is a great responsibility. I do hope that we may always try more to make her good than clever. She has been twice in a great passion, beating everything and screaming dreadfully, but she is generally the most sweet tempered little thing, letting us take away her playthings without crying. She has got such a nice little perambulator which was Nora Playfair's and which Harry bought for her from them. It has a black leather hood which puts up and down like a grown-up carriage and has a pane of glass behind. She likes riding in it very much, but has a strong objection to being taken out. I was trying to get a kiss for Grandmamma and Grandpapa but she turned over onto her face and laughed every time I put my face near, so I gave it up.

We have bought all the furniture in the shamba including a nice little iron cot for baby, which I am very glad to have as she seems inclined to fall out of her berceaunette, lying often with one leg and arm over the sides and trying to lift herself over. I think dear Mother need not fear our being murdered by the Arabs here - the natives of Zanzibar are quiet people and the Northern Arabs who come for slaves etc. are only here a few months a year, besides which the Sultan has many reasons for wishing to be in the good graces of the English Government. It is not very well to go into the streets without arms or armed servants, as they draw their swords on the slightest provocation, and greatly despise people who they fancy are defenceless. Of course, I mean for the purpose of intimidating, not hurting them.

My dear love to Maggie and congratulations, also to Emma, hoping that all is well. Tell dear Hannah Baker that I was much concerned to hear of her baby's accident and only hope he is no worse. Our dear love to you all. Harry has no time to himself now, he is working very hard. The book-keepers here have been very inefficient and the present one isn't very clever, giving Harry a good deal of work. Captain Fraser is talking of going to Bombay this week and very likely to England too, so that Harry will be master of this large business here till he comes back, including the sugar factory and plantation at Kokotony, the oil mills at Shangany and the orchella weed and cotton cleaning, to say nothing of the building and launching of two cargo boats here and all the outdoor and office work. Of course, there are Europeans in all these departments and Mr Bishop who was here before has come back from Bombay to do the outdoor work under Harry of course, but he will have his hands full I imagine and a long way to go back and forwards to the shamba.

I hope you will send this long letter to Tom and Artie and excuse its having been written at so many times as to be very fragmentary. We are enjoying excellent health and have just got over the hottest season and the rains are coming on. The cow gives very good milk and baby is looking very well indeed. My love to Dr & Mrs Ryott and everybody else who asks after your most loving sister.

Elsie H Jacob

Notes:
1. Kokotony/Mkokotoni: about 23 miles from Zanzibar city.
2. "Dr Steer": by 1870 the Reverend Doctor was Bishop Steere of the Universities Mission to Central Africa, well-known for his handbook on the Swahili language.
3. White Muscat donkeys: these were much prized riding animals, worth more than a horse.
4. *The Lyra*: H.M.S. *Lyra,* a British man o' war, was well known around the coast of Zanzibar for intercepting the slave ships.
5. Colonel Playfair was in the Diplomatic Service for the Foreign and India Office.
6. Tantalus: a son of Jupiter. For revealing his father's secrets he was punished in Hades with a raging thirst, and the water and fruits that he tried to reach always slipped from his grasp.
7. gum copal: a hard aromatic resin obtained from various tropical trees for the making of varnishes and lacquers.
8. attar of roses: essential oil from the damask rose used as a base for perfume.
9. da capo: a nice musical reference meaning to go back to the beginning and start again.

A box of goods from England was much delayed by being sent round the Cape of Good Hope, and Bartholomew Smith is reproached. Elizabeth lyrically describes the natural beauties of Zanzibar and the clever little ways of baby Nora. But the most exciting passages are about the capture of the Arab slave ships. Communications were so slow that Elizabeth had no way of knowing that her brother Tom had died on 4th April.

St Patrick's

Island of Zanzibar

June 7 1865

My very dearest Mother & Father

We were delighted the other day to get dear Father's letter via Seychelles dated 16th March, and to hear of you all after so long an interval. I don't suppose that we feel so anxious about your being well as you do about us, but still it is delightful to think that you are just as we left you. Only remain so, and that is all I ask. I don't want any of you altered, even for the better, but I mustn't say that, seeing that it is a thing to be thankful for that you are not likely to be altered for the worse.

I often wonder whether you will find me very different after knocking about the world so much. If it has not made me wiser and more thoughtful it is my own fault, for certainly that is the tendency of it, particularly when one has husband and baby to take care of and be anxious about in these anxious climates, for I can assure you that, well as we are, we have many serious thoughts about how long we shall remain so, and how much more uncertain life is (humanly speaking) here than at home, of which we are continually reminded.

But to return to Father's letter, I cannot tell you how disappointed we were to get the information of my box being sent round the Cape, it inconveniences me more than I can tell you, for I am almost destitute of dresses and I had been counting the days until it should come. You can have no idea of the destruction of clothes here, I can truly say that I don't think a single day passes in which I don't tear my dresses more or less against these frightful doors, etc., that have nails sticking out (as necessary parts of their construction) in all directions, and everybody does the same, to say nothing of the dhobies having absolutely destroyed every washing dress and jacket past all hope of redemption.

Father will realize what false economy the saving of £8 in freight is, when I tell him that I have had to buy some dresses in the bazaar, getting them with great trouble, for which I paid 2/- [10p] a yard all round. Four were common coarse but strong prints and two alpaca worth about 4½d or 6d a yard at home, horrible to look at and the lining for the latter (without which they would wear about as well as tarlatans) cost about 1/6d a yard. Well, after this there is the cost and trouble of making. I make the body and pay the tailor about £1 to make the skirt, and to add to my troubles I heard this morning that the only tailor who can work properly for me is dead, and really I haven't time to put a stitch in for myself.

It is as much as I can do to keep dear baby supplied with things and look after the house, garden and yard, for I think I told you that Ahmed has been discharged and sent to Bombay. He drank so dreadfully since he came here, so that I am manager now, our head servant being quite a young Portuguese named 'Bastian, who has not done butler's work before. Harry felt parting with Ahmed very much indeed, but it didn't seem right to keep him here where he had such great temptation, besides that, he was perfectly useless and lost all his self-respect.

We are now staying at the shamba and hope to remain here pretty continuously and make it our house. It is a great distance from business but the exercise really seems to do dear Harry good, a five mile ride in the morning and the same distance in the boat in the evening. The climate here is so delicious and the life is so free and happy that one feels almost like a seabird. I wonder whether you can imagine this fine high long room with four large open windows (innocent of glass or anything but shutters) almost overhanging the sea at a height of about 25 feet, which is now breaking in lovely clear green waves against the bank edge six feet from the house, so different to those at English seaside places. I often wonder how it is that the sea spray doesn't hurt the shrubs and trees and ferns that overhang our little terrace and garden edge. I have seen orange trees near here that dip their branches into the sea water every high tide without seeming any the worse for it, and all along the seashore creepers trail over and hang in the sea,

171

washing about like seaweed. Oh, this is surely one of the loveliest places in the whole world.

Besides its four seaward windows which give a distant view of the African coast and the extreme end of the Mountains of the Moon, or rather of the Maseen Peaks which terminate them, this room has two looking to Zanzibar and the beautiful reaches of the coast leading to it and the islands that guard the harbour which are most literally described by Tennyson as "Summer isles of Eden lying in dark purple spheres of sea". With a telescope I can see Harry's boat from the time when it pushes off from just below the office door to when it reaches the bottom of the steps leading up into the garden here. On a day like this after the rains, the colours are almost dazzling from the burnished golden green of the palm tree fronds waving and glittering against an azure sky, to the wonderful iridescent sea which is like a mixture of peacock tails and rainbows sprinkled with diamonds.

Beside the tall 60 & 70 feet coconut palms which surround us we have a row of precious and beautiful Pemba palms whose leaves are of a yellower green than the other and the fruit every shade of yellow and golden brown. The beauty of them is that one can reach the branches of nuts with a stick. We like the water of these nuts best of all, it is deliciously sparkling and refreshing and a little acid in taste. These edge the garden on the land side before you get under the orange trees and with the light acacias and the stiff but beautiful almond trees, shade the smaller plants and shrubs nicely. This is like an almond tree [small sketch of a tree], and each leaf is about as big as a meat-dish, only the trees are much taller in proportion than my drawing. They are not all so stiff as this but that is the typical shape, and some are exactly so, but I must leave off talking about trees.

Do you know that dear baby was very ill after I wrote to you last about a month ago, so ill that Dr Seward who was going to Seychelles with his wife and child for his and their health sake, said that he should not go unless he could persuade some doctor to come and take his place, so Dr Pendreth of the *Rapid* came and only left us today to return to the boat which has been out slaving without him. It was very kind of the Captain to let him come and he has been most kind. We thought Nora was teething, her gums swelled and she had almost every ailment you can imagine besides which they feared convulsions, but Dr Pendreth immediately ordered me to wean her, leave off her medicine and give her chicken broth in her milk, as she was suffering from insufficient nourishment. I did this and she began to get better directly, the diarrhoea gradually abated and now thank God, she is one of the fattest, healthiest looking small babies you can imagine, with a little rose colour in her cheeks which is very unusual here. All signs of teeth have passed away, her gums are not lumpy and apparently she will never have a tooth! The doctor says he thinks she will not be so ill again, as now she is so much stronger to bear teething when it comes.

She sleeps all night and a great deal in the day, here at the shamba the cold sea wind makes one so sleepy. She can do such delightful things now. She can give smacking kisses, only she always does it at the wrong time, first gives a wet kiss and then shuts her mouth and makes a loud smack - to her great delight - for she goes on rehearsing long after. She also says tata when she is told and dada and mama at her own sweet will, but it seems to me that she doesn't know which is which - she often says dad-dada to me, oh, she is such a darling. Harry is going to draw her he says, with her little shirt on, sitting on the bed with her legs very far apart to balance her fat little body.

She has such a sweet expressive little face with a broad smooth square forehead just like Harry's, lovely dark eyes with black eyelashes ditto, ditto, the dearest little retroussé nose and kissable mouth and small decided chin; all so full of character. She has a great perception of the ludicrous and when she is sitting up and Saburi making antics in front of her, she falls flat on the couch with laughing. I think I must have described her fifty times before - her hair is just beginning to grow perceptibly and be parted, it is about an inch long of a lovely light golden brown that is sure to go dark to match her brows and lashes.

Before we left Zanzibar [city] we had reason to be very thankful that Dr Pendreth was living with us. Mr Peebles the book keeper was taken ill with a very severe kind of fever, not belonging to Zanzibar (whose fevers are of the mildest intermittent order). He was in bed more than three weeks and had to have all his hair cut off. He is now with us at the shamba but Harry has given him leave to go to the Seychelles in the *Rapid* to recruit [recover]. He is such a bad bookkeeper that Harry will be most thankful to get rid of him for a time, altrough it will entail upon Harry the severest office drudgery, besides the apparent necessity of his being in three places at the same time, for there is nobody now to look after the machinery at Shangany and the sugar plantation at Kokotony. Mr Rae the engineer had no sooner seen Captain Fraser's back turned, than he is proceeding to take himself off to England without giving any reason to anybody, so there is nobody now but Harry and Mr Bishop to do everything, and if they don't soon knock up, it will be little less than a miracle.

Indeed, I am very, very anxious - it is so many months before we can let the firm at home know the want of help. Two of the under engineers have died since we came, one of drinking, one of malaria fever, caught at an unhealthy place called Moira, and I am very much afraid of Harry going to Kokotony, although that is not so bad a place by any means, being elevated. So now I think I have told you all my troubles and of course one can't expect to live anywhere without them. Oh, no I haven't! Naval officers are my present grievance. They worry me to death now I am the only lady (ie English woman) on the island, Mrs Seward being at Seychelles at present. They called in town at the rate of sometimes 9 or 10 a day, there being at present 4 men-of-war hovering about here, and since we came to the shamba we have had two officers here, and two more are coming tonight. They <u>will</u> be invited, this is such a delightful place, and they drink a great deal of wine etc. which I tell Harry I think is the reason they like visiting. I don't have anything to do with giving it to them, I can assure you. They make free enough in asking the servants to bring it as we should ask for water. As long as Harry doesn't see the harm of it I can only remain neutral, but I disapprove of it most heartily as might be expected from my "broughtens-up" [upbringing]. It is one comfort that Harry doesn't join them, he only takes very little at dinner.

The Captain of the *Highflyer* who is senior officer here now, asked us to luncheon on board and I enjoyed going very much as I had never seen the new kinds of Armstrong guns and all the beautiful orderly appointments of a man-of-war, but you don't know how near we are sometimes to the horrors of this anti-slavery, and therefore as they think greatly to-be-proud-of warfare. The *Wasp* sent off two of her boats to capture a dhow containing slaves and they overtook her just by our shamba, only nearer Zanzibar. This was before we came here this time. They generally disarm the crew without much bloodshed, but the captain of this slaver, a Northern Arab, vowed he would die rather than be taken by a couple of boats, so as the boats came up and tried to board her in the dark, they fired a volley over their side and wounded many of our sailors, killing the coxswain.

Well, the two officers, one of whom was a boy midshipman, commenced to climb the sides, followed by their men, the Arabs all the time chopping at their hands with their swords so that the principal officer got nearly all his fingers cut off one hand, and nearly all were wounded on their arms. But the worst was when they got on board and found themselves far outnumbered by a crew of the fiercest Arabs that ever come here, some of whom fought hand to hand with them, and nearly all of whom they killed. The first lieutenant killed six or eight and the little middy whom I don't know I am sorry to say, struck 5 or 6 times at a great big fellow about twice his own height and a splendid swordsman, and not only guarded himself so as not to be fatally wounded, but cut through the big fellow's turban, skull and all and left him dead upon the deck. You must remember that all this time the remainder of the Arabs were down below striking up through the beams of the unplanked deck at the men's legs, that is the way they got their worst wounds.

However, they took the dhow after killing the captain, containing in her hold about 300 slaves, and she was going to take in 200 more near our shamba, nearly all of whom were stolen, and she was only about 150 tons burden, so you may imagine how tightly they were packed. Nobody in town heard anything of all this during the night although the noise was fearful, on account of the wind being away from us, but next morning we saw them handing the poor wounded men and the two who were killed up the *Wasp's* side. They took the slaves to Seychelles to liberate them. I have not heard if any marines have died since, but I know that many were dangerously wounded because we had prayers for them in church and the Bishop himself went at their own request to be with them on the voyage, he is dearly loved by the poor seamen.

In consequence of the absence of so many Englishmen, Dr Steer the Bishop's chaplain, was the only Britisher in the island besides our own household to take dinner together on the Queen's birthday [24th May] and wish Her Majesty long life and happiness and prosperity to our dear old Fatherland.

It is quite true dear Father that there are 20,000 slaves brought into Zanzibar every year who are re-sold and reshipped for the north, principally Muscat and the Persian Gulf. They are brought from the Sultan's territories on the mainland [of Africa] and of course we cannot prevent his moving them about from one part of his kingdom to another, but it is equally absurd to suppose that having allowed him by treaty to bring them here again, we can prevent their owners from selling them again. In fact out of 20,000 we catch about 1,000 annually which is the total result of that great naval establishment here, excepting of course that the Arabs wouldn't let us remain here long if there was not some visible safeguard for us in the harbour or near it.

I am looking forward with apprehension to a great calamity which is within three weeks of us. We are nearly at an end of our flour in Zanzibar and it will be weeks and perhaps months before ships can get here from Bombay to bring some. No wheat grows here and though there is plenty of maize, Harry says that one can't make edible bread of it without preparation, and there is not even the means of grinding it! So we shall soon have no bread, no pastry, no flour puddings and to add to our misfortunes there have been no potatoes in Zanzibar for the last three weeks. We eat yams (vile) and sweet potatoes (far from pleasant) and we have a good many biscuits, mostly fancy ones and horrid they are, old and musty and tasting of rancid butter and made by Peek Frean & Co. who make the worst biscuits in the world, and those we must live upon I suppose with meat and curry and rice.

I have just remembered that I didn't tell you that Nora plays at bo-peep most beautifully. We have a red quilted curtain in the town house instead of a door to my little room and very often we see a little fat hand take hold, very cautiously, of the edge, and then it is whisked aside. A little head comes suddenly in and if you look at her and say 'bo' you hear a laugh and the little head as suddenly disappears. If you pretend not to see, she makes a little cough and puts her head further and further in until you see nothing but the top of it and she nearly falls out of the ayah's arms. How I wish she could peep at you - she gave me a kiss for grandpapa and grandmama and smacked her lips a dozen times afterwards, the dear old pet she is.

Harry will send you the remainder of our bill either this mail or next. At present I am the happy possessor of about six rupees - so I can't send it even if bullion would go by post. Dear Father's is a most interesting letter but I have gossipped so long about ourselves that I must soon leave off. I am very glad that dear little Artie is so happy at school. I hope he will soon be raised from his lowly position in class which however isn't half a bad thing for him as he gets so much easier lessons. You must not be at all anxious at my saying the ayah has fever or any of the servants - all Portuguese have it and very often - once every month or two - both here and in India. I reproved Bastian the other day for disobedience and in consequence of his being afraid he was taken ill with shivering about 10 minutes after and had fever for two days. Harry says they can get really ill almost any time. Dr Pendreth went down to see Bastian, for I thought he was shamming, and said he had got real fever! And if the ayah has a fit of crying about anything she would have fever perhaps for days as likely as not. I don't know about using wet sheets in this intermittent fever, dear Father, one can never tell when the cold fit will come on when the pulse lowers very suddenly after the feverish spell, and I think it might be dangerous to lower the pulse artificially.

You must know they don't give any medicine in this fever except an aperient to begin with which is always needed and when the fever has gone, quinine for several days. Fever can easily be warded off by quinine if you take it in time when you feel the first symptoms and before you feel any heat. I am happy to say I never needed it. Harry has taken a little quinine since he came here, and this treatment seems to be a safe and certain cure and as simple as possible and so I can manage the ayah quite well.

I enjoyed the note from America and will try to answer it. I didn't expect to see dear old Aunt Mary again. I fear I shall find very few of the old people left when I come home but I should like to see Aunt Esther again. I hope that long ago you have recovered from your little ailments and that Pollie, Gulie and Tom are well as thou doesn't mention them. Why Maggie didn't write to me after baby was born I can't imagine. Wasn't she glad of that dear child coming who I hope someday will know and love her. With the assurance dear old people and young ones that we are all quite well and that I never felt heartier and hungrier in my life (if I only had anything to eat), I am your most loving daughter and sister and friend, Elsie.

PS. This is a most interesting island and I believe that Harry means to write an account of it some day. I cannot arrange my facts or thoughts at all, besides, I am so _very_ busy from six o'clock in the morning until dinner time at 6 in the evening that I couldn't write it if I could.

Back in England, Tom Smith was taken seriously ill and died on 4th April, a month before his 16th birthday. The certificate records the cause of death as erysipelas, which is an acute streptococcal skin infection with fever and purplish raised lesions, especially on the face. Before antibiotics this was a serious condition and could ultimately lead to blood poisoning. The family were distraught, and letters of sympathy from relatives and Friends arrived from all over the country. It seems ironic that Tom should be taken when the Jacob family were in constant peril from tropical diseases. This letter from Henry's brother Isaac Jacob is typical of many addressed to Bartholomew and Isabel Smith.

Stockton on Tees
April 7th 1865

My dear friend

The card which I received by this morning's post has indeed introduced me into feelings of near [close] sympathy with thee and Isabella Smith, and suffering as I am acutely from the loss of a beloved son of the same name, I think I may in a peculiar degree understand and appreciate what you are now suffering, but how different it must be to those who unlike me, have been endeavouring before their trials to do the work of the Great Head of the Church upon earth, and so may not have to endure the bitter reflection that had obedience kept pace with knowledge it might have been spared.

Now my dear friend I am sure that all who know thee must acknowledge that thou earnestly strives to do the Master's work upon earth and I can but commend thee to him and remind thee that we none of us know how soon the veil which divides us from immortality may be drawn aside and place us in the presence of the Saviour, restoring us also to the society of those loved ones from whom it has hitherto separated us.

With dear love to Isabella Smith
thy affectionate friend
Isaac Jacob

See Appendix 1 for list of letters of condolence.

My dear Father

Elisa has asked me to send the enclosed in payment for the box (balance of a/c) gloves, etc. etc. My poor darling is in sad distress having just received your letter conveying the sad intelligence of the death of our brother Tom. She is I believe, writing herself. I am in great haste but I need not tell you how deeply I sympathize with you in this terrible bereavement. E often told me about her dear brother, and although I did not know him personally I often looked forward to the pleasure of meeting one whom my dear wife loved so much and was so proud of.

Pray excuse this very hasty note, I am overwhelmed with business for the mail.

Your affectionate son H Jacob.

Tom Smith 1849-1865.

If it was written, the letter from Elizabeth promised by Henry after the news of Tom's death has not survived. With careful and devoted nursing Elizabeth recovers from malaria. Quinine was well-known as a useful medicine to reduce the fever of malaria, even before the cause of the disease was discovered. A dose of alcohol was prescribed as a cure-all for everything, but she is not keen to take it because of her temperance principles.

Zanzibar, June 29 1865

My dearest Father and Mother

We have no letter of yours to answer since the sad one that reached us at the beginning of the month but I don't like to let a mail go by without sending you news of us, knowing that you will prefer a short letter to none.

You will see by the address at the top that we have left St Patrick's and I daresay you will wonder, knowing that we felt settled there, but the fact is that I got rather a sharp attack of malaria fever there, and while I was at the worst, Dr Seward came with a boat, had me carried into it just as I was, bedding, mattress and all, and brought into town. I had the fever on me continuously for three days and nights and Harry gave me splendid hot packs twice a day during that time with the Doctor's full consent and approval, and every time they got me a short refreshing sleep and a moisture on my burning skin, so that although the fever returned I got the good of them and I have no doubt that they saved me from a much longer and worse attack. I was troubled with the most distressing sickness, but the Doctor was able to relieve it and I was only in bed a week altogether. I am thankful to say my strength is coming back more every day.

Dear Harry is just such another good nurse as Father and was the best and tenderest that could be imagined, to me he seemed never to tire, but nearly got knocked up. Some time ago he also had a slight attack of fever, so I hope we may both consider ourselves acclimatized. We ought to be most thankful for quinine - it is the one preventive of fever if you take it in time. I am to take two doses a day for a while now. I am taking a wine-glassful of beer as medicine at the Doctor's request and find it most nauseous and will soon leave it off, as I shan't long need a tonic or stimulant I hope. The Doctor has been very good in not giving me drugs as he knows I am no medicine taker, and that is the reason I gave in about the beer, that and Harry's asking me not to object, so you must not think my principles are getting lax, for indeed they are not.

Dear baby I am happy to say is as fat and jolly as Friar Tuck and as full of mischief. She is so active we dare not leave her anywhere but on the floor, and there she sits for hours a day, as upright as possible playing with her poor little bits of toys, shells and so on. If we put her on a couch or chair she immediately throws herself down on her stomach and slides off backwards, no matter how high it is, and she does it instantaneously, so that it is not safe for us to turn our backs. She has just been taking hold of me with both hands and giving me such big wet kisses, because she wanted me take her. It was so funny while I was poorly and in bed, she wouldn't so much as look at me and begged to be taken away, but directly I was well, she was just as fond of me as ever, indeed, I think more so,

Since Mrs Seward came back from Seychelles quite a colony of English ladies seem to be here. Two new ones have come - the Bishop's sister, Miss Tozer; a friend of hers, Miss Jones, and Miss Tozer's maid, so the poor Bishop has been fairly inundated. Miss Tozer came to see me when I was poorly, she is a very kind creature, not very young, but very ugly with reddish hair and a kind of light reddish brown eyes and no lashes or eyebrows. She has projecting teeth and a nose as thin as a lath and also reddish as is her complexion, and she dresses frightfully. Miss Jones I haven't seen but they say she has a long beard. It is queer what plain-looking women come to Zanzibar for Mrs Seward is as far from beautiful as I am and Mrs Playfair was the same. I think I am rather improved with being so thin, I can tell you I have no spare flesh on my bones by this time.

The Bishop's system of religion is a queer mixture. He lives very sparingly and leads a very self-denying ascetic life like an old monk missionary, but at the same time he prizes above all things his altar cloths and episcopal toggery generally. He is getting sent out to him by his old associates a Bishop's throne and no end of purple and fine linen robes, his surplice and scarlet and black D.D. hood not being half grand enough, and he has besides his Bishop's lawn sleeves which he sports sometimes. This seems to be his one weakness, but he is a very good man in other ways and spends nearly all his time over his little heathens, now 24 in number, all living under his roof and getting the best of secular as well as religious instruction. Some of them can already do sums beautifully and they can all say the Lord's Prayer, etc. besides which they are taught to use brushes and combs and become clean and decent members of society.

Mr Peebles has gone away in the *Lyra* for a change of air, hoping that he may come back fit for work again, and Mr Bishop is at Kokotoni so that Harry is doing all the office work at present and we are living alone in this big town house. I am going down with Harry to the other end of the town to see the three great hydraulic presses working for expressing coconut oil. They are not yet in full working order but when they are, Harry expects to make about five tons of oil a day. There will be some pleasure in really manufacturing something to send home and when the sugar machinery gets to work at Kokotoni there won't be much difficulty in filling up the ships that they send out from Smith Flemings.

This island is covered with coconut trees and they bear two or three crops of nuts a year, so they anticipate no difficulty in procuring copra, as the dried coconut kernel is called, enormous as is the quantity that will be consumed, only Harry says that it will raise the price very much. They are going to buy it by contract.

We were dreadfully disappointed at having to leave the shamba and now the oranges are ripening and I was just getting the garden into order, and cleaning out all the dead leaves from the inside of the long trellis-covered walk in the garden. Mr Gully, who was staying with us when I got the fever, was helping me. He is a very nice fellow indeed, second officer of the *Pantaloon* and comes from Ackworth, having been born at Ackworth Park, the lodge gates of which we have so often passed. He said that he had never met a Yorkshire girl abroad before, and we had great talks about dear old Yorkshire, Charlesworth's and the school. Harry was also getting all the steps mended about the house and I and a little tailor boy were making pink chintz valences for all the sitting room windows, six in number, but I don't think we shall soon venture to live there again. We had also got a croquet ground levelled under the orange trees and all our hoops driven in. Isn't it a proof of the fact that "Man proposes and God disposes".

How often I thought, especially when I was ill, of dear Tom's having died so lately and wondered whether I was going already to join him. I prayed very much to be quite willing either way, and I seemed to have a little faith sometimes that Jesus was all sufficient and that I needn't fear, in spite of all my shortcomings. But I am very glad to be able to take care of baby a little longer, and to be a companion for darling Harry in this lonely place. It was well that Tom didn't live to have a wife and baby and then die. That would have been worse to bear. As it is I hope you are comforted dear ones as time comforts us all when there is nothing but hopelessness in our grief. We have only too many temptations to dullness and melancholy here, but this is a thing we must strive against and I hope some day to see you all again that are left in our dear old Fatherland.

You must try not to feel unduly anxious about our health. We will take extra care not to get damp or anything of that kind. I hope that dear Pollie, Gulie and Artie are well and you, dearest ones, the same.

Much love to you all
Your loving Elsie.

Baby kisses your photographs nearly every day and knows which is grandmamma and which grandpapa.

For the sake of their health, the Jacob family has been invited to live on one of the Sultan's ships in the harbour, although they hope to go back to the shamba at St Patrick's when the monsoon is over.

H.H. Ship *Victoria*
Harbour of Zanzibar, July 26 1865

My dearest Pollie

I am so sorry to hear that you have been so long without hearing from us. I write, I think, by every opportunity, which I imagine is about once a month at the farthest, but of course we can't always send our letters the same way. Sometimes they go round by Bombay, but if we can we always send them via Seychelles, from whence it is only a month home. Thy most welcome letter, dear Pollie, dated May 1st came about a week ago, together with one from Hannah Baker. Please thank her greatly for remembering me and <u>showing</u> it by writing - those were all the letters we got although we were expecting two or three mails, and dear Harry hasn't heard from Ireland I should think for three months - Maria Taylor never writes now.

You will see by the superscription of this that we are living afloat instead of ashore and find it a great improvement during this most unhealthy season. The Doctor in whose hands I have been several times since I wrote last, I am sorry to say, prescribed a cruise out to sea, but I objected as Harry couldn't have gone and he needed a change as much as I did, so Dr Seward said this would do nearly as well and Harry asked the Sultan, through the Consul, and he willingly gave us leave. You must understand that the *Shah Allum* is one of his ships of war, a very fine old frigate belonging originally to the East India Company but now 40 years old and nearly superannuated. The accommodation is excellent - a fine large sitting room, an outer room where ayah and baby sleep, a stern gallery with the Sultan's camp bed in, where we sleep, and several little bedrooms, bathrooms etc., and the whole well ventilated and pleasant. If we are hot, there is a large poop overhead where the wind is strong enough.

The Captain, or Nacoda as the name is here, is a very nice kind Arab who says he is most happy to accommodate us and that the whole of his crew are at our service. His name is Abdullah-ben-somebody-or-other and I was wishing you could have seen us sitting talking Hindostani yesterday morning, trying each to be most polite. He had on a beautiful black coat trimmed profusely with silver and crimson, and he wears a silver hilted scimitar fastened to his belt with yards of silver chain. Some of the crew were fighting with sticks this morning and as I am rather afraid of the Arabs getting their blood up and stabbing each other with their knives as they often do, I went to them and told them that if I heard any more noise, I would tell the Nacoda, who would flog them all round when he came, and they were quiet directly, for you must know that the Arabs give the English credit for always keeping their word.

We had a little dinner last night. Our guests were the Captains of the *Highflyer* and *Wasp* and the Commander of the *Lyra* and we had a very pleasant evening. Mr Peebles has come back from his cruise no better and the Doctor says he has got liver, and must go home instantly, so he goes to Seychelles tomorrow. Poor Harry is fated to do all the work. Mr Rae the engineer is also going home to get married, so the machinery will also fall to Harry, and Mr Bishop will spend most of his time at Kokotoni [where] the sugar is growing splendidly and exceeds the Mauritius average of saccharine matter in spite of everybody's assertions that the sugar cane wouldn't grow here. Captain Fraser alone was certain that it would.

I forgot to tell you that we got a most providential supply of flour - an American ship came in with some the <u>very day</u> the other was finished in the island, and now we have excellent bread. We also got some potatoes from Bombay, and better still, Mr Bishop says that those he planted as an experiment at Kokotoni are answering splendidly. The only drawback is the excessive luxuriance of the tops. Cabbages too, grow so tall no one can make them have hearts, they sprout straight up four or five feet. I shall try potatoes at the shamba, if they answer at Kokotoni. We hope to go back to the dear little house at St Patrick's as soon as this monsoon is over, it is one of the healthiest places on the island when the wind is off the sea.

We had a big picnic there the other day and asked all the Europeans here and all the officers of the men-of-war, about 25 came and we greatly enjoyed the day. Our servants went the night before to get things ready, and I can assure you we required some providing for, besides ourselves, 25 who were all ravenously hungry. There were about 20 English sailors who manned the boats and some of the little negroes whom Miss Tozer brought from her brother's to enjoy themselves. The Bishop himself would not give his boys a holiday, so did not come. We wandered about the garden until ten o'clock then had a big breakfast, like an English dinner, then went under the orange trees and tried to cut down a coconut tree which stands in the avenue, but couldn't for want of proper tools, and Domingo the cook wouldn't let me have his meat-axe. We wanted the tree to get the cabbage out of the top which makes a very nice salad raw, and a vegetable of the most delicious flavour cooked. It is a mark of delicate attention to offer it to your guests, because it requires you to waste a tree to get it.

We also played at various games, duckstone etc., and came in the house at noon to get some fruit and cake. In the afternoon the gentlemen leaped and vaulted and there was great competition between the various ships. However, baby's friend Mr Theobold did the best, he is a very nice little fellow, one of the *Wasp* lieutenants, who comes in and plays with baby very often indeed and she likes him enormously and claps her hands and "shakes her waist" as the ayah calls it, when he comes. She has grown wonderfully in good looks and intelligence lately and she has such pretty ways of being delighted. One is of laughing out loud and clapping her hands ecstatically, which she seemed to do without being taught, and makes quite a noise I can assure you with her little fat palms. Another and the most amusing is when she squeezes her hands tight together into her stomach and her chin down and her shoulders up and then gives a great laugh down to herself. I'm sure nobody taught her that and it is the most ridiculous thing I ever saw.

There is a great danger of her getting spoiled here - all the Captains and officers who have bairns at home and who hardly ever see an English baby, love her and pet her so much and she, at any rate, appreciates their gilt buttons. One gentleman brought her two squeaking dollies from Mauritius, another a coach and horses, and two picture books, but she hates dolls and has dismembered the one I gave her instantly. The only thing she will do with them is to take them one foot in each hand and use their smooth bald heads as battering rams against the floor. I am afraid she will be a dreadful Tomboy as I was. But all this time I didn't tell you that she got a tooth on her 9th birthday (the 21st) and is getting another today which makes her a little cross and sleepless all day, but she sleeps all of every night. She has also learnt to creep at last, which she manages by raising herself forwards or sliding along the ground for a change. She is looking as fat and rosy as an English child lately, the little precious, I hope she may keep so, but this is a digression from the shamba.

We had dinner at four o'clock, partly hot and partly cold, and after that it was time to set off, as it was near sunset, so Captain Bowden took us ladies, Mrs Seward, Miss Tozer, Miss Jones and self in his little boat and we rowed part of the way and after dark got stuck on a sandbank, and sailed off again and got in early, which was my object as I had never left baby before for so long. I found all right and went to bed at 8 o'clock very tired, for I had had fever the day before. Harry and the other gentlemen in the larger sailing boat didn't get in until 10 o'clock as they had a head wind. Everybody says they had a truly jolly day. The oranges were ripe and there were plenty of Pemba coconuts and we told the sailors to eat as many of one and drink as many of the other as they liked.

I wish you could see the orange trees now, although we have given away hundreds of baskets full there seem as many as ever. They are quite ripe and golden amongst the dark leaves, sometimes hanging in bunches of a dozen, never having been thinned in winter, speaking English-wise. As for us, this up to October is the cold season and the weather begins to be healthy. When the heat comes the cloves ripen and sweeten the air with their aromatic scent. If we are not better during this next season than we have been for the last month or two, we shall soon give up Zanzibar as a residence I can tell you, but we have little doubt that we shall be all right again in the dry weather.

I have had nothing fresh the matter with me, only fever hanging about and the Doctor says the malaria is still in my system, or was until I came off here. I feel quite well today, I am thankful to say. Harry too is greatly better - he and I were having fever on alternate days, to our great discouragement of mind and exhaustion of body, and the ayah was no better, but we hope for better things. You would be amused if you could see how gaunt I am - only weigh just over 9st. and that is a small weight for me. I weighed 10st. when I came at Christmas, and all my big bones show, but my appetite has come back and I shall soon pick up again if all be well. So don't be anxious about us, everyone has more or less trouble with their health at first, but many live here a long time without any apparent damage to their constitutions, and both of us owe the best of these to our dear fathers and mothers.

The next page is missing, but it sounds as though Elizabeth was just rounding off her letter. She may have written on a small scrap of paper which has been lost.

Elizabeth feels safer living on the Sultan's ship in Zanzibar harbour in spite of the loyal salutes. She is very disappointed that their box <u>still</u> hasn't arrived from England as she is quite out of dresses. Her descriptions of the baby are delightful to read, but there is some regret that her parents haven't yet made contact with Henry's family in Ireland. An outbreak of smallpox at home and in Zanzibar makes her thankful that the family have all been vaccinated.

H.H.S. "Shah Allum"
Harbour of Zanzibar, Aug 24 1865

My dearest Father and Mother

I am writing to you this time although I have a letter of Gulie's to answer, because it seems a long time since I wrote to you, and still longer since we had a letter from darling Mother. I hope she feels by this time as though she could write again and comfort our hearts with the sight of her dear well-known hand.

Did my last letter make you very anxious about our health? I hope not, for I have nothing but good news to give of us now and I really hope that it may last, for the feverish season is very nearly over, and we do not mean to go on shore again until the north east monsoon sets in, unless our good friend Abdullah, the captain of this ship, turns us out before which isn't likely. We enjoy living on shipboard greatly, the cabins as well as the deck are so airy and spacious, very different from the general run of ships. The only drawback to our pleasure is the constant firing of the big guns, fifty of which form the complement of this fine old frigate. For instance, the Sultan goes off in the *Wasp* for a cruise - bang go 21 guns just under our feet; the English consul goes up to Bombay, and is saluted by 11 ditto for himself and 21 for our Queen; the English vice-consul comes in a quiet way to get dinner with us and gets 9; the French consul ditto, so that we are getting shy of asking anybody, finding that they are considered the Sultan's guests as well as ours, and treated accordingly.

To add to my misery for I hate the terrible firing on my own account as well as baby's, I am expecting a royal salute to be fired today, as it is the Arabic new year's day, and the greatest of festivals. Harry is going to send a present of Brussels carpet to Abdullah and 3 goats to his crew to kill and eat for dinner, as they consider flesh meat the greatest of treats. I am disgusted at the idea of having them killed on board, but one gets used to all sorts of horrors here. For instance, two sailors were flogged here the other day in sight of the cabin door and in hearing too, which was worse when they howled, there was one consolation, they certainly deserved it.

The ship lying nearest to us in the harbour is the *Victoria*, one of the ships which is going with the [1]Sultan to Bombay on the 20th of this month, and they have a very stupid careless old captain, Hallal by name, and of course numbers of accidents. The other day he sent a lot of "longshore" men up into the rigging and in consequence two fell out of the crosstrees and were killed, one in the morning and the other in the afternoon. We did not actually see them fall, but we saw one of the corpses being handed over the side. The day before yesterday a lot of gunpowder exploded there, frightening us considerably, but I did not hear that anyone was killed.

That reminds me of another thing that I think very dreadful, and that is that the powder magazine, containing I believe some hundreds of tons of powder imported both by Fraser's and others, stands right amongst the negro houses at the other side of the creek. The other day in one of the frequent fires which occur amongst these careless people and dry thatched houses, the very house adjoining the magazine was blazing and sparks flying in all directions. It was a very miracle that all Zanzibar wasn't blown into the sea. Harry, with all other Europeans, is making efforts to get it stowed far out in the country, but the Sultan is an idle careless man and very difficult to move. This idea of going to Bombay seems a tremendous undertaking to him and he is selling off all his moveable goods nearly, to raise money enough to go, and also to buy new things there. He has never seen a carriage, or a carriage road for that matter, and Colonel Playfair induced him and other Arabs to make this trip, hoping that this place might profit by it ultimately, perhaps to the extent of his importing some road-makers from India.

I think I told you that the streets are hardly wide enough for two people to walk abreast (indeed two ladies can't) and that we have nothing wider than a footpath in the island. Indeed, the paths are so narrow that the ayah can't drag baby's perambulator beyond

191

the limits of the garden at the shamba. I was going to tell you when I spoke of the Sultan's selling off his things, that we went with the Sewards one day before the auction to look and see what we liked that our husbands might bid for them. The secretary and brother-in-law of the Sultan, Suliman bin Ali, met us there and told us to put aside what we liked, that the auctioneer might know. We thought it rather a curious proceeding; however, I chose a paraffin lamp with a white china shade, four vases - two beautiful large ones and two small, a set of glass plates, etc. Well, the next morning came a man with a hamper and a note as follows from Suliman bin Ali -

"That what you thogt is good to you.
Will you be kind to keep it,
From you frind Silamen bin Ali
I am you truly SBA"

Wasn't it kind of him, but Arabs would give you anything you admired, and we never expected less to get things without paying for them. We have kept the note as a curiosity as I fancy there are not many Arabs in the world who can do as much as write one at all.

I have not told you yet how glad we were to get your dear letters, at least your <u>letter</u> and those from Ireland. We were anxiously expecting the *Wasp* back from Seychelles with the mail and when on Saturday night a sail came in sight, how anxiously we kept the telescope fixed upon her, and it wasn't until she turned round the point into the harbour that it turned out to be the *Pantaloon*, the difference being that the latter is full-rigged which we could not tell from the barque rig of the *Wasp* while she was head-on. We were certainly a little disappointed, but next day just as Harry was going off to tiffin on board the *Pantaloon*, I espied her and she had got in. The letters had come on board and I had read them before Harry had got back to take me to evening church.

The *Wasp* brought very bad news of Mr Peebles who went in her as far as Seychelles on his way to England, the doctor thinks he won't live to get there. He was sent out here very delicate and consumptive and has got now an abscess in his liver. He was always obviously unfit for the climate and very foolish and obstinate and careless into the bargain. Harry sent him home almost the very day he had the doctor's opinion, so there is no blame to him that it was very likely too late.

The ship brought no box for me, and Harry says he thinks it is entirely lost. I am so vexed with dear Father for sending it round the Cape. There is no communication between the Cape and Mauritius, and it is nobody's business to forward it to the Seychelles, even if it ever gets there. I wish you would send everything overland whatever it costs, Harry says that it will be quite as dear this way if we ever get it, with all the charges made by the people at the different places.

I am dreadfully badly off for dresses as you may imagine, all my thin ones worn out long ago and my <u>only</u> silk almost one great stain, with having to go everywhere by sea. The ladies here wear nothing but dark silks every day, everything else is very little good and I want one or two good silks very much but H says it is no use asking for them as they are never likely to get here. I wear alpacas and prints out of the bazaar and am not fit to be seen beside the other ladies not so well off by any means as we are. The simple reason is that they constantly get out a few fresh things overland and get them regularly, whereas I have been waiting for <u>eight</u> months until I saw the contents of the box to guide me as to what else I wanted. Now enough of grumbling, but I do feel a little ill used when I have to dine out in an alpaca dress, as happens constantly.

We are getting quite dissipated and idle as we always are when the ships are in. The officers are so glad to be on shore and so weary of the sea that one can't help trying to entertain them and make their stay pleasant, and they are very hospitable in return. We went off to tiffin on board the *Pantaloon* last Tuesday and it turned out to be a dinner and lasted all the afternoon. After that we went in four boats for a sail and great fun it was seeing huge Dr Achison sitting alone in the little wee dinghy, the smallest boat, and completely filling up the stern. At half-past six we came on board and found <u>our</u> dinner ready, and got some of the officers to stay and help us eat it, although of course nobody was hungry. Then yesterday Mr Gully, my Yorkshire friend, and Dr A. came on board to tiffin and made me come ashore to the house to play billiards with them, and we made raids into the office to try to get

Harry out. We presently succeeded and then Captain Purvis and the other officers gathered up and we set off in two boats for another sail, the Captain and I in his gig and the rest in the pinnace and we sailed most beautifully almost round and round the big boat and came on board bringing five of them to dinner.

Today we are to go to dine with dear old Captain Bowden on board the *Wasp* and afterwards to tea at Mrs Seward's. Tomorrow there is a monster picnic to French Island to which everybody is going, and after that luckily for me, the *Pantaloon* sails for Seychelles to bring our next mails, and the *Wasp* goes off cruising on Monday. I say 'luckily' for I have a dozen little plain dresses cut out in jaconet muslin for baby, who is now as big round the waist as her mother, saving one inch, and a half dozen little shirts and lots more wanted, and of these only <u>one</u> has got made in a week. However, we are quiet enough between times and I mean to make up for my disgraceful idleness soon.

I wish you could see the dear child now for she has grown in the last two months almost out of knowledge, and is no longer a baby but a most independent little mortal with the fattest hardest cheeks and legs and arms, creeping in all directions, puffing like a steam engine and getting up on to her feet with the greatest ease, indeed, doing everything but walk alone. She pulls herself along (walking) by anything, and when she gets tired sits down so suddenly with such a plop. She is just like a monkey for imitating and mimics the sailors whenever she can get a bit of rope or string to pull, bending her back as though she were handling the rigging and singing out "Ah illah" Arab fashion, with just their intonation. We had a big cry the other day because she was not allowed to join some sailors who were hauling a big spar on board and keeping time by singing and stamping as negroes do. She got so excited and would not be pacified until I gave her the end of the thick coir rope which was lying on the deck, when she was quite happy chanting "Ah illah" and fancying she helped by lifting it up and down, getting very red in the face with her exertions.

I am thankful to say she is perfectly healthy and never frets, she roars twice a day at being taken out of her tub and that is all we hear of her except laughing and trying to talk. We have begun to call her "Totty" because one day when Mrs Seward, who always calls her Totty, had been here, baby began saying "To-tee", "To-tee" in such a pretty sing song and did it almost without stopping all next day, so we picked it up from her and now she knows it is one of her names. She has a bad memory and soon forgets the words she learns, but I never knew any child learn so quickly. She will say almost any letter of the alphabet after listening to me or the ayah and watching our mouths. First she sets her little absurd mouth the right shape and a long while afterwards the sound comes. She can say "papa", "ayah" when she likes and yesterday the ayah taught her to say "cat", but she hardly ever says mama, she generally says "papa" for us both. When I try to make her call me by my name, she sits before me with her laughing obstinate little face, and every time I say "mama" she deliberately says "papa" until we both burst out laughing.

She has two fine bottom teeth, larger than any of Minnie Seward's are now, but no signs of any others being near at hand. They certainly are coming very slowly, as also her hair, she has a good deal really but it is so fine and light it hardly shows, and I am afraid it will be a long time before she needs the round combs I got for her from Bombay. Did you ever know anyone talk so determinedly about even a first baby! Mother will say I am worse than Maggie was. Neither she or Rachel ever write to me, are they grieved because the marriage they disapproved of has proved to be by so much the happiest and best and rightest thing I ever did, or ever shall do I expect. They should have given me credit for knowing exactly what I was about and they oughtn't to cut me now my wisdom is proved.

Our Irish Mother says she wrote to you when she heard of dear Tom's death and got no reply. I am so sorry about it for she is a loving sensitive creature and says she longs for some intercourse with you. She evidently feels slighted just when she had done such a difficult thing as to be a little demonstrative and she has had to endure so much of that kind of thing since their fortunes went somewhat down in the world that I am especially sorry that any apparent neglect should come from you, though I am quite sure you never intended it. They are also evidently a good deal grieved about your not visiting them, isn't it too bad to go again to the Lakes when you could so easily have gone to Ireland instead without any more expenditure of time or money. I can't understand your being so halfish [half-hearted] about getting to know people who are almost part of our own family now, if they could have done so they would not have left the matter so long in your hands I know. The reason I am so sorry is that it is likely to prevent very cordial intercourse afterwards, which I was hoping we should all have enjoyed together in years to come. It is always difficult to forget that people left off getting to know one as long as they possibly could.

I am afraid you will think I am making myself very unpleasant today, but indeed I feel so full of love to you all and so does Harry. He knows you quite well by this time and says you are just the sort of people he would be fond of which I should rather think you are, for he is just like you except having knocked about the world and perhaps being less particular about some outward observances in consequence, but just as true to the spirit of goodness for all that, and full of respect for opinions that differ from his. He has, as he says, the gift of seeing with equal distinctness the two sides of every question, which is a quality I haven't got at all. I am always a violent partizan - though I hope I have learnt something from him, the dear wiseacre.

He wants to know if Pollie and Gulie will let him kiss them, he says that every time he looks at the smooth fat cheeks in the photographs and I tell him they are much softer than mine. He says he is rather sorry he didn't ask Pollie to marry him instead of me, when I tell him how much cleverer she is in her intellect. Really it is true what he says that I am the greatest old stupid in the world. Since I left England and got no new books or magazines and no time to read them if we had, my capacities and conversation have sunk rather below the ordinary level, and are limited to sewing, cooking, talking gossip, coaxing Harry and baby, and scolding the servants!

It will be very pleasant for Pollie to have John Hall at the lakes. I am greatly interested in my new brother-in-law elect and am only sorry I didn't foresee the necessity of cultivating his acquaintance. Do you know what happened the other day? Two young American tourists came here in an American merchant ship and although we met them twice, once at the American Consul's and once at a large dinner at the Sewards, we never found out that one

196

was a Friend, just come over from Philadelphia and no doubt well acquainted with all our cousins belonging to the same Quarterly Meeting. The Sewards told him that we were Quakers just as he was going away and hadn't time to come and see us again, and we never heard till he had gone, wasn't it provoking, and we are the first of the sect whoever set foot here. His name was Mr Brown.

A great event happened in Zanzibar the other day at the British consulate - the first English wedding that ever took place here. I told you that Miss Tozer the Bishop's sister brought out a very nice maid about two months ago. Well, to Miss Tozer's intense aggravation, for she had paid her passage out and found her most useful, she was married last Saturday to one of our head men, McCall, the engineer in charge of our presses in Shangany. They sent us a large piece of bride cake, and very far from nice it was - so I gave it to the servants.

I am very sorry to hear so bad an account of the boys [2]Hills. I liked them very much. I suppose it is Kate Donkin whom he was engaged to before that, Gulie means, when she says that Teddy is married to an innkeeper's daughter. As to Charlie's escapade I don't understand it at all.

We don't know at all how much our letters cost in postage as they come in a big box with all the business letters and are paid for en masse by Mr Brooker of Seychelles. There is no post to Zanzibar I suppose you know, they are merely brought across as a favour from there by any of the men-of-war. If you asked Mr Barley the postage to Seychelles he would tell you in a minute as the P&0 steamers run there - a Post Master ought to know that Seychelles is the nearest postal station to Zanzibar - he is the greatest ignoramus in such matters, I remember, that ever existed.

We were greatly concerned to hear of your having had smallpox in the house, God grant you may all be kept safe from it. It has been pretty bad in Zanzibar, there is no lymph here to vaccinate anybody with, it is very rarely that it will keep its virtues long enough to "take" here after coming from England or India. Dr Seward once got some that took in one instance, and if the natives would have been vaccinated the "pus" might have been kept in a constant supply, but they all refused to allow themselves or their children to be done. Now that smallpox has come upon them, they

197

come in hundreds to Dr Seward and beg to be vaccinated and he has to tell the poor foolish creatures that as they refused to be done before it is impossible now. None of the cases that he has tried lately came to anything and he says it may be years before any will take again. Isn't it a sad thing to be so isolated as not to be able to get vaccine. I mustn't go on any longer as I must write to Ireland today.

My dearest love to all as if named and a kiss from Totty to Grandmamma and Grandpapa, etc, etc. Your Elsie.

Notes:
1. The Sultan: The government of India had invited the Sultan to pay a state visit to Bombay. He took three of his warships, the *Victoria*, a frigate of 40 guns, and two smaller ships, the *Ishander-Shah* and the *Nadir-Shah* .
2. The Hills boys: Edward and Charles. Probably the sons of Bartholmew Smith's sister Sarah [b. 23.11.1809] who married James Hills in 1835.

Alas, the box from England was lost in a shipwreck off the Cape of Good Hope, South Africa. Already Henry's letter suggests that they have had enough of this life in the tropics so far from home, but he is hoping for some leave, at least.

Via Bombay
Zanzibar August 30th 1865

My dear Father

You will see by the enclosed letter which I received yesterday from Mauritius, that our box has been at the bottom of the sea for some time and no chance of our ever seeing it now. I do not know whether it was insured or not - but if it was, will you be so good as to ask your London agent to try and recover the amount. If it was not insured there is no help for it.

We hardly see our way at present to asking you to send another box. Elisa has managed to supply her immediate wants with coarse articles bought in the bazaar, and we shall try to get a dress or two for her from Bombay. I am writing by this mail to London in order to arrange if possible to get a little furlough home next year, but cannot tell at present whether I shall succeed. In this state of uncertainty about our prospects we don't care about getting anything else out from home and will try to rub on a few months longer. Do not begin to calculate on seeing us next year, or you may perhaps be disappointed as I do not at all know whether I can be spared, but I shall do my best to obtain the indulgence.

Pray excuse this short letter - I am busy with others to go to Bombay by a native vessel tomorrow, and have not time for more. E. would unite with me in dear love to you all were she present.

Your affectionate son
H. Jacob.

No.13237

                                   Port Louis, Mauritius
                                         29th July 1865

H. Jacob Esqre.
Messrs H.A. Fraser & Co.
Zanzibar

Dear Sir

In reply to your letter of the 7th ultimo, which reached us on the
24th instant, we regret to have to inform you that the case to your
address shipped at Southampton per SS *Briton* had been tran-
shipped to the *Athens* at Cape Town and has been lost in that unfortunate steamer, which as you will ere this have learnt, was totally
lost in Table Bay during a fearful gale which occurred there on the
17th May last.

Protest, with all Documents attached, has been forwarded from
Cape Town to London, for the purpose of settling the claims on
the Underwriters, and reference to it can be had, on application
to the London Agents of the Union Steam Ship Co., Messrs
Falconer & Mercer, 3 East India Chambers, Leadenhall Street.

Hoping you were covered by Insurance, we remain,

Dear Sir
Your obedient servants
Blyth Brothers.

Desperation is setting in - no box, no new clothes, no books, illness, limited social contacts, a feeling that they have been abandoned, and then a near catastrophe.

Per *Aden* to Bombay On board the *Shah Allum*
Harbour of Zanzibar Sept 18 1865

My dearest Father and Mother

Although it is not a month since I wrote and I have neither a letter to answer nor much news of any kind to communicate yet I know it rejoices your loving hearts to get any letter from us however short and uninteresting.

You see we are still on board the ship of our hospitable friend Abdullah bin Manala, and continue to find it the best safeguard against fever, for I am thankful to say that for nearly two months, and that in the most feverish season, I have been quite free of my old enemy and the ayah also, and although Harry is not quite so fortunate, having to pass his days ashore, yet he keeps pretty well and what fever troubled him at times is much milder and yields readily to quinine.

Dear little baby has been suffering again with her teeth for the last fortnight and has lost a good deal of flesh in that short time, but she is better again this last day or two although still restless and fretful for a child. She is a most patient invalid and tries to smile and be a little cheerful even when in most pain. She makes me love her so that I feel half brokenhearted at not being able to help her out of her trouble in some way. I think her teeth are coming with unusual difficulty. She has got none since the first two - her gums swell and go down again in the most trying way. It seems almost hopeless to think of all that are to come, but we must be patient.

I think we all love her more since she had such a narrow escape from drowning the other evening. It makes me shudder to think of it. We were going ashore late the other evening (to sleep out of the ship on account of a great many guns being expected to be fired very early next morning, saluting the Sultan on his going to Bombay) and we could not get a boat till nearly ten o'clock when it was pitch dark. We took the little sleeping darling out of her cot and wrapped her up head and all in my white Indian chudder.

Harry carried her down the accommodation ladder, as there was a great heavy swell on the sea and I was nervous, and gave her into the hands of our Portuguese servant Bastian. He stood up on the thwarts of the boat to receive her and had just turned round and was carefully stepping down by the light of a lantern, when the boat gave a fearful lurch and he and baby toppled backwards into the black narrow space of sea between the boat and the ship's side, leaving nothing but a brilliant bubbling mass of phosphorescent water to show where they had disappeared.

Harry's first impulse was to plunge in after them but fortunately he had presence of mind to wait a few moments and see whether they would appear in the same place, which all depended on the boy's presence of mind in remaining quite still and not struggling or letting go of baby, as I fully expected he would. However, in less than half a minute the black and white head appeared, <u>both</u> thank God, and Bastian instantly with the greatest presence of mind, lifted her high up out of the water so that Harry caught the little dripping thing by her clothes and she was soon in his arms, screaming with fright, but not a bit worse. That good fellow had held her so fast in his arms that her little mouth had been pressed against him and she hadn't apparently swallowed a drop of water. The little under flannel was hardly wet in front.

Oh, Mother, nobody else I think can understand what I felt when I heard her cry and found she was not choked or half dead as I fully expected. Even after she was got out, sooner than we had dared to hope, there was still the danger of her being ill from the cold, shock and fright, particularly as she had been feverish and ill with her teeth. In less time that it takes to tell it, she was stripped of her wet clothes and wrapped in a big warm blanket which I called out for first thing when I saw her come up from the water, and in a couple of minutes she was sitting in her hot bath, poor little darling, with wide open frightened eyes and a white face, but quite herself with only a bit of seaweed hanging over her face to tell how far down she had been.

When I think how many chances there were against her being saved, first the darkness, secondly, the narrow space which made it almost a miracle that one of the two didn't strike against anything in falling, thirdly, the heavy sea which threatened to swing the boat up against the ship side or to wash them up under the boat, and fourthly, the many chances against the servant's keeping fast hold of the baby and not struggling in the water. I hope we shall never feel thankful enough to God who took such wonderful care of our little one. The blank horror I felt during that half minute that we were childless I shall never forget, and Harry too had the same dreadful feeling for a minute that the little one had gone suddenly and irrevocably away for ever, and so she would have done hadn't that Bastian been not only a good fellow but a good swimmer, which made him hold on to the baby with one hand and paddle with the other, which brought them up to the surface much sooner than would have been the case otherwise. He, poor fellow, ran about getting the hot water in his wet clothes, crying bitterly all the time until Harry sent him away to change them, which he did in half a minute, and then came back to watch, evidently thinking it all his fault, until I told him how pleased we were with the way he had behaved.

Afterwards Harry gave him a ten dollar piece to comfort him and reward him for his plucky way of acting and his evident forgetfulness of himself when he came to the surface and thought of nothing but restoring baby safe and sound. He had some difficulty afterwards in getting into the boat but the boatmen helped him and Harry, dear old fellow, stayed with baby in his arms to give him a haul, before he ran up the steps to me with her.

What makes us more thankful about this is another accident of something the same kind by which one of our German carpenters lost his life. Yesterday a boat full of Fraser's employees, and another boat belonging to the Captain of the *Aden*, went out picnicing to an island called Chumbi at the south entrance to the harbour. On returning one young man named Edward who helps Harry at Malindi, fell overboard and others jumped in to help him. This poor fellow Boorman who was sleeping at the bottom of the boat, awoke suddenly, and being a good swimmer and seeing the melée in the water, jumped in, in spite of the warning of one of his fellow workmen who knew him to be delicate (in fact he had a heart complaint). He swam bravely for a little and then suddenly his head sunk under water and he floated helplessly until they hauled him into the boat, when he became sensible [conscious] again and told them to take him to Dr Seward, and then died in the boat. Wasn't it dreadful, all the others got back safely, for a wonder, for it is believed they were all nearly the worse for liquor. Last night Harry sent to French island to get his grave dug and this morning at sunrise followed the melancholy burden to the grave, the third of our men who has been buried there since we came. We fear and yet expect to hear by next mail that Mr Peebles, the late book keeper in the office is also amongst those who were and are not, so you see we have plenty of warning about the uncertainty of life, perhaps especially here, although climate had nothing to do with this last poor fellow's sudden death - all so different to the lingering carefulness and tenderness of an English funeral.

Harry told you I think that my box is lost in Cape Town bay. It is very grievous to lose it after waiting 9 months for my things, while other people write home and get the same in 9 weeks, and you never send us a new book. I haven't had anything new to read for months, and both Harry and I find it one of the greatest of minor trials. I do so wish too you had done as I asked about sending gloves regularly. I thought it would trouble you so little, but you only did it once. I could cry sometimes when I think how little you who have everything seem to care about us, who have nothing except the bare necessities of life, and yet who are willing to pay everything if anybody cared to get and send things to us, with an exact amount of what we owe.

I am making baby some plain morning dresses now, of jaconet muslin, the best I can get here, but of such vile quality that I grudge every stitch I put into it. I am sending to Bombay for a few little things but of course we pay more than twice the English price for everything there. Still, anything is better than sending home and waiting for the best part of a year.

The Sultan of Zanzibar went off to Bombay last week with the elite of the Arab nobility and a "very great train" of riffraff in the shape of a mongrel Persian and English rigged bodyguard, band of fifes and tom-toms, etc, but we must hope the best of the effect of even the semi-civilization of India upon their weak minds. That is the only thing that has happened I think since I wrote last.

And now dearest ones at home, goodbye, and don't mind my being so cross about not getting things, we are so very badly off and have been for many months. Dear love to Pollie, Gulie and Artie, our _only_ brother now, and more than all to yourselves whom I long to see with a very great longing. I should like to be at home at Pollie's wedding! When is it to be? Next year? Dearest love from your big son Harry and your loving daughter, Elsie.

[Written across the first page]
Totty is fast asleep or she would send kisses. She is so funny with her little Hindostani words. When she is hungry she calls out so pitifully and continually "Bhooa, bhooaa" which is her way of expressing "bhooka, the Hindostani word for "hungry". She can also say "Papa, jata" - Papa is going, but she is much quieter lately. She will soon be 11 months old and since she is ill and looks thinner and paler she is more like a little angel than ever with her dark blue eyes and long black lashes and pale golden hair which curls just a little like tiny wreaths of yellow smoke about her head, it is so thin and light. That reminds me to tell you that I have lost nearly all my hair and it is still falling off fearfully. I have been obliged to cut it within about 4 inches of my head but there is a heavy crop of new hair coming and the Doctor says it is only fever and that it is pretty sure to be all right in time when all the old has fallen off and the new hair grown. Meanwhile, I am just like Hannah Sturdy! Don't tell her I said so.

Note:
Pollie's wedding: Pollie (Mary Ann) Smith and John William Hall were married on 1st August 1867.

This is the last letter of the series from India and Zanzibar. After all the disasters and privations, the near drowning of Nora must have been the final straw to convince them to return home to England.

Closing the Box

After the accident on board the Sultan's ship *Shah Allum* in Zanzibar harbour, the family must have decided that life in the tropics was too hard for them to endure any longer. Then the trail went cold. In letters from relatives and Friends on the occasion of the Golden Wedding Anniversary of Isabel and Bartholomew Smith on 25th April 1889, I discovered that Elizabeth and Henry Jacob had emigrated to America and now had four more children, Isabel, Henry, Arthur and Dorothea.

But where had they been during the intervening period? Research at the Friends Historical Library in Dublin and a birth certificate, revealed that they returned to England at the end of 1865 and that a daughter named Isabel Lucy after her two grandmothers, was born at Thirsk on 21st July 1866 over her grandfather's shop in the Market Place. Photos of the three elder children, Nora, Isabel and Henry when they were about 6, 4 and 2, were taken in Thirsk by Joseph Robinson Clarke, a well-known photographer in the town from 1870 onwards. A letter dated 4th June 1872 from Isabel Smith to her son Arthur, reads, "Carlo [the dog] came back with Lizzie, but he doesn't settle happily with us at all..." The letter hints that Isabel hadn't been very well and Elizabeth had come to keep her mother company, but it's not absolutely clear and there are no references to Henry or the children which could clarify that it is Elizabeth Jacob. It seems that the two boys were born in England, Henry in 1868, and Arthur in 1869, while we know from her letter that Dorothea was born in Richmond, Virginia in January 1877. Other research suggests that the boys were born in the "State of New York" in the late 1860s. It's difficult to know what to believe, but all records are only as accurate as the person giving the information. Further research of original sources will

Elizabeth Harris Jacob 1840-1916.
Photo: JR Clarke, Thirsk c1870.

Honora Elizabeth Jacob 1864-1932.
Photo: JR Clarke, Thirsk c1870.

Isabel Lucy Jacob 1866-1933.
Photo: JR Clarke, Thirsk c1870.

Henry Jacob 1868-1928. Son of
Elizabeth and Henry Jacob.
Photo: JR Clarke, Thirsk c1870.

be necessary. The family probably emigrated to America in the early 1870s - but this is only my guess!

Chataigne's Directory of Richmond, Virginia, in 1885, records Henry JACOB as a draughtsman with the Chesapeake and Ohio Railway, a householder of 717 West Main Street. On the next line is Henry JACOB Jr. a clerk, also with the Chesapeake and Ohio Railway, at the same address. Next door at 719 West Main Street lives John F JACOB. Another member of the family? There are two other JACOB entries for 723 West Main Street which lead one to wonder if the family emigrated to be near their kinsfolk.

The same street directory for 1888 records Henry Jacob father and son again, but now includes Miss Honora E JACOB, a teacher, address still 717 West Main Street. This is the baby Nora who was born in Karachi on 21st October 1864.

Golden Wedding:
Bartholomew Smith
1814-1897
and his wife Isabel (née
Oddie) 1814-1893.
25 April 1889.

On their retirement Isabel and Bartholomew Smith moved from Thirsk to Weston-Super-Mare (Somerset) for the gentler climate. Their Golden Wedding was an occasion of great celebration among family and Friends, with cards and letters from well-wishers arriving from all over the country and abroad (see Appendix 2). From Richmond, Virginia, on 12th April 1889 Elizabeth wrote sadly to say that she wouldn't be able to join them, but Nora was coming to visit them in the June.

My dearest Father and Mother

I hope these letters of ours will reach you on or about your Golden Wedding day, as we want you to receive our congratulations through the mail - as we are so unfortunate as not to be able to offer them in person. For years I have been planning to spend your fiftieth anniversary with you but "Man proposes and God disposes" and it would only have been half a pleasure after all to have gone to England by myself and of course all the family could not have gone.

We are so thankful that you have lived so long and so happily and that you are both so healthy and likely to live a great while longer to be a comfort to your children and children's children, for it is a comfort to know that you are there. Even if we cannot see you, we can hear about you occasionally. Nora has taken her passage today in the Cunard steamer *Bothnia* to sail on the 19th of June, so that if nothing happens untowardly she will be in England on the 25th or 26th of June. Her school closes on the 14th and she will leave Richmond on the 17th probably. She is looking forward with great pleasure to seeing you all and I cannot help envying her the trip. I hope I may still be able to come at some future time.

We have had quite a bother from an attack of German measles that we think Bel caught at a Mission school. It went right through the family and most of us were quite ill with it. Dolly was the only one that did not suffer from it - but Harry and Arthur both escaped very easily. Dolly was confirmed at Grace Church last Sunday week. There was rather a large class and the church was crowded. While Nora had measles Bel taught her class for her - she found it rather hard work as there are fifty children in her grade and they do not belong to a very civilized class of the community, but are rather a rough crowd.

We are going to have a family photograph taken for our present to you and will send it by Nora. I wish we could send you a Golden present - the best we can do is to put a gold frame on the photograph! Nora is writing to Arthur [Arthur Smith, Nora's uncle and Elizabeth's younger brother, not to be confused with Arthur Smith Jacob, her son] and the rest of the children will send you the news so I will close my small share of the family congratulations wishing you every happiness and a most pleasant anniversary.

I am your loving daughter
Elsie.

From Henry Jacob to his in-laws, 14th April 1889
My dear Father and Mother

I must add a few lines to Elisa's letter with congratulations upon your golden wedding - and regrets that we cannot join your other children and grandchildren in celebrating it. For years we have both hoped against hope that in some way we might be able to be present, and at one time it seemed as if Elisa at least would be able to go, but we have had finally to give it up to our great disappointment. All we can do is send our dearest love and best wishes. You must think of us as longing to be with you but prevented by a hard fate.

Just now it looks as if we might have to move still further away. The Head offices of the Company have been moved to Cincinnati [Ohio] and although some of the officials will remain here it seems as if it would be to my interest to go too. The matter is not decided yet and we are very averse to moving, especially as both Harry and Nora have employments here, but I have to decide between a permanent position in Cincinnati and one here which <u>may</u> be permanent and <u>may</u> only last a limited time. In any case we should not think of moving the household until I have been to Cincinnati myself and seen how the land lies. E. would stay at least until Nora has gone and then we would decide as to the future. We shall know more about it in the course of a few weeks.

With dear love to all, I am your affte. son
H. Jacob.

From Dorothea Jacob, 12th April 1889
My dear Grandfather and Grandmother

I am very sorry that I cannot go with Nora to England and see you. Mother and Papa intend to have a family group taken and send it to you by Nora. I am writing this letter in hopes that it will reach you on your Golden wedding-day. I expect to go to the High School in February; I was twelve years old last January, and when I go there I will be thirteen. Bell caught Rosiola [Roseola] at a mission school and everyone has had it, papa and mother included. I believe it is what is called in England, German Measles, but we are all quite well now.

We have had an electric line of street-cars in Richmond for about a year, and now we are going to have them throughout the city. A convict escaped from the carts which they were pulling; he was called upon to halt, and not obeying, he was shot, but not seriously hurt. This happened today but I forgot to say so.

It is exceedingly hot today and has been for two or three days back. We were hoping for rain this evening, but it did not rain enough to settle the dust; it may rain tonight though. Bell and Harry are preparing a very nice tennis-court in the field next door.

With dear love and best wishes for you both, I remain your little unseen grandchild,
Dorothea Jacob.

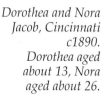

Dorothea and Nora Jacob, Cincinnati c1890. Dorothea aged about 13, Nora aged about 26.

211

On the next fold of paper a note from Nora Jacob:
My dear Grandparents,

Dolly has left me only half a sheet for my congratulations on your anniversary, but as I shall be fortunate enough to offer them in person, that does not make so much difference. All the others are envying me my good fortune, and we are all very disappointed that the Mother has had to give up her proposed journey. Uncle Arthur has drawn such an enticing picture of an English spring as to make me long to see it, but not being a free agent I cannot get to Weston before the end of June. We have had endless pleasure from Uncle Arthur's present of photographs. It must be charming to bring all the pretty part of your holiday back with you and keep it to look at in the future.

I see the Mother has promised that we are to give you all the news. I do not know what there is to give; that we all join in the most loving wishes for you on your golden wedding day can be no news.

Ever your most affectionate granddaughter
Nora Jacob.

From Isabel Jacob, 13th April 1889
My dearest Grandpapa & Grandmamma

I must write you a short letter in Mother's to wish you lots of good-luck & happiness on this joyful anniversary - your golden-wedding day. It would be so nice, & we should be so happy to be with you at this time of all others, but as it is an impossibility we will have to content ourselves with saying by letter what we could say <u>so much</u> better by word of mouth. And I am sure that of all the grandchildren, none will think of you more lovingly on that day than those you have never known away out here in America!

Mother was so much disappointed not to be able to come over this spring - & we all wished it above everything - but we are sending Nora later on, as a kind of substitute - this I know she cannot make up to you for not seeing Mother. We are going to have a "family group" taken & send to you by Nora so that you can get some sort of an idea of what kind of a looking family we are, taken as a whole! We enjoyed getting the photos Uncle Arthur sent us so much. They made us feel as if we knew you & your surroundings a great deal better than we ever did before. Nora is very anxious to have a camera & take some photographs, but as yet she hasn't succeeded in purchasing one - & indeed there is nothing about here worth photographing. The country here is quite flat and uninteresting.

I wish so much I was coming to England with Nora - I know I would enjoy it immensely - for I am a thorough American & have a great admiration & respect for everything "English". And I am sure the voyage would not make me sick at all - for tho' I haven't done much travelling by sea, since I can remember, what <u>little</u> I have done has agreed with me splendidly. We were so unlucky as to have half the hyacinths stolen out of our garden last night. Flower-thieves in Richmond have become a regular <u>institution</u>, & it is almost impossible ever to have any flowers in your front garden.

Give my best love to Uncle Arthur & Alie [Alicia Milner, her cousin, the daughter of Gulielma]. Uncle Arthur & I used to keep up a desultory kind of correspondence - but now he <u>never</u> writes to me!

With very much love for you both, I am your loving Granddaughter
Isabel L Jacob.

A typical example of the many other letters written to Isabel and Bartholomew.

Glenmore Cottage, Lisburn (Ireland)
April 24 /89

My dear Uncle and Aunt

We wish to let you know that were not unmindful of you at this time; & I could not think of allowing so important an event as the fiftieth anniversary of your wedding day - your golden wedding - to pass by without a line of congratulations & good wishes. Eliza will be sorry not to be with you at this important time - the only one of your children left out at this festival gathering. We hear that her eldest daughter is shortly coming on a visit to you, & we do hope it can be arranged for her to come & see us, as well as her other Irish relatives.

Rachel sent us just lately photographs of you standing in your garden & which we suppose to have been taken by Arthur.We like best the one with the larger figures - you look real nice; & as Rachel did not say we were to return the photos I have no notion of doing so. We hope you have had a good winter & that both of you have been free from colds. Our winter was a very mild one for which the skaters and sliders were not thankful.

We are having a stormy April so far - nevertheless, we spent Easter Monday in our favourite Collin Glen & brought home a most ridiculous quantity of primroses. Two of our boys spent Easter in Birkenhead with our friends the Heatons. We have good accounts from Harry who went into Richardson's New York house at the end of last year.

With our love to all the circle gathered to do you honour on this great day & and all good wishes for yourselves, I am your loving niece
Margaret Davies

My dearest Father (from Elizabeth, no date but probably early May 1889)

We received some days ago the beautiful souvenirs of your Golden Wedding and should have written at once to thank you for them

214

but have been in the very unusual condition of having no servant, which precludes, on my part and Bel's, anything but drudgery, as Nora and Dolly are away at school all day and we have all to do. A tolerably good cook came in today so we are more at liberty.

Your cards were so tasteful and well got up that everybody admired them and thought the poetry beautiful. We were thinking of you all on the 25th and hoping that you had a better day than we had here - it was a pouring wet day and I was very much afflicted with neuralgic headache and we had no servant, so it was not a [1]white stone day for us by any means, but I hope that everything was as pleasant as good weather and good company could make it at your home at Weston.

We are all hoping to go tomorrow and have our [2]family group taken for your edification. We have been planning it for so long but something has always prevented it, but as it is the [3]Washington Centennial and a general holiday, I hope we may be able to

Arthur Smith Jacob
c1890.

collect our scattered forces and carry the photographic studio by assault. You will be surprised at the appearance of Arthur's head which looks as if he had just escaped from the Penitentiary. It is the custom here for boys to have all their hair cut off at the beginning of the warm season, and he went and had his cut without our knowing it or we should have stopped him until after the eventful picture was taken, as of course he looks much stranger to your eyes than to ours. I cannot say that I admire the style at all.

Everything is in the first fresh greeness of spring. The park which is opposite our house is lovely with the young elm and linden trees and various flowering trees such as the tulip tree, Judas tree, Japanese cherry, and Paulownia. The Magnolias which are the pride of the Richmond streets will not be in bloom for about a month yet - all the streets are shaded by beautiful trees, some very fine old ones, but mostly young elms and maples and ailanthus.

Nora is looking forward with much pleasure to seeing you all. I hope she will find travelling alone as little disagreeable as she expects. I hope the Siddonses will see her on board ship if her father or Harry cannot do so. All send dear love and many thanks for the wedding cards.

With dear love to Mother, Arthur and yourself,
I am dear Father your loving daughter
Elsie.

Notes:
1. White stone day: to be remembered with pleasure. The Romans used a white stone or piece of chalk to mark their lucky days on the calendar.
2. Our family group: has this photo survived?
3. The Washington Centennial: to commemorate the inauguration of President George Washington on 30th April 1789.

****

A wonderful autograph book among the family archives was given to Isabel Milner "with the love & best wishes of her affectionate Uncle, Arthur Smith Christmas 1884." It contains popular poems and improving verses and many beautiful illustrations.

Arab gentleman of Zanzibar.

This Isabel (born 1871) was the daughter of Gulielma, Elizabeth's sister. It seems that Nora Jacob took the book back to America from her visit to her grandparents as the Jacob family have all made a contribution, Henry jnr. on 3rd October 1889; Elizabeth on the next page; "Lovingly by your cousin, Isabel L Jacob, Richmond Virginia Aug. 8 1890"; from Dorothea on 9th August 1890; from Arthur Smith Jacob on 13th August, and a pen and ink drawing of an "Arab gentleman of Zanzibar, Sketched by Uncle Harry - with love and best wishes for the little niece he has never seen - Cincinnati Aug. 1890". She would have been a young woman of 19 by then! Later entries show that the authograph album returned to England, whether by hand or by post is not known. Elizabeth's mother died at Weston-Super-Mare on 30th May 1893, and her father on 28th January 1897, in his 83rd year.

Henry Jacob died 30 March 1905 at Spencer Avenue, Norwood, Ohio, U.S.A. Of the children, Nora died in 1932, Isabel in 1933, Henry in 1928, Arthur in 1924 and Dorothea in 1931. Records show that Isabel married Benjamin Taylor by whom she had two daughters named Dorothy Cockayne and Isabel Irwin; and Dorothea married Charles Courtney Wharton, and had three children, Dorothea Cecilia, Iris Virginia and Henry.

In the 35th Ackworth Old Scholars Association Report (1916-17) is the following obituary notice:-

Isabel Irwin Taylor aged 2½ and Dorothy Cockayne Taylor aged 4.
Daughters of Isabel Lucy (Jacob) and Benjamin Taylor c1900?

Eliza Harris Jacob, *née* Smith: (scholar 1851-3), was the eldest daughter of the late Bartholomew and Isabel Smith, of Thirsk, and widow of Henry Jacob, of Cincinnati, Ohio, U.S.A., where she died April 21st, 1916, aged 76 years.

****

The shop of Bartholomew Smith & Son, Market Place, Thirsk, passed to the Hall family through the marriage of Mary Ann Smith and John William Hall. Many of their descendants live in Yorkshire, some still in Thirsk. The draper's shop closed in 1971, when it was claimed in the *Guinness Book of Records* to have been the oldest drapery business in Great Britain. Gulielma Smith, my great-grandmother, married Robert Alsop Milner in 1868 and their living relatives number about 40, scattered all over England and in America. Are there any descendants from Elizabeth and Henry Jacob out there? It would be lovely to know!

Without the box of letters I would never have journeyed on this voyage of discovery, learned so much about the Jacob, Smith, Hall and Milner families, and been in touch with so many relatives, some for the first time. Charts of the immediate ancestors and descendants as far as I know them, can be found at the end of this book. A family history is never finished. Only yesterday I heard of two babies recently born to be added to the story, and tomorrow I am taking my manuscript to the publisher. Yes, really! But I have got to stop somewhere even while the story continues .....

****

STOP PRESS!

August 2000: Carlisle Knowlton, of Connecticut, USA, phoned me to say that he is a direct descendant of Elizabeth Jacob. His mother is Isabel Irwin Taylor, Elizabeth's granddaughter, the little girl illustrated on page 218 opposite. He is thrilled, and so am I!

Henry and Elizabeth Jacob, 1890.

The Jacob family in 1882, left to right: Elizabeth aged 41; Henry Snr. aged 45; Honora aged 17½; Isabel aged 16; Henry Jnr. aged 14; and Arthur aged 13. Except for Henry Snr. whose photograph was taken in Baltimore, Maryland, USA, all the others were taken at Farmville, Virginia, in "C.H. Erambert's Photographic Studio".

Dorothea Jacob aged 5, 1882.

Honora Jacob 1886, to her Grandmamma, taken in Richmond, Virginia, by G.S. Cook; Isabel Jacob (no date) to her Uncle Arthur, photograph by Campbell & Co. of Richmond; and Henry Jnr. to his Grandmother, August 1885, photograph also by Campbell & Co.

Appendix 1

Letters from Friends and Relatives on the death of Tom Smith April 1865

Emily C Brown (née Spence)	No. 9 Dockwray Square (North Shields). Emily Brown was the daughter of Deborah Smith, Bartholmew's sister.
Elizabeth H Crosfield	Oaklands, Aigburth, Liverpool.
Elizabeth Davies (née Oddie)	9 James Street, Birkenhead. Isabel Smith's sister.
John Davies, husband of above	
Henry Hipsley	Holgate, York.
Henry Howard	Salem Cottage, Thirsk.
Isaac Jacob	Stockton on Tees (Henry Jacob's brother).
Henry Jacob	Zanzibar.
Cousin Elizabeth Oddie (addressed to Gulie)	The Mount, York (Quaker girls school).
J. Oddie (Isabel's nephew)	Albert Place, Chelmsford, Essex.
Thomas Ollis	Osbaldwick, York.
Hannah Peirson (née Smith)	Bartholomew's sister, who married Thomas Peirson, and moved to America in 1849.
Jane Proctor	Polam Hall, Darlington (Quaker girls school)
G. Richardson	Royal Lancaster School.
George Satterthwaite	Ackworth School (Quaker), near Pontefract. Teacher at the school, who arranged for Arthur to be sent home to Thirsk with Mr Pumphrey of Newcastle.
H. B. Sewell	Norton (writing to "My dear Cousin").

John Spence	Wakefield, husband of Deborah Smith, father of Emily Brown, father-in-law of Gulielma Spence.
Gulielma Spence (née Riccalton)	Kendal (daughter-in-law of John Spence, above).
William Taylor	Anthony Harris & Co. Coal, Coke & Iron Exporters, Middlesbro' on Tees.
B. Thompson	York.
Fielden Thorp, B.A.	20 Bootham, York. Fielden Thorp was headmaster at Bootham (Quaker boys school) where Tom had been a pupil.
Henry Wilson	Sunderland.
Jas. Whitworth	Whitworth & Company, Wholesale Tea and Coffee Merchants, 28 Mincing Lane, London.

Appendix 2

Friends and Relatives writing on the occasion of Isabel and Bartholomew Smith's Golden Wedding, 25 April 1889

The Smiths had retired to St. Cuthbert's, Southside, Weston-Super-Mare, Somerset. Their son Arthur took photos of the couple and sent them to relatives and Friends all over the country, much to everyone's delight. On the celebratory day the family and guests all went to Cheddar Gorge. This is a list of most of the letter writers whose names and addresses could be deciphered.

S J & M E Alexander	Posilip, Weston-Super-Mare.
George Baker	Guttenberg House, Clevedon, Somerset.
Mrs Bell	The Hall, Thirsk.
Charles Brown	Clevedon, Somerset.
E Brown (niece)	Arundel Villas, Wivelscombe, Som.
John H & M Buchanan	Sowerby, Thirsk.
James Clark	Street, Somerset.
Henry E Clarke	1 Kings Road, Doncaster.
M J Dale	Sowerby, Thirsk.
Margaret Davies (Isabel's niece)	Glenmore Cottage, Lisburn (Ireland).
Allan B. Hall (grandson)	1 The Terrace, Carlton Hill, Leeds.
Mabel Hall (granddaughter)	Ackworth School (nr. Pontefract, Yorks).
Marie Hall (granddaughter)	Ackworth School.
Jed (John Edward) Hall (grandson)	Ackworth School.
John William Hall (son-in-law)	Thirsk (father of the children, above).
C J Jackson	5 Fairmount, Manningham, Bradford.
Elizabeth & Henry Jacob and family	Richmond and Cincinnati, America.

Joseph L Johnson — Torville, 30 Westbourne Park, Falsgrave, Scarborough.

Octavia Kingsley (to Arthur Smith) — South Kilvington.

Sarah M Knight — 3 South Parade.

Isabel Milner (granddaughter) — Park Terrace, Thwaites Brow, Keighley.

Felix Milner (grandson) — Friends' School, Great Ayton.

Wilfrid Milner (grandson) — Friends' School, Great Ayton.

J. Oddie (nephew) — 10 Crookham Road, Fulham, London SW

Lucy Oddie (sister-in-law) — The Grove, Bowerham Lane, Lancaster.

Rachel Oddie (niece) — Ackworth School, nr. Pontefract, where she was a teacher.

Mary Ann Peirson (niece) — Mowbray Cottage.

E Peirson (niece) — Mowbray Cottage.

Mabel Priestman (niece) — Pierremont, Bradford.

John Rhodes — Thirsk.

Edith Brearey(?) Robinson (also on behalf of her sisters Minnie and Nellie) — West Bank, Scarborough.

"Sam" (nephew aged 55) — 73 Victoria Road, Headingley, Leeds.

Robert Skilbeck — Thirsk.

John Taylor (cousin) — "Sunbury", 208 Denmark Hill.

William Taylor — Redcar.

Fielden Thorp — 18 Blossom Street, York. In 1897 he was treasurer of the British Temperance League.

Sarah S Tyzack — Sowerby House, Thirsk.

Robert Walton — South Terrace, Sowerby, Thirsk.

Sara M Watson (niece) — Willesboro', Hales Road.

Ellen M Wedmore — Stoneleigh.

Elizabeth A Wilson (niece) (and sister Sophie). — The Green

Clara J Worsdell — 28 King Street, Lancaster.

A Ellis Wood — 7 Mowbray Place, Thirsk.

Family Chart of
Henry & Lucy Jacob of Ballitore

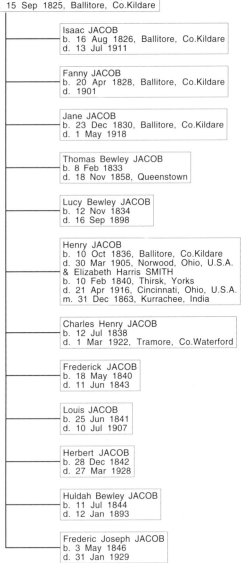

Henry JACOB
b. 21 Jul 1797, Clonmel, Ireland
d. 31 Aug 1871, Ballitore, Co.Kildare
& Lucy BEWLEY
b. 13 Aug 1802, Ballitore, Co.Kildare
d. 28 Oct 1883, Mountmellick, Ireland
m. 15 Sep 1825, Ballitore, Co.Kildare

Isaac JACOB
b. 16 Aug 1826, Ballitore, Co.Kildare
d. 13 Jul 1911

Fanny JACOB
b. 20 Apr 1828, Ballitore, Co.Kildare
d. 1901

Jane JACOB
b. 23 Dec 1830, Ballitore, Co.Kildare
d. 1 May 1918

Thomas Bewley JACOB
b. 8 Feb 1833
d. 18 Nov 1858, Queenstown

Lucy Bewley JACOB
b. 12 Nov 1834
d. 16 Sep 1898

Henry JACOB
b. 10 Oct 1836, Ballitore, Co.Kildare
d. 30 Mar 1905, Norwood, Ohio, U.S.A.
& Elizabeth Harris SMITH
b. 10 Feb 1840, Thirsk, Yorks
d. 21 Apr 1916, Cincinnati, Ohio, U.S.A.
m. 31 Dec 1863, Kurrachee, India

Charles Henry JACOB
b. 12 Jul 1838
d. 1 Mar 1922, Tramore, Co.Waterford

Frederick JACOB
b. 18 May 1840
d. 11 Jun 1843

Louis JACOB
b. 25 Jun 1841
d. 10 Jul 1907

Herbert JACOB
b. 28 Dec 1842
d. 27 Mar 1928

Huldah Bewley JACOB
b. 11 Jul 1844
d. 12 Jan 1893

Frederic Joseph JACOB
b. 3 May 1846
d. 31 Jan 1929

See Family Chart
Henry Jacob and Elizabeth Smith

Family Chart of
Bartholomew Smith and Isabel Oddie

Bartholomew SMITH
b. 13 Mar 1814, Thirsk, Yorks
d. 28 Jan 1897, Weston-Super-Mare
& Isabel ODDIE
b. 29 Jan 1814, Southport ?
d. 30 May 1893, Weston-Super-Mare
m. 25 Apr 1839, Warrington, Lancs.

Elizabeth Harris SMITH
b. 10 Feb 1840, Thirsk, Yorks
d. 21 Apr 1916, Cincinnati, Ohio, U.S.A.
& Henry JACOB
b. 10 Oct 1836, Ballitore, Co. Kildare, Ireland
d. 30 Mar 1905, Norwood, Ohio, U.S.A.
m. 31 Dec 1863, Kurrachee, India

See Family Chart
Henry Jacob and
Elizabeth Harris Smith

Mary Ann (Pollie) SMITH
b. 24 Nov 1841, Thirsk, Yorks
d. 1911, Thirsk, Yorks
& John William HALL
b. 28 Jan 1842, Studdon, Allendale, NML
d. 2 Mar 1929, Thirsk, Yorks

See Family Chart
John William Hall and
Mary Ann Smith

Gulielma SMITH
b. 4 Aug 1846, Thirsk, Yorks
d. 6 Nov 1909, Bristol
& Robert Alsop MILNER
b. 5 Feb 1840, Hanley, Staffs
d. 15 Mar 1931, Bristol
m. 15 Apr 1868, Thirsk, Yorks

See Family Chart
Robert Alsop Milner
and Gulielma Smith

Thomas SMITH
b. 25 May 1849, Thirsk, Yorks
d. 6 Apr 1865, Thirsk, Yorks

Arthur Harris SMITH
b. 13 Sep 1854, Thirsk, Yorks
d. 8 Apr 1928, Thirsk, Yorks

Family Chart of
Henry Jacob and Elizabeth Smith

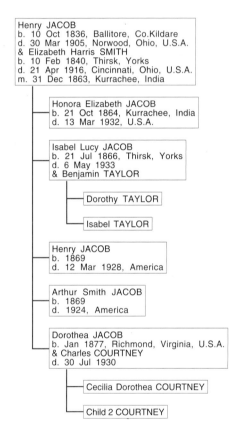

Henry JACOB
b. 10 Oct 1836, Ballitore, Co.Kildare
d. 30 Mar 1905, Norwood, Ohio, U.S.A.
& Elizabeth Harris SMITH
b. 10 Feb 1840, Thirsk, Yorks
d. 21 Apr 1916, Cincinnati, Ohio, U.S.A.
m. 31 Dec 1863, Kurrachee, India

Honora Elizabeth JACOB
b. 21 Oct 1864, Kurrachee, India
d. 13 Mar 1932, U.S.A.

Isabel Lucy JACOB
b. 21 Jul 1866, Thirsk, Yorks
d. 6 May 1933
& Benjamin TAYLOR

Dorothy TAYLOR

Isabel TAYLOR

Henry JACOB
b. 1869
d. 12 Mar 1928, America

Arthur Smith JACOB
b. 1869
d. 1924, America

Dorothea JACOB
b. Jan 1877, Richmond, Virginia, U.S.A.
& Charles COURTNEY
d. 30 Jul 1930

Cecilia Dorothea COURTNEY

Child 2 COURTNEY

John William HALL
b. 28 Jan 1842, Studdon, Allendale, NML
d. 2 Mar 1929, Thirsk, Yorks
& Mary Ann (Pollie) SMITH
b. 24 Nov 1841, Thirsk, Yorks
d. 1911, Thirsk, Yorks
m. 1 Aug 1867, Thirsk, Friends Meeting House

Winifred HALL
b. 24 Dec 1868, Thirsk, Yorks

Allan Bartholomew HALL
b. 9 Jul 1870, Thirsk, Yorks

Isabel Mary HALL
b. 12 Nov 1871, Thirsk, Yorks
d. 10 Jan 1945

Mabel Susan HALL
b. 18 Sep 1873, Thirsk, Yorks

John Edward (Jed) HALL
b. 3 Sep 1875, Thirsk, Yorks
d. 1947
& Helen GRUBB
bp. Clonmel, Ireland
d. 1961
m. 1904

Margaret HALL
b. ca 1906

John Philipson HALL
b. ca 1908, Thirsk, Yorks
d. Apr 1995, Ripon, Yorks
& Joan Wigham EDMUNDSON
b. 8 Oct 1907

Roderic Smith HALL
b. 17 Dec 1909, Thirsk, Yorks
d. 3 Jul 1989
& Olive Miriam Constance HAYWOOD
b. 31 Oct 1911, Essex
m. Oct 1934

See Family Chart
Roderic Hall and
Olive Haywood

Mary Lecky (Molly) HALL
b. ca 1912
& John FOTHERINGHAM

Christabel HALL
b. ca 1914
d. 3 Apr 1999
& Sam LODER

Marion (Marie) HALL
b. 20 Feb 1878, Thirsk, Yorks
d. 1961
& John Edgar EDMUNDSON
b. 22 Apr 1879
d. 17 Sep 1920, Roxburgh
m. 29 Jul 1903, Thirsk, Yorks

Joan Wigham EDMUNDSON
b. 8 Oct 1907, Thirsk, Yorks
& John Philipson HALL
b. ca 1908
d. Apr 1995, Ripon, Yorks
m. 1931

Kathleen Mary EDMUNDSON
b. 28 Feb 1905

Norah Gertrude EDMUNDSON
b. 22 Jun 1906
& Gerald Grover BROWN
m. 1933

Arnold Watson EDMUNDSON
b. 6 Feb 1911
& Henrietta BEECHAM
m. 1935

Robert Alsop MILNER
b. 5 Feb 1840, Hanley, Staffs
d. 15 Mar 1931, Bristol
& Gulielma SMITH
b. 4 Aug 1846, Thirsk, Yorks
d. 6 Nov 1909, Bristol
m. 15 Apr 1868, Thirsk, Yorks

Family Chart of
Robert Alsop Milner
and Gulielma Smith

Alicia MILNER
b. 3 Jun 1869, Carlisle
d. 1935, Thirsk

Isabel MILNER
b. 8 Aug 1871, Keighley, Yorks
d. 15 Mar 1961, Hitchin, Herts

Wilfrid MILNER
b. 9 Mar 1875, Keighley, Yorks
d. 20 Jan 1929, Bristol

Felix Kirk MILNER
b. 9 Dec 1876, Keighley, Yorks
d. 29 Jan 1956, Didcot, Berks
& Gwyneth May GOODGER
b. 24 May 1875, Wolverton, Northants
d. 4 Apr 1950, London
m. 12 May 1900, Worcester Register Office

See Family Chart
Felix K Milner and
Gwyneth Goodger

Gulielma MILNER
b. 4 Feb 1879, Keighley, Yorks
d. 1959, Hitchin, Herts

Robert Ewart MILNER
b. 27 Nov 1880, Keighley, Yorks
d. 11 Dec 1954, Bristol

Philip Arthur MILNER
b. 8 Sep 1882, Keighley, Yorks
d. 9 May 1928, Leeds, Yorks
& Edith BLUNSOM
b. 30 Apr 1885, Kettering, Northants.
d. 5 Jan 1970, Evesham, Worcs.
m. 21 Jun 1910, Kettering, Northants

See Family Chart
Philip Milner and
Edith Blunsom

Kathlene Gladys MILNER
b. 22 Jul 1884, Keighley, Yorks
d. 15 Jul 1890, Keighley, Yorks

Bernard Clare MILNER
b. 22 Feb 1887, Keighley, Yorks
d. 28 May 1941, Bristol
& Marion Bessie (Marie) HICKING
b. 11 Feb 1895
d. 23 Feb 1964, Bristol
m. 16 Aug 1919

Denis Bernard Milner
b. 21 Oct 1926

Lorna Harris MILNER
b. 11 Oct 1890, Keighley, Yorks
d. 19 Nov 1966, Didcot, Berks

230

Family chart of
Roderic Hall and Olive Haywood

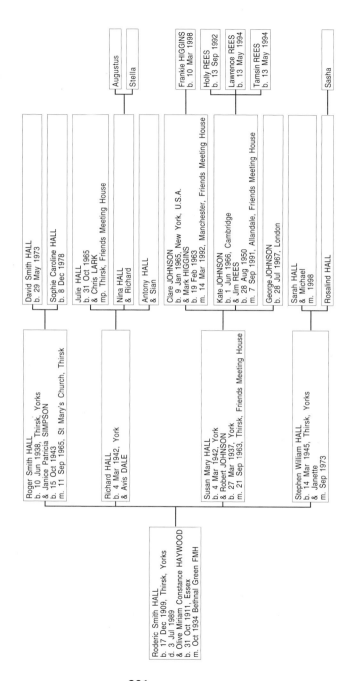

Roderic Smith HALL
b. 17 Dec 1909, Thirsk, Yorks
d. 3 Jul 1989
& Olive Miriam Constance HAYWOOD
b. 31 Oct 1911, Essex
m. Oct 1934 Bethnal Green FMH

Roger Smith HALL
b. 10 Jun 1938, Thirsk, Yorks
& Janice Patricia SIMPSON
b. 15 Oct 1943
m. 11 Sep 1965, St Mary's Church, Thirsk

David Smith HALL
b. 29 May 1973

Sophie Caroline HALL
b. 8 Dec 1978

Richard HALL
b. 4 Mar 1942, York
& Avis DALE

Julie HALL
b. 31 Oct 1965
& Chris LARK
mp. Thirsk, Friends Meeting House

Nina HALL
& Richard

Antony HALL
& Sian

Augustus

Stella

Susan Mary HALL
b. 4 Mar 1942, York
& Robert JOHNSON
b. 27 Mar 1937, York
m. 21 Sep 1963, Thirsk, Friends Meeting House

Clare JOHNSON
b. 9 Jan 1965, New York, U.S.A.
& Mark HIGGINS
b. 19 Feb 1963
m. 14 Mar 1992, Manchester, Friends Meeting House

Frankie HIGGINS
b. 10 Mar 1998

Kate JOHNSON
b. 1 Jun 1966, Cambridge
& Jim REES
b. 28 Aug 1950
m. 7 Sep 1991, Allandale, Friends Meeting House

Holly REES
b. 13 Sep 1992

Lawrence REES
b. 13 May 1994

Tamsin REES
b. 13 May 1994

George JOHNSON
b. 28 Jul 1967, London

Stephen William HALL
b. 14 Mar 1945, Thirsk, Yorks
& Janette
m. Sep 1973

Sarah HALL
& Michael
m. 1998

Rosalind HALL

Sasha

231

Family chart of
Felix K Milner and
Gwyneth Goodger

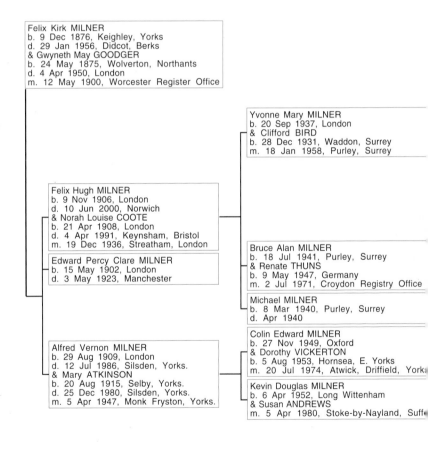

Felix Kirk MILNER
b. 9 Dec 1876, Keighley, Yorks
d. 29 Jan 1956, Didcot, Berks
& Gwyneth May GOODGER
b. 24 May 1875, Wolverton, Northants
d. 4 Apr 1950, London
m. 12 May 1900, Worcester Register Office

Yvonne Mary MILNER
b. 20 Sep 1937, London
& Clifford BIRD
b. 28 Dec 1931, Waddon, Surrey
m. 18 Jan 1958, Purley, Surrey

Felix Hugh MILNER
b. 9 Nov 1906, London
d. 10 Jun 2000, Norwich
& Norah Louise COOTE
b. 21 Apr 1908, London
d. 4 Apr 1991, Keynsham, Bristol
m. 19 Dec 1936, Streatham, London

Edward Percy Clare MILNER
b. 15 May 1902, London
d. 3 May 1923, Manchester

Bruce Alan MILNER
b. 18 Jul 1941, Purley, Surrey
& Renate THUNS
b. 9 May 1947, Germany
m. 2 Jul 1971, Croydon Registry Office

Michael MILNER
b. 8 Mar 1940, Purley, Surrey
d. Apr 1940

Colin Edward MILNER
b. 27 Nov 1949, Oxford
& Dorothy VICKERTON
b. 5 Aug 1953, Hornsea, E. Yorks
m. 20 Jul 1974, Atwick, Driffield, Yorks

Alfred Vernon MILNER
b. 29 Aug 1909, London
d. 12 Jul 1986, Silsden, Yorks.
& Mary ATKINSON
b. 20 Aug 1915, Selby, Yorks.
d. 25 Dec 1980, Silsden, Yorks.
m. 5 Apr 1947, Monk Fryston, Yorks.

Kevin Douglas MILNER
b. 6 Apr 1952, Long Wittenham
& Susan ANDREWS
m. 5 Apr 1980, Stoke-by-Nayland, Suffk

232

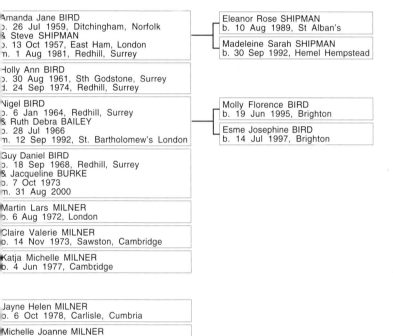

Amanda Jane BIRD
b. 26 Jul 1959, Ditchingham, Norfolk
& Steve SHIPMAN
b. 13 Oct 1957, East Ham, London
m. 1 Aug 1981, Redhill, Surrey

Eleanor Rose SHIPMAN
b. 10 Aug 1989, St Alban's

Madeleine Sarah SHIPMAN
b. 30 Sep 1992, Hemel Hempstead

Holly Ann BIRD
b. 30 Aug 1961, Sth Godstone, Surrey
d. 24 Sep 1974, Redhill, Surrey

Nigel BIRD
b. 6 Jan 1964, Redhill, Surrey
& Ruth Debra BAILEY
b. 28 Jul 1966
m. 12 Sep 1992, St. Bartholomew's London

Molly Florence BIRD
b. 19 Jun 1995, Brighton

Esme Josephine BIRD
b. 14 Jul 1997, Brighton

Guy Daniel BIRD
b. 18 Sep 1968, Redhill, Surrey
& Jacqueline BURKE
b. 7 Oct 1973
m. 31 Aug 2000

Martin Lars MILNER
b. 6 Aug 1972, London

Claire Valerie MILNER
b. 14 Nov 1973, Sawston, Cambridge

Katja Michelle MILNER
b. 4 Jun 1977, Cambridge

Jayne Helen MILNER
b. 6 Oct 1978, Carlisle, Cumbria

Michelle Joanne MILNER
b. 12 Feb 1983, Lancaster, Lancs.

Family chart of
Philip Milner and Edith Blunsom

```
                                        ┌──────────────────────────────────────────┐
                                        │ Charles Ewart MILNER                       │
                                        │ b. 27 Nov 1912, London                     │
                                        │ d. 14 Sep 1981, Horseheath, Cambridge      │
                                        └──────────────────────────────────────────┘
                                        ┌──────────────────────────────────────────┐
                                        │ Gladys Joan MILNER                         │
                                        │ b. 8 Feb 1915, Bristol                     │
                                        └──────────────────────────────────────────┘

                                        ┌──────────────────────────────────────────┐
                                        │ Cicely Edith MILNER                        │
┌──────────────────────────────────────┐│ b. 11 May 1918, Bristol                    │
│ Philip Arthur MILNER                  ││ & Lionel Lindsay WEST                      │
│ b. 8 Sep 1882, Keighley, Yorks        ││ b. 21 Aug 1919, Crawley, Sussex            │
│ d. 9 May 1928, Leeds, Yorks           ││ m. 14 Sep 1940, Sidcot, Somerset           │
│ & Edith BLUNSOM                       │└──────────────────────────────────────────┘
│ b. 30 Apr 1885, Kettering, Northants. │
│ d. 5 Jan 1970, Evesham, Worcs.        │
│ m. 21 Jun 1910, Kettering, Northants  │
└──────────────────────────────────────┘

                                        ┌──────────────────────────────────────────┐
                                        │ John Philip MILNER                         │
                                        │ b. 17 Dec 1922, Darlington                 │
                                        │ & Margret ROSEEN                           │
                                        │ b. 23 Apr 1929, Sweden                     │
                                        │ m. 27 Jan 1951, Kil, Sweden                │
                                        └──────────────────────────────────────────┘
```

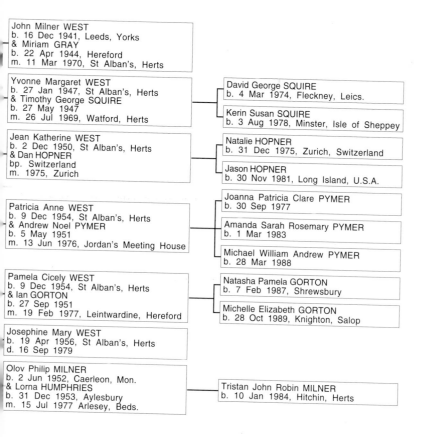

John Milner WEST
b. 16 Dec 1941, Leeds, Yorks
& Miriam GRAY
b. 22 Apr 1944, Hereford
m. 11 Mar 1970, St Alban's, Herts

Yvonne Margaret WEST
b. 27 Jan 1947, St Alban's, Herts
& Timothy George SQUIRE
b. 27 May 1947
m. 26 Jul 1969, Watford, Herts

David George SQUIRE
b. 4 Mar 1974, Fleckney, Leics.

Kerin Susan SQUIRE
b. 3 Aug 1978, Minster, Isle of Sheppey

Jean Katherine WEST
b. 2 Dec 1950, St Alban's, Herts
& Dan HOPNER
bp. Switzerland
m. 1975, Zurich

Natalie HOPNER
b. 31 Dec 1975, Zurich, Switzerland

Jason HOPNER
b. 30 Nov 1981, Long Island, U.S.A.

Patricia Anne WEST
b. 9 Dec 1954, St Alban's, Herts
& Andrew Noel PYMER
b. 5 May 1951
m. 13 Jun 1976, Jordan's Meeting House

Joanna Patricia Clare PYMER
b. 30 Sep 1977

Amanda Sarah Rosemary PYMER
b. 1 Mar 1983

Michael William Andrew PYMER
b. 28 Mar 1988

Pamela Cicely WEST
b. 9 Dec 1954, St Alban's, Herts
& Ian GORTON
b. 27 Sep 1951
m. 19 Feb 1977, Leintwardine, Hereford

Natasha Pamela GORTON
b. 7 Feb 1987, Shrewsbury

Michelle Elizabeth GORTON
b. 28 Oct 1989, Knighton, Salop

Josephine Mary WEST
b. 19 Apr 1956, St Alban's, Herts
d. 16 Sep 1979

Olov Philip MILNER
b. 2 Jun 1952, Caerleon, Mon.
& Lorna HUMPHRIES
b. 31 Dec 1953, Aylesbury
m. 15 Jul 1977 Arlesey, Beds.

Tristan John Robin MILNER
b. 10 Jan 1984, Hitchin, Herts

235

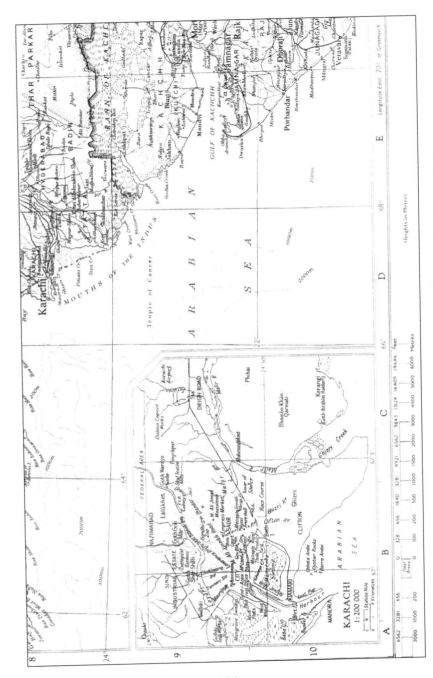

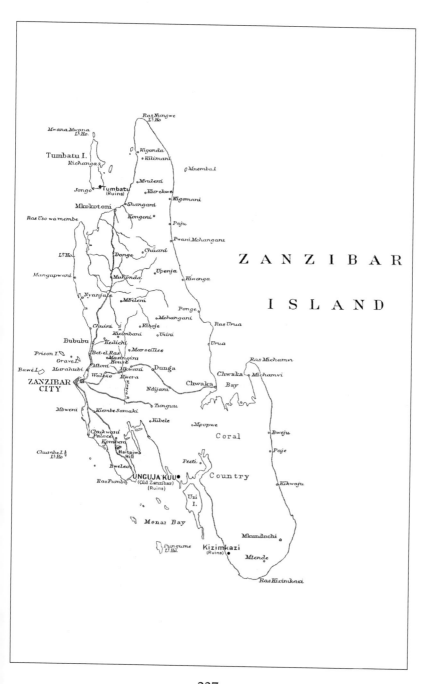

Bibliography and References

Barr, Pat, *The Memsahibs: The Women of Victorian India* (1976).

Best, Geoffrey, *Mid-Victorian Britain 1851-70* (1979).

Burton, Sir Richard, *Zanzibar: City, Island and Coast, Vol. I* (1872).

Dictionary of Quaker Biography, from the library of the Religious Society of Friends, Euston Road, London.

Drabble, Margaret, Ed. *The Oxford Companion to English Literature* (1985).

Family Records Centre, 1 Myddelton Street, London EC1R 1UW, for civil registers of births, marriages and deaths from 1836, and census returns. On the internet: www.pro.gov.uk/about/frc/default.htm

Forster, E. M., *A Passage to India*. First published 1924. Penguin Books 1989. This novel most delicately captures the atmosphere of India during the period of the Raj.

Harding, Cooper, and Wyon, Peter, *Around Thirsk: Britain in Old Photographs* (1995).

Harrison, Brian, *Drink and the Victorians: the temperance question in England 1815-1872* (1971).

James, Lawrence, *Raj: The Making and Unmaking of British India* (1997).

Macmillan, Margaret, *Women of the Raj* (1988).

Pearce, Major F.B., *Zanzibar: The Island Metropolis of Eastern Africa* (1920).

Robinson, Jane, *Angels of Albion: Women of the Indian Mutiny* (1996).

Sykes, Marjorie, *An Indian Tapestry: Quaker Threads in the history of India, Pakistan & Bangladesh* (1997).

Wigham, Maurice J., *The Irish Quakers: A short History of the Religious Society of Friends in Ireland* (1992).

Wyon, Peter, & Foggitt, William, *Thirsk Past & Present* (1980).

Index

The frequent references to Thirsk, Kurrachee (Karachi), Bombay and Zanzibar are not indexed.